Growing Up Suburban

Growing Up Suburban

by Edward A. Wynne

Foreword by James S. Coleman

University of Texas Press
Austin and London

Drawing by Seanna Wray, age 13

Library of Congress Cataloging in Publication Data
Wynne, Edward A   1928–
Growing up suburban.
Includes bibliographical references and index.
1. Suburban schools—United States. I. Title.
LB1566.W94   370.19'346'0973   77-3905
ISBN 0-292-77538-5

To Judith F. Wynne, my wife
Every page reflects her advice, patience, and love

Contents

Tables

Foreword

The discourse on education in recent years has been notable for its selective perception. Almost without exception, it has focused on inequalities in education, on the "disadvantaged" and the "delinquent," and on various pathologies, either of the educational system or of the young people who pass through it. Implicit in this discourse is the notion that somewhere, in the middle classes, in the schools which have numerous National Merit Scholarship finalists, in the clean, safe, and open suburbs, is the ideal from which these other schools and these other young people deviate. Among these undisadvantaged, nonproblem youth, all is presumed to be well; and if only the disadvantaged children could be transformed, and their school environment transformed as well, all educational problems would be solved.

I have perhaps overstated the case; there are anomalies that sometimes give us pause: the increasing numbers of runaways from middle-class families; the high drug use in the fresh, open, nonblighted, well-to-do California schools (higher than anywhere else in the country); the great increase in suicide rates among middle-class young people. Despite these disturbing facts, there is among most commentators an implicit assumption something like that I've described.

Yet all is *not* right in the schools with ample budgets, educated parents, and bright children. The daily diet of activities for children in this "ideal" setting may well be far from that which will serve them best for becoming adults. It is the merit of this book that it refuses to make the assumption I've described. It asks instead what is wrong even in nonproblem schools, what is wrong even for nonproblem children. This book, in short, asks the fundamental questions—not about how we are raising some children better than others, and some with greater opportunity than others, but, rather, about what is going wrong when there are no longer constraints imposed by tight school budgets, slow learning, poor health, and low income. If we fail when these constraints are gone, then the failure is immeasurably worse. It is a failure to know and to act: to know how to make young people's youth most productive for their futures, and to act on that knowledge. It is no longer a failure that can be remedied "if only there were enough money, or enough time, or enough reading skills." It is a failure that can be explained only as a defect in the society of adults: an incapacity for wisely bringing young people into adulthood.

Wynne raises the fundamental question in this book, the question of what a child needs to become an effective adult. He then asks just how schools now satisfy these needs, or fail to, and how they might come to do so in the future. The book is part of an awakening that is slowly taking place, a recognition that the function of schools is no longer the simple one of teaching cognitive skills. Ever since public schools began, their task has been defined in much the same way it was at the beginning, in terms of the cognitive skills of reading, writing, and arithmetic. Even in the most recent wave of program evaluations in education, the issue at question is nearly always "Did the children's achievement in reading and mathematics increase?"

This single-minded focus on cognitive function of the schools may be responsible for the lack of concern with middle-class suburban schools. Children in these schools perform adequately in standardized achievement tests in mathematics and reading; thus there are no perceived problems. Unexamined is the question of whether the youths in these schools are gaining the other qualities they will need as adults, and whether the school is aiding or impeding this acquisition.

Very likely the reason that such questions remain unexamined is that these "other" aspects of becoming adult are presumed to be learned in the family and in other contexts outside school. This presumption was probably not too incorrect some years ago, when the family was multifunctioned, a production unit as well as a consumption unit, a unit with a large number of members and relatively stable composition. But as the family has been eroded over the years, that presumption can no longer be reasonably maintained. And the presumption that these other aspects of becoming adult were learned outside school was not misplaced when school was a relatively short period of time in most young people's lives: a portion of the day for a portion of the year from ages six or seven to fourteen, that is, to the seventh or eighth grade.

But the multifunctioned full-blown family and the minimal school are relics of another day. The school is now multifunctioned and full-blown, while the family has become minimal. Yet in this new context, when more and more of a young person's time, for an increasing number of years, is absorbed by the school, when the family has fewer and fewer functions by which it can bring about education in noncognitive areas, there has developed no new set of educational principles by which schools can be organized. There are efforts in this direction, and there is emerging a recognition of what is necessary. It is to this developing discourse that the present book will contribute. It is probably the most comprehensive contribution to this discourse to date. It raises precisely the right questions for education of the future, and it even begins to offer some answers. It will, I hope, help focus the national discourse in education on the fundamental problems which exist for all children who grow up in a society like our own.

James S. Coleman
University of Chicago

Preface

It is likely that this book will quickly become obsolete. It is an early work on an important, dynamic subject that will inevitably become the focus of growing concern. And, as an early work, it may be surpassed by future events, more data, and increasingly refined analyses. Still, there must be a starting place.

The most definitive current bibliography on suburbs contains over twelve hundred entries.[1] About 10 percent of its entries apparently relate to suburban education or child rearing, and most of those are concerned with the political and economic conflicts that have arisen around suburban schools or with simple statistical comparisons between student cognitive learning in suburban and urban schools. Only between five and ten of the entries even touch on the relationship between the suburban social and physical environment and the child-rearing patterns in suburban neighborhoods and schools. Even these works usually discuss the matter in an unsystemic or brief fashion; for example, none of the studies discusses the connection between local observations and the data for regional and national suburban development. In other words, we have not paid serious attention to the quality of suburban childhood and adolescence; nor have we considered the long-range trends that shape that quality. It is as if we have ignored the developments uniquely affecting the largest pool of children and parents in America.

Of course, we do know that suburban children are in schools and colleges and that—as measured by achievement tests—many of them are doing reasonably well. But these raw facts do not tell us about the kinds of children and adolescents being reared in suburban environments or about the kinds of adults they become. Furthermore, as this book will demonstrate, many suburban environments are historically unique communities: the level of technology, affluence, and economic development underlying the modern suburb did not exist before (let us say) about 1950. Technically, we can call such communities post-industrial environments: essentially, their structural patterns and the life styles of their residents apply forms that are typical of post-industrial America. In effect, we have raised our first post-industrial adults. And it seems likely that unique environments might produce unique effects on the children reared in them. Still, we have not yet begun to seriously consider what these unique effects might be. Nor have we begun to consider whether any unusual effects appearing in suburban children have implications for children being raised in other American environments.

We can be sure that the quality of suburban childhood and adolescence will become a topic of growing importance. This book is an effort to contribute a theoretical framework to this concern and to propose potential solutions to the complex problems it identifies.

Growing Up Suburban

*To escape isolation, a person must be able to become a member of
a group, and this is not just a problem of finding a group. The
capacity for relating one's self easily to other men and women is
not inborn, but a result of experience and training, and that experience and training is itself social.*
—George C. Homans[1]

CHAPTER 1
Why Worry about Suburban Children?

As children mature, they should attain increasing competency in meeting the central challenges of adult life: finding satisfying work, earning a living, initiating and carrying through a successful marriage, raising healthy children, maintaining friendships, and participating in community life. We should not assume that competency in meeting such challenges is necessarily related to academic skills —beyond some minimal level. In other words, prolonged attendance in typical modern schools and colleges is not enough. To really achieve such competency, children and adolescents must be raised in environments that stimulate them to develop adaptive and realistic attitudes, significant coping skills, and the potential for judicious and profound commitment. Many suburban environments fail to provide such stimulation.

We must first recognize that more American children live in suburbs than in either central cities or rural areas.[2] This pattern of suburban growth is a comparatively new historical phenomenon. For instance, in 1950, 25 percent of American families lived in suburbs; in 1970, the figure was 37.25 percent.[3] In 1972, the Bureau of the Census made a population forecast for the year 2000, based on two alternative assumptions. The forecast estimated that between 1970 and 2000, depending on the assumption applied, the suburban population would increase by 72 to 84 million above its 1970 figures.[4] Suburban growth will thus continue to be the dominant national population trend. But the phenomenon of population growth is only one of many special elements that bear on suburban child rearing.

Post-Industrial Environments

Modern suburbs are unique primarily because they are post-industrial environments. David Riesman gave currency to the term "post-industrial" to characterize the major elements that make contemporary American work and life different from the earlier industrial society, just as industrial America was different from the previous agricultural society.[5] "Post-industrial environments" are physical and social environments which are strongly affected by the special factors that characterize post-industrial society. Even as we have locations we describe as agricultural environments (a farm or a farming town) or industrial environments (a factory or people traveling together in a subway train) we also have post-industrial environments.

When such social scientists as Riesman and Daniel Bell talked about America becoming a post-industrial society, they understood that this "becoming" would not occur all at once.[6] Some American environments would be becoming post-industrial while others were still industrial and still others were primarily agricultural. But the expectation is that the proportion of America called "post-industrial" will grow and the earlier forms will decline.

Suburbs are a segment of American life pervaded with post-industrial characteristics because most of them have been built since 1950, that is, after the time that post-industrial influences began to prevail in our society. In contrast, older residential environments—cities, farm communities, and suburbs created before World War II—contain many characteristics of industrial or agricultural life. Still, some post-industrial characteristics are found in most communities; and to the extent such characteristics do exist, the problems now affecting modern suburban child rearing will begin to appear there also.

But what do I mean when I call a modern suburb a post-industrial environment? Let me present a definition. A post-industrial environment is an environment in which:

- The design, structure, and operation of the environment—be it office, library, or community—rely heavily on contemporary technology.
- The technology is more concerned with the management and processing of information than the actual production of consumer goods; thus, the technology relies on such devices as the computer, television, telephone, and microfiche.
- The activities undertaken involve the coordination of many large, widely dispersed, often decentralized organizations with complex decision-making processes; most of these organizations are profit making and some of them are government agencies.
- The inhabitants have relatively high levels of income and cognitive knowledge.
- The intense interpersonal cooperation practiced among its inhabitants is based on an elaborate network of remote, specialized, and abstract systems.
- The inhabitants attach special importance to the values of privacy, emotional self-control and flexibility, rational analysis, individualism, and the attainment of material goods, physical health, and comfort.

Although this definition can apply to many modern service and production organizations, its relationship to a residential environment, such as a suburb, is not quite so clear. And so let us now take this definition and apply it to a modern suburban environment. Concurrently, we will discuss some of the characteristics of personal relations in such environments. Finally, we will try to understand how such unique environments shape the children that are being reared within them. We may incidentally also develop a better understanding of how post-industrial characteristics affect American child rearing in communities beyond modern suburbs.

Post–World War II suburbs are usually based on modern technology. Often the homes are prefabricated. They may be air-conditioned. They use modern heating systems. Their construction does not facilitate maintenance by their occupants but requires the employment of technicians. In particular, the suburban residents are expected to get about via auto rather than by walking (often there are no sidewalks) or using mass transportation. This large-scale suburban reliance on the auto and express highways is a post–World War II phenomenon. Before that time, suburbs were typically constructed around railroad stations (an industrial transportation system),[7] commuters would walk to the station and residents staying at home during the work day would walk to shop or to visit. Between 1960 and 1970, passenger miles traveled by autos in suburban and urban areas increased 74 percent, while passenger miles traveled on public transportation remained static or declined (during a period when suburban areas were growing). Again, between 1960 and 1970, the proportion of suburban families owning autos went from 82 to 87 percent, while the central city proportions went from 62 to 68 percent.[8]

This reliance on the auto and the availability of the telephone to assist communication have naturally stimulated residential dispersion in suburbs. (And, as we will see, this dispersion has affected human relations in such environments.) Thus, in 1970, the national population density for central cities averaged 5,957 persons per square mile; the average density for the suburban area around those cities was 242 per square mile.[9] These data are somewhat deficient, since they include both developed and undeveloped suburban land; however, data are available for the Chicago area which compare population density in the city of Chicago with the density in surrounding suburban townships (and excludes unincorporated areas). In 1970, density in Chicago was 15,477 per square mile; for the townships, it was 1,030.[10] Another national study disclosed that "the roughly 50 million U.S. [central city and suburban] residents added between 1950 and 1970 consumed an estimated 0.4 acres per person, in contrast to 0.2 acres per person used by [central city and suburban] residents in 1950."[11]

Modern institutional arrangements pervade the design, financing, construction, and merchandising of suburban developments. This process has encouraged developers to take advantage of economies of scale. To do this, they have designed communities aimed at comparatively homogeneous groups of buyers: buyers with generally comparable income levels or with approximately similar family status, for example, families with young children, swinging singles, or older and retired persons. Such designs have been facilitated because one developer can amass the resources to manage a large parcel of land. The homogenization has also been assisted by the development of the shopping center (a classic post-industrial institution), which, in turn, relies on the ability of the shoppers to travel by auto. The existence of the shopping center has made it possible for developers to plan communities where no trade or service agencies are in sight or within walking distance of the typical home.

Some of the outcomes described above are demonstrated by the tendency of adults with particular patterns of employment to concentrate in particular suburbs, as shown in table 1, which presents the 1970 employment patterns of residents of the city of Chicago

Table 1.
Chicago Area Adult Employment and Residence, 1970

	Professional/ managerial	Clerical/ sales	Craftsmen/ operatives	Laborers/ farmers	Service
Chicago	17.8%	30.1%	34.1%	5.1%	12.8%
Barrington Hills	57.3	19.8	10.6	6.1	6.1
E. Chicago Heights	4.5	12.1	45.2	11.3	26.9
Evanston	39.8	33.4	12.9	2.6	11.4

Source: Northeastern Illinois Planning Commission, *Suburban Factbook*, pp. 21, 25.

and three of its suburbs. Suburban homogeneity, however, is more than vocational. The child-rearing orientation of many suburbs results in the tendency of householders not oriented to child rearing (e.g., retired persons) to live in other communities. Thus, in the city of Chicago, 10.6 percent of the population was 65 or over in 1970. By comparison, the percentage of persons 65 or over in the Chicago suburban area was 7.5. However, there was wide diversity among individual Chicago suburban communities: 18 percent of the Berwyn population was 65 or older, while 4.1 percent in Palatine and 3.1 percent in Bloomington were 65 or older.[12]

The definition mentioned affluence as a post-industrial characteristic, and suburban residents are typically more affluent than residents of central city areas. In the city of Chicago in 1968, 23.3 percent of the families earned $15,000 a year, while 41.5 percent of the residents of the Chicago suburbs were at or above this level. But this matter of affluence must be qualified. *Not all suburban residents are affluent.* Average figures covering millions of persons obviously cover hundreds of thousands of persons living at lower income levels. But this book is focused on persons living in newer suburbs, and more affluent residents tend to concentrate in such communities. As a result, the most significant contrast in family income levels is not between suburb and city, but between individual suburbs. For instance, in the Chicago area, 74 percent of the families in the suburban community of New Trier earned $15,000 or above in 1969, while only 18.5 percent of the families in the suburb of Kanesville were at that level.[13] One government report summarized this medley of developments in the following terms: "suburban communities are typically internally homogeneous, but differ from one another along social and economic lines, with the rich in some, and the less affluent in others. Variations among suburbs are becoming as important as those between the central city and the suburbs as a whole."[14] Of course, the very word *affluence* calls for definition. Affluence does not imply the extinction of material or physical desires, but simply a level of possessions and conveniences considerably higher than that enjoyed by nearly all persons in other societies. Thus, suburban reliance on the auto is a sign of growing affluence. Members of the modern suburban family may say they "need" one, two, or three cars, but the "need" exists because they can afford to *choose* to live in an environment that presumes they will have such autos. And a man who chooses to live in an environment that "requires" him to own an airplane or to buy a $300 suit may feel pressured by the costs of his living style. Despite that pressure, we still should call him affluent.

Affluence is reflected in the conveniences (and amusements and distractions for children) found in many suburban homes, the fact that families live in private homes which they own rather than in apartments or in rented housing, the lack of economic pressures on children to earn money, and the ability of families to afford expensive and prolonged schooling (and school taxes) for their children.

There is much cooperation among residents of modern suburbs, just as there is among residents of many communities. But suburban cooperation is of a relatively complex and abstract type. A particular suburban family is likely to have its residence located in a number of political subdivisions: a sewer district, a school district, a congressional district, a county, a township. There are other significant, but more informal, divisions: churches people attend, the local paper they take, the shopping center at which they regularly buy, the country club to which they belong, the golf course or recreation center they use, and the subdivision in which they live. Yet, in some way, most of these different systems must work together—cooperate—if this particular family is to lead a satisfying life. Of course, complaints are often heard about the lack of cooperation among such systems, but the complaints are really part of the cooperative process and will often bring the systems back into conjunction. It is remarkable, indeed, that the innumerable systems are as responsive as they are. This profusion of systems is caused by a variety of post-industrial forces: widespread transportation and fast communication, which enable institutions to exercise control and provide service over apparently dispersed areas; the rapid pace of suburban development (due to affluence and technology), which has made it harder to consolidate existing institutions; and the use of many resources in suburban development, which has required the assistance of a great number of specialized agencies—a typical suburban house might represent the contributions of five thousand agencies and businesses, whereas a settler on the prairies in 1876 might have been able to identify only one hundred entities in any way connected with his home. But the peculiar truth is that, the greater the variety and scope of cooperation involved in an enterprise, the more abstract the particular acts of cooperation become. The postman who hands us the mail can be an acquaintance or friend; the telephone system that permits us to talk to someone in Berlin is a remote and impersonal institution.

It is not difficult to see how post-industrial values pervade modern suburbs. The high value attached to privacy is obvious: for example, detached homes, separate rooms for most family members, private transportation, family friends who usually live out of the neighborhood, and merchants who have only fleeting contacts with their customers. Ironically, at one stage in American history the impersonality of the city was contrasted with rural life; however, traditional urban impersonality is perhaps more "personal" than that in many modern suburbs. For example, customers in suburban stores often receive polite and prompt service. However, "personal" service means service directed at the particular needs and style of the customer. How personal can a supermarket or fast-food store be? Children hanging around a city candy store perhaps receive more personal service—and, incidentally, have less privacy—because of the attentions of the store owner. In other words, privacy can be equated with superficial contacts. Thus, we may have many contacts with other human beings but still have privacy if those other persons lack the incentives or opportunity to know us in depth.

Self-control and personal flexibility are obviously important in modern work. In modern suburban environments self-control is the norm, and rarely are there occasions that encourage the dramatic display of emotions. There are few street festivals, conspicuous wakes and funerals, or occasions for the dramatic public release of anger. As a result, adults normally display their strong emotions in carefully structured situations. These patterns of self-discipline thus make for a degree of flexibility; the self-control permits people to successfully adapt to unusual situations. Rational analysis is evinced by the emphasis on "good," college-oriented schools; clubs that foster programmatic (rather than social, religious, or ethnic) activities; the maintenance of quality libraries; and the stress on independent (rather than partisan) politics. The importance of individualism is evinced by the tendency to approach issues with rationality—which implies a willingness to accept differences—and by the modern suburban community's sympathy with privacy.

Material goods, comfort, and health are important to suburban adults because they are major reasons for the efforts adults make to move to and remain in the suburbs. Suburban life represents the large-scale application of material resources, such as express highways, air conditioning, elaborate recreation equipment. And, apparently, cleanliness and privacy foster comfort and health. Of course, most persons in most societies desire goods, comfort, and health, but they also sometimes honor conflicting values. For instance, in some societies, social prestige (which is different from wealth), the maintenance of social networks, or religious or aesthetic expression are all viewed as superior to the attainment of possessions. And, in other cultures, forms of mortification, such as scarification, adult circumcision, and fasting, are often valued more highly than comfort or apparent physical health.

Not too surprisingly, the rapid development of the technologies, systems, and values that pervade modern suburbia in particular (and post-industrial life in general) has revealed a number of significant contradictions between these elements. (And, as we will see later, these contradictions have important implications for suburban child rearing.) Privacy and individualism are not consistent with cooperation, since cooperation is based on either informed expectations about the conduct of others or some system for controlling that conduct. Of course, self-control (which is essentially practiced to please others) is also not consistent with individualism. Perhaps one can create special definitions for these diverse terms that reconcile their apparent inconsistencies. Still, it is evident that, in the ordinary lay sense, they involve contradictions.[15]

Now, let us consider the operational effect of such contradictions on post-industrial suburbs. The fact is that such suburbs have the *appearance* of privacy and individualism; however, cooperation and self-control are maintained by a variety of post-industrial agencies. Zoning codes, mortgage lending requirements, the need for residents to maintain predetermined income levels (which usually requires holding demanding jobs) are all indicators that most modern suburban residents have gone through a careful screening process which limits their capability for dramatic individualism and restricts their privacy in many particulars. Another contradiction is the contrast between the adults' world of work and their home environment. Most job environments are relatively heterogeneous, peopled with clients, secretaries, students, witnesses, top-level executives, and day laborers—persons of all ages and ethnic groups. Yet the adults who work in such worlds come home to suburban communities that are perhaps the most homogeneous in human history— and, of course, far more "commonplace" than the much derided Gopher Prairie or Winesburg. Another contrast between work and home is that, while the adult is subject to great demands at work, there is little constructive and essential work to be done around the house. Food preparation can be simplified. Much maintenance must be done by outside specialists. While "make-work" projects can be developed at the home, there is little of the natural urgency stimulated by a leaking roof or the need to carry groceries from the store, to chop wood to heat the house, or to tend a garden that helps to feed the family. All these "genuine" chores are handled by buying goods or services with money earned away from the home.

The existence of such contradictions is not automatically bad. One element of maturity is to learn to adapt to some significant degree of diversity (and this ties in with the post-industrial value of self-discipline). The novelty often associated with diversity can even be stimulating. But there can be too many contradictions, and when that obscure boundary is passed, the anxiety level begins to rise. Whatever the adult response to such contradictions, we can be sure that children have less tolerance for real or apparent contradictions than adults.

Child Rearing in Post-Industrial Suburbs

But how do these post-industrial elements and contradictions affect the nature of child rearing in modern suburbs (and other post-industrial communities)?

Children in post-industrial suburbs are uniquely isolated from diversity. Until the children are old enough to drive a car, their out-of-school life is limited to the experiences that (1) are within walking distance, (2) they are "ferried" to, or (3) may be available via bicycle in some seasons and for some age groups. Bedroom communities in post-industrial suburbs have been designed precisely to create such limitations. Usually the children are isolated from stores, factories, service stations, or persons of different income or age levels. In a historical perspective, such isolation is relatively unusual. Although we talk about the constraints on modern urban children, crowded central cities have existed since Rome or Alexandria. The word *ghetto* describes a residential pattern perhaps one thousand years old. The truly new "invention" is the post-industrial suburb, which relies on a technology that has been applied on a large scale for no more than twenty-five years.

The lack of stimulation for children in many suburbs—a sign of their extraordinary safety—has further encouraged parents to leave their children alone—what is there that can harm them?—and thus has lessened both adult-child engagement and monitoring. Or, conversely, the sterility has compelled adults to contrive and manage activities to occupy the young; there is little middle ground for letting the young manage their own play, while some adult (otherwise involved in housework or paid employment) can keep an eye on them.

The level of suburban affluence has diminished the number and intensity of the household chores done by children, and, while many suburban children hold part-time jobs, the money is often seen as "nice" compared to "essential." This fact can affect the quality of realistic, on-the-job learning.

The rational, large-scale level of their parents' geographically remote work makes it hard for suburban children to see work as either comprehensible or interesting. Nor do they find simple images of tangible work activities in the complex modern institutions that provide efficient services to many suburbanites—supermarkets, teams of doctors and aides, branches of quick-service food chains.

The communications technology of post-industrial society—television, telephones, stereo equipment—and the toys that affluence affords also have an effect. They provide systems with which children and adolescents can be occupied without coming into contact with other persons, or which let them restrict their circle of acquaintances (via reliance on the telephone) to persons with similar values and style of living. In other words, these systems foster withdrawal and/or the avoidance of diversity.

But perhaps the most important suburban post-industrial characteristic from the point of view of children and youths is the school. In this book, the word *school* includes all formal educational institutions that regularly deal with high proportions of suburban children: such institutions can range from preschools through colleges. Thus, future remarks about "suburban schools" must be treated as applicable to all such institutions, unless the context suggests another interpretation.

Suburban schools are typical post-industrial institutions. They are often large; individual high schools frequently enroll several thousand students and have hundreds of teachers on their faculty. As does post-industrial work, the schools stress highly abstract cooperative work. In other words, individual students are assigned to particular classes or programs that have been designed to permit particular teachers to deliver planned packages of knowledge to properly prepared students. Such assignment systems rely on complex record keeping, decisions of counselors, deliberate requests by individual students or their parents, and use of diagnostic tests. The systems are guided by data collected on complex forms, maintain elaborate schedules, and oftentimes rely on the assignment of students by a computer. This process supposedly enables individual students (and their parents) to receive the greatest help from the system. Like the cooperation offered by the phone company compared to that of the mailman, abstract cooperation may be profound and genuine, but young people probably need more tangible evidence to recognize they are being helped and cared for.

The faculties in these schools are often highly specialized: they include teachers, reading specialists, counselors, psychologists, security guards, clerks, and administrators. And, among the teachers at higher grade levels, each teacher typically specializes in one academic discipline or even in one topic (*American* history). Such specialization is steadily "creeping down" into lower-level schools, where it is presented as the way to greater efficiency.

Because of the diversity of specialists, the large numbers of students, and the variety of programs, most individual students deal with many different adults during the course of a day or school term, and individual adults similarly deal with hundreds of students. Also, since students (after elementary school) are often regrouped (to assist efficient teaching) from one period to the next, and from term to term, the students are often surrounded by shifting pools of their age-mates. But, while the composition of such pools of students is unstable, the pools are still peculiarly homogeneous, since such homogeneous grouping facilitates rational cognitive instruction: the precise package of knowledge can be presented to the right group of users.

Like other post-industrial institutions, school systems are broken down into many subdivisions to assist specialized treatments. The nature of these subdivisions varies among communities, but they can include preschool, kindergarten, elementary school, junior high, senior high, junior college, or senior college. Many schools further subdivide their students into different programs or ability tracks. This diversity of subdivisions makes it difficult for a family to develop strong ties to an educational system or any of its units: there may be too many institutions for it to relate to, and their children's enrollment in each institution may be too brief either to provide a basis for communication or to offer an incentive to develop a relationship (why bother to become familiar with a two-year school?). A school system comprised of such a diversity of institutions will have difficulty in presenting a consistent body of aspirations and standards to the maturing students who pass through. The students, too, may begin to control their emotional "investments" in a series of short-term relationships. The age segregation just described is further intensified by the ability grouping typically practiced in the separate schools. This segregation is applied to assist focused instruction, which is directed at the apparent ability levels of particular groups of students. As a result of the combination of age and ability segregation of students in each school, students are rarely in close touch with large numbers of students with much greater or lesser capabilities. Thus, they cannot be urged to act as models or helpers to far younger or less able students; nor can they easily ask for help from much older or more able students.

The specialization of the school has generally confined students to the role of cognitive learners. They are rarely, if ever, expected to assist in the support or maintenance of the school or to help other students, although the school is providing them (at little or no economic cost to them) with expensive and valuable services. It is true that some students do engage in athletic or other extracurricular activities which provide help or amusement for others or bring prestige to the school. Still, it appears that the level of prestige attached to such activities has gradually tended to decline in suburban high schools. This impression is supported by the evidence that modern colleges (except when enrolling extraordinary athletes) have placed increased emphasis on test scores as admission criteria —as compared to personal references and student activity records. This shift in criteria has undermined one of the reenforcers for such nonacademic activities.

The post-industrial values that were touched on earlier have also influenced the structure of suburban education. In some ways, schools do provide their students with a comparatively high degree of privacy. That is, very few of the students or faculty in modern schools know much about the personal life or serious feelings of one another. Of course, it is true that some teachers and classes may stimulate students to express their personal "values" or views about significant public events. But it is unrealistic to perceive these activities as exchanges of deep views, that is, intrusions into privacy. The exchanges occur in an environment pervaded with formalistic, transitory relationships and in which the students are subjected only to modest interpersonal demands (that is one effect of a homogeneous social environment—people are all alike).[16] Under these circumstances, deliberate in-class discussions about values are highly artificial. Students with even modest insight will recognize that it is foolish to open oneself up before such casual groupings, and so there will not be discussions on how students feel about their parents' divorce, their ambivalence about drugs, or their fear of blacks (or whites). Students who are naïve enough to be "open" will be "punished" as their confidences are passed on elsewhere, or their ignorance put down outside the classroom. Furthermore, such school-structured discussions about feelings and public events take place among a group of youths and highly select adults (school-teachers). Given the limited experience of this pool of human beings, one can wonder about the validity of their views about how to govern South Africa, prevent inflation, or correct drug abuse. In other words, the nature of the school environment supresses consideration of the true knowledge and concerns of students and encourages discussion about remote ("safe") matters which they can really know very little about. All of this increases the students' privacy. However, it is hard to see how truly individualized programs can be designed or conducted unless they are directed at real needs and feelings of particular students: this requires a diminishment of privacy. Furthermore, genuine intrusions by adults into the privacy of comparatively young persons probably should be conducted under the informed supervision of their parents (the persons ultimately responsible for their protection); but, given the comparatively remote relations between parents and the typical school, it is hard to see how such supervision can occur.

The high value that post-industrial adults attach to prolonged formal education has magnified the impact of school on their children. The adults make sacrifices to enable their children to give undivided attention to school. If the school produces many college-bound graduates, they will give it a favorable evaluation. They will vote for comparatively high school taxes and assume, by reason of such taxes, that their children are receiving quality schooling. And, if their children are apparently doing well in school, the expectation will be that everything else is fine. These patterns make it harder for suburban schools to receive healthy, broad-based criticism.

The school apparently gives great weight to individualism. It talks about individualized programing, uses tests and counselors to identify individual skills, and "individually" evaluates the work of each student. But, much of this "individualism" is rather specious. That is, when two to three thousand comparatively young persons are put in one building at the same time, it is essential that many common conventions be articulated and followed. Furthermore, the students are being prepared to earn a living as adults who are usually paid to produce some good or service that someone else wants—a world in which individualism is not usually rewarded. And, of course,

American adolescents are notoriously peer oriented. Thus, while they individualistically reject school dress codes, they all wear the jeans, hair styles, or eyeglasses promoted by current pop figures. Usually, when the theme of individualism is being bandied about, a careful listener can find that the users are subtly watching each other, to ensure they are staying in step. Actually, there is nothing "wrong" with people being relatively group oriented. Such an orientation makes social life possible. The problem arises when people who are highly group oriented cannot recognize that they are. This phenomenon can generate a great deal of psychic confusion. And so we see, in the post-industrial school, an aggravated version of the dichotomy that pervades adult suburban life: a high degree of abstract cooperation coupled with a naïve dedication to individualism. This dichotomy can be even more confusing to children than it surely is to adults.

Because of its size—and, to some degree, its impersonality—the school necessarily demands a great deal of self-restraint from its students. A person cannot operate successfully in a large, relatively bureaucratic institution without developing a fairly high level of reserve.

Obviously, suburban schools give great emphasis to material wealth, comfort, and physical health. They often have elaborate facilities for students, and they strive to provide well-qualified (and paid) staff and to maintain low teacher-pupil ratios. Great care is taken to protect the students from physical danger and stress. Sometimes, one might assume that suburbanites believe their educational systems must be working well—because, after all, look at all the money they are spending.

In sum, the various contradictions underlying post-industrial life obviously pervade the school. Students are implicitly promised individually prescribed "treatments" and then are told their privacy will not be invaded. They are told that individualism is an important value; they are then placed in environments where they are expected to engage in massive cooperative efforts. Furthermore, it is evident that the students' parents (and probably the students) expect or hope they will grow up to hold well-paying jobs, so they can acquire valuable goods and services as adults: they must perform services which will be valued highly by others. At the same time, the students are told they must become "individuals" and, in effect, not be too beholden to others. Again, they are told that formal knowledge (book learning) is important. Yet it is obvious that their eventual success as adults may depend more on their ability to live with ambiguity and to practice self-restraint than on their vocabulary or test scores.

Still, the contradictions just sketched are essentially an extension of those affecting post-industrial adults—although those contradictions probably press more severely on the young than on their parents. But there is one other contradiction that especially affects the young: the expectation that they should learn to control their emotions in an environment that provides them with no productive system of emotional release. In other words, for almost all post-industrial adults, no matter how much self-control is expected of them, there are circles of understanding friends and other systems of release and reassurance. Furthermore, the adults—because of having matured—have an emotional foundation that should enable them to develop permanent and enriching relationships. Unfortunately, the environments around post-industrial children provide them with fewer occasions for structured emotional release—of love, joy, or sorrow—than those around their parents. And all common sense tells us that children need more structured occasions for the release of such emotions than do their parents. It is through such structured experiences in our youth that we develop the power to provide our own systems of self-controlled release as adults. This is what is meant by healthy self-control—not the abolition of emotions, but their reflexive redirection into rewarding channels. But we cannot learn such redirection without the help of "training systems," systems that provide us with occasions to feel strongly, to share those feelings with others, and at appropriate moments to use them to motivate us to attain prosocial goals. Through such occasions, we gradually become adults who redirect our natural tensions into conduct that helps ourselves and others. Such adults can joke about frustration, cry with joy, conceal their fear, and console someone in sorrow. However, none of this involves the extinction or ignorance of feelings.[17]

In particular, the social environments around suburban children are emotionally barren because they are (1) more homogeneous than those around their parents (and homogeneity deprives people of emotion-stretching experiences), (2) largely populated by young persons who have had few occasions to develop or test their emotions, (3) pervaded with transitory relationships that discourage serious emotional engagement, and (4) lacking in tangible cooperative activities aimed at producing goods or services for actual users or buyers (and such responsibilities stimulate emotional maturation). Many young persons maturing in such environments will tend to hide their emotions, or fear them, or have an excessive or unhealthy fascination with them, or occasionally release them in awkward or sometimes harmful fashions. But at this point, a question will undoubtedly come to mind: if many suburban environments present barriers to healthy emotional maturation, how is it that we are not seeing widespread disorder among suburban children?

Acts of Alienation among Youth

We must recognize that there are many serious signs of disorder and alienation among American children, as shown by the following data, which represent the most recent available information about many important trends relating to youth alienation.

Between 1950 and 1974, the annual suicide rate for white males, aged 15–19, went from 3.7 per 100,000 members of the cohort born alive to 11.9 per 100,000.[18] The pattern of increase was persistent and incremental. During these same years, the overall national suicide rate for adults remained comparatively constant, ranging from a high of 12.1 to a low of 9.8. No other age group had an increase in suicide rate between 1950 and 1974 equal to the rate presented above. (Between 1950 and 1974, the rate for white females, aged 15–19, went from 1.9 to 3.3.)

There is evidence of increased drug use by the young. In 1971, 30 percent of all college students surveyed in a national sample reported having used marijuana in the last thirty days; in 1970, 28 percent of a similar sample had reported such use. This use and experimentation extends to other, more powerful drugs. Seven percent of the respondents in the 1971 sample reporting having used cocaine.[19]

The issue of trends in drug use is complicated, for we do not have data about the national level of drug use by youths before the late 1960's. However, we do have some trend data from the late 1960's forward. The most thorough data cover San Mateo County, California, school students for every year from 1968 through 1976.[20] A suburb of San Francisco, San Mateo County has the second highest per family income level among California's fifty-eight counties.[21] Table 2 contains the San Mateo data on marijuana use among certain high school grades.

These data reveal a stabilization of use at a comparatively high level. It is also significant to recall that, nationally, arrests of males under 18 for narcotic law violations increased 1,288 percent be-

Table 2.
*Percentage of Marijuana Use among Male San Mateo
County High School Students, 1968–1976*

| | One or more uses in past year | | Ten or more uses in past year | | Fifty or more uses in past year | |
	Grade 9	Grade 12	Grade 9	Grade 12	Grade 9	Grade 12
1968	27	45	14	26	na	na
1969	35	50	20	34	na	na
1970	34	51	20	34	11	22
1971	44	59	26	43	17	32
1972	44	61	27	45	16	32
1973	51	61	32	45	20	32
1974	49	62	30	47	20	34
1975	49	64	30	45	20	31
1976	48	61	27	42	17	30

Source: San Mateo County, *Summary Report*, 1976, p. 6.

tween 1960 and 1972.[22] The most recent report of the National
Institute on Drug Abuse concluded that "there is no indication of
any recent decline in the annual prevalence of any drug, with the
possible exception of psychedelics."[23]

There are also data on increased use of alcohol by youths. A survey in one community reported that the percentage of seventh grade
boys who began drinking during the previous year increased from
52 percent in 1969 to 72 percent in 1973. This increase is consistent with equivalent increases reported in other surveys. This
adolescent drinking is not simply tasting; in 1974, 25 percent of
the eleventh graders covered in a survey of a national sample reported being drunk four or more times during the past year.[24]

The use of cigarettes has also increased. While smoking is, of
course, widespread among adults, it is still a dangerous practice.
Typical data disclose that between 1969 and 1975, in a national
sample of females aged 13–17, the proportion of respondents who
smoke a pack or more of cigarettes a day rose from 10 to 39 percent.[25]

The San Mateo data, referred to earlier, also provide evidence of
the breadth of use of stimulants and depressants by children and
adolescents in one community. Students were annually asked between 1969 and 1976 if they had "significantly used" any of the

following substances during the past school year: alcohol, amphetamines, LSD, marijuana, or tobacco. The surveys covered students from the seventh through the twelfth grades. These data are given in table 3.

Some trend data about delinquency cases are also available. Between 1957 and 1972, the rate of delinquency cases (per 1,000 child population aged 10–17) disposed of in U.S. juvenile courts went from 19.1 to 33.6.[26] Drug cases were a significant, but not central, element in this increase. There are also data about increased antisocial conduct in schools. One survey reported that, in the sample of schools studied, assaults on teachers increased 85 percent between 1970 and 1973. During the same period, the weapons confiscated from students by school authorities in the schools surveyed had risen 54 percent.[27]

The increase in self-destructive and antisocial conduct has extended to the area of sexual relations. Venereal disease increased among both sexes aged 15–19 between 1956 and 1974. Reported cases of gonorrhea (per 100,000 members of the cohort) rose over 200 percent, while cases of syphilis increased 100 percent.[28] Between 1950 and 1974, the estimated number of illegitimate births for unmarried white females aged 15–19 went from 5.1 per 1,000 such females to 11.1.[29] The increases in venereal disease and illegitimacy occurred during a period of widespread availability of antibiotics, medical services, and contraceptive information and materials. It is also significant that, between 1970 and 1972, the number of females under 18 arrested for violent crimes increased 388 percent, while the proportion of males under 18 arrested increased by 203 percent.[30]

We should also consider the student unrest, building takeovers, and other youthful disorders of the late 1960's and early 1970's. Student disorder has occurred in America in the past, but the most recent wave involved a higher proportion of our youth cohorts and more drastic forms of destructive conduct. For example, during 1969 and 1970, over 8,000 bomb threats, attempted bombings, and bombings were attributed to student unrest.[31] In 1970, nine of the top sixteen names on the FBI's most-wanted list were youthful activists, wanted for such crimes as bombings, murder, and bank robbery.[32]

Attitudes Evincing Alienation

A number of pieces of attitudinal trend data are available to help us interpret this alienated conduct. Many of the populations sur-

Table 3.
San Mateo County, California, Student Use of Harmful Substances
(Table Reports "No Significant Use" of Following Substances:
LSD, Alcohol, Amphetamines, Marijuana, and Tobacco. Cited Rates
for Male and Female Students Are per 100 Responses)[a]

	1969	1970	1971
Males			
Grade 7	na	80.9	74.2
Grade 8	na	65.1	58.6
Grade 9	56.9	57.5	50.5
Grade 10	48.5	46.4	43.3
Grade 11	40.5	39.2	34.2
Grade 12	32.8	36.7	30.7
Females			
Grade 7	na	84.8	80.5
Grade 8	na	71.2	64.6
Grade 9	60.3	61.0	52.4
Grade 10	56.9	49.4	45.9
Grade 11	49.2	43.4	43.1
Grade 12	45.5	44.2	42.3
Standardized Rate[b]			
Total Grades 9–12	48.8	47.2	42.9
Total Responses[c]	25,883	35,148	35,701

Source: San Mateo County, *Summary Report, 1976,* p. 8.
[a]"Significant use: Alcohol—10 or more occasions; tobacco—10 or more occasions; Marijuana—10 or more occasions; LSD and amphetamines—3 or
more occasions in past twelve months.
[b]Standardized rates of use for senior high schools are computed using equal
proportions for each of the eight class/sex groups. This eliminates distortion
because proportions of classes or sexes have changed between years.
[c]Total number of responses used in tabulations for the year specified.

veyed are essentially upper-middle-class youths, who may have
been raised in post-industrial environments.

Between 1948 and 1968, successive freshman classes at Haverford College, in Pennsylvania, took the Minnesota Multiphasic Inventory test.[33] A sample of the students' responses reveals the steady
and incremental decline in attitudes that are sympathetic to cooperative and group activities: more and more, the students evinced

1972	1973	1974	1975	1976
71.4	68.0	68.7	71.7	74.7
55.3	52.6	50.7	57.0	59.4
48.6	42.1	45.3	46.0	51.6
39.6	36.3	35.1	37.8	41.3
34.4	32.4	31.3	31.8	31.4
27.2	29.8	27.3	26.2	29.8
77.2	73.6	71.2	75.9	79.1
59.7	55.6	56.1	60.0	59.5
51.6	46.7	44.4	46.6	49.0
42.6	42.3	39.9	36.4	31.7
38.9	37.7	36.4	35.9	34.8
36.5	35.5	31.7	32.5	34.6
39.9	37.8	36.4	37.1	38.8
31,251	27,388	28,232	28,303	20,848

attitudes consonant with withdrawal from contacts or responsibilities connecting them to others, as shown in table 4.

This growth of withdrawal attitudes among Haverford students was coupled with an apparent simultaneous increase in egoistic attitudes: between 1948 and 1968, the proportion of such students who thought they could work great benefit to the world if given a chance rose from 40 to 66 percent, while the proportion of those

Table 4.
*Haverford College Sample MMPI Items for Classes, 1948–49
through 1968–69*

Item	Percentage answering affirmatively							
	1948	1952	1956	1960	1961	1965	1967	1968
When I was a child I didn't care to be a member of a crowd or gang	33	35	35	38	49	58	19	47
I could be happy living all alone in a cabin in the woods or mountains	23	28	34	38	33	35	42	45
I am a good mixer	77	49	48	63	60	58	38	43
I like to go to parties and other affairs where there is lots of loud fun	65	56	55	53	44	40	38	40
At parties I am more likely to sit by myself than to join in with the crowd	23	35	40	27	44	38	47	50
My worries seem to disappear when I get into a crowd of lively friends	71	69	73	68	58	65	56	55
If I were in trouble with several friends who were equally to blame, I would rather take the whole blame than to give them away	63	56	50	57	47	43	33	45

Item	Percentage answering affirmatively							
	1948	1952	1956	1960	1961	1965	1967	1968
When a man is with a woman he is usually thinking about things related to her sex	29	37	15	27	35	28	36	43
I enjoy reading love stories	55	49	35	25	44	30	18	25
I like dramatics	80	74	73	75	60	73	67	65
I would like to be a singer	51	47	37	36	33	38	31	23

Source: Heath, *Growing Up in College*, p. 63.

17-year-olds who thought they knew more than experts rose from 20 to 38 percent. It was not clear how these increasingly withdrawn and introverted students could render such benefits without human interaction or could acquire the experience incident to becoming so knowledgeable.

Other data about youth attitudinal trends show that the Haverford patterns are representative of trends displayed by successive cohorts of late adolescents on many college campuses. Attitudinal tests were administered to students at Dartmouth in 1952 and 1968 and at the University of Michigan in 1952 and 1969.[34] Several similar questions were asked the students at both colleges. They were asked whether "human nature is fundamentally more cooperative." Agreement declined from 66 and 70 percent, at Dartmouth and Michigan respectively, to 51 and 55 percent. Another question asked them to say if "most of what I am learning in college is very worthwhile." Agreement declined from 67 and 74 percent, respectively, to 58 and 57 percent. Again, the students were asked to identify private and public institutions (e.g., school, church, family) that they felt related to. The number and intensity of summed identifications declined from 296 and 259, respectively, to 269 and 206. A third group of studies on students' attitudinal trends were conducted at several unnamed private colleges between the early

1950's and 1966.[35] Those studies showed shifts on an attitudinal expression scale evaluating student desire for impulse expression from 41 (proimpulse) to 54 percent, and a decline in the proportion of students describing the need to be liked as "very important" from 48 to 26 percent.

A series of surveys of a national sample of college-age youths was taken between 1969 and 1973.[36] Unfortunately, these surveys do not replicate the questions asked in the Haverford, Michigan, or Dartmouth studies; nor do they cover equivalent populations. Still, they show a continuation of the trends toward egoism and withdrawal. Among the college students surveyed in 1973, the importance of "privacy" as a value increased from 61 to 71 percent. At the same time, the respective importance of "religion" and "patriotism," two values which stress the individual's obligation tr, extrapersonal concerns, declined from 38 and 35 percent to 28 and 19 percent. The series also showed a continuing pattern of gradual dissemination and acceptance of college youths' views among noncollege youths. In general, the views disclosed in the survey demonstrate an enlargement of expectations about the rights of students and citizens, and a lessening of expectations about the responsibilities of these same persons.

An Interpretation

It is understandable that the attitudes just described can lead to the alienated reactions that have been enumerated. We can also sense how post-industrial environments around the young—such as those already sketched—could form such attitudes. Still, at this time, we do not have enough precise data to make a firm statement about what proportion of these symptoms are occurring among children reared in modern suburbs. All we can say for certain is that many of the symptoms encompass whites as well as blacks, that they developed increasing intensity during a period (1950–1972) of growing prosperity for all social classes, and that there are data to show that some of the symptoms (e.g., marijuana use) were more prevalent in post-industrial environments than in central cities. In other words, some of the traditional "explanations" of such youth disorder—that it occurs mainly among poor blacks, that it is the outgrowth of increasing poverty, or that it is largely a central city matter—are belied by the data. The extent to which such disorder is the outgrowth of growing suburbanization remains to be definitely determined.

Causes for Misperceiving the Suburbs

The relationship between post-industrial suburbs and alienation among youth is obscured by forces beyond the simple lack of data. As already noted, many suburbs are more akin to traditional small towns than to post-industrial environments. Typically, such suburban communities were built before World War II and were dependent on a railroad station.[37] In 1950, most suburbanites lived in such communities. Consequently, when we date the modern suburb from (let us say) 1950, we mean that after that date the proportion of suburbanites living in older suburbs steadily declined. Still, in 1955, perhaps 80 percent of suburbanites lived in older suburbs, and today the proportion is perhaps 45 percent. Thus, many contemporary suburbanites are still not living in suburbs that can be described as post-industrial. (Of course, we can forecast that, by perhaps 1985, 90 percent of suburban residents will live in post-industrial suburbs.) Therefore, research on suburban children—if it does not distinguish between children or young adults from industrial compared to post-industrial suburbs—will not generate data to demonstrate the significant future trends that will affect suburban children.

Another obstacle to accurate assessment is that some kinds of child-rearing difficulties take time to be recognized. By the second or third grade of elementary school, we can perceive if substantial reading problems are occurring among students. But if we are concerned with broader areas of personality development, serious symptoms (e.g., drug abuse, delinquency) may not begin to appear until late adolescence—fifteen or more years after a child is born (and raised) in a "harmful" environment. But fifteen years ago—in 1962 —perhaps only 10 percent of all American children were living in modern suburbs. And so the current proportion of recently matured or adolescent children fully raised in post-industrial suburbs—compared to the total youth cohort—is still relatively small, although that proportion will grow dramatically. (By the year 2010, perhaps 25 percent of the adults in America will have been raised in such environments.)

In considering the forces that shape our vision of suburban child rearing, we cannot ignore the meaning that suburban life has for many American parents. Often, the move to the suburbs involved an initial sacrifice for such adults. One of their motives was to give their children a more satisfying and safer environment than they had had as children. In other words, the parents assume—though they were probably not raised in modern suburbs—that such suburbs provide ideal child-rearing environments. And there are ample data to show that adults suburbanites are generally pleased with their environment.[38] It is cleaner, safer, more spacious, and relaxed. Unfortunately, there is no indication that these virtues—beyond a very modest threshold level—have much to do with raising emotionally healthy children. However, it is true that these benefits do, in the short run, diminish certain child-rearing demands on parents. But after the parents commit themselves to suburban life, it would be extremely distressing for these adults to discover that post-industrial suburbia was seriously flawed as an environment for child rearing. This discovery would dramatically undermine their life plans. In other words, many examinations of suburban child-rearing structures are tied to the expectation that nothing is wrong that cannot be corrected by a little tinkering. This expectation suggests that nothing seriously wrong can be permitted to be perceived.

Assumptions about the excellence of modern suburban schools are also a barrier to adequate perceptions. In one sense, these assumptions are correct. Most teachers prefer teaching in suburbs than in central cities, and suburban schools can be more choosy in hiring. Suburban buildings usually have more up-to-date and elaborate equipment. The concept of the excellence of suburban schools is sustained by data about the superior academic performance of students and graduates of the schools: typically, their achievement test scores are superior to those of urban pupils, and they obtain more college scholarships.[39] However, this sign of excellence neglects to separate the effects of school quality from the many assists such students receive as a result of the superior economic and educational level of their parents: a large body of research suggests that such superior pupil performance would be displayed in central city schools with central city teachers if the central city pupils came from families such as those that populate modern suburbs.[40]

Our ambivalence about the meaning of adulthood and maturity has also obscured our vision. For most of human history, children were raised in environments which were "experience rich and information poor."[41] In other words, the inevitable social processes surrounding a typical youth in an American frontier community, a Midwest farm, or a nineteenth-century city would promote emotional maturity and the growth of judgment. However, the low level of community intellectual resources in the agricultural and industrial environments of the nineteenth century handicapped citizens in the attainment of significant cognitive and formal knowledge. Books were often comparatively rare and expensive, education was abbreviated, and leisure time for studying and information gathering was limited. Post-industrial society, at some subconscious level, is driven by these deprivations experienced in the distant past and equates increased formal schooling of youth with the attainment of maturity.[42] And it assumes that the experiences that foster true adult maturity will "naturally" occur, as they did in the past. As a result of these misconceptions, we tend to measure the adequacy of child-rearing environments in terms of the formal cognitive information they provide the young, such as the "quality" and length of schooling or the accessibility of books and media. We are reluctant to ask: are the young adults who have grown up in post-industrial suburbs adequately equipped to assume genuine adult roles? We are more prone to ask: are they good at reading, writing, mathematics, and other cognitive skills? Until the former question is asked, we will not be able to fairly evaluate the meaning of modern suburban life for children.

A Proposition

The burden of this book is that the many unique characteristics of post-industrial suburbs affect children and adolescents in historically unique ways. The number and proportion of American children involved will tend to further increase, as, probably, will the intensity of the suburban effects. These effects confront suburban schools, and the colleges suburban students attend, with a series of obscure, but powerful, issues. The key element is the articulation between youth and adulthood. The issues arise from the impact of post-industrial systems on the youths' attitudes. Modern suburban environments do not provide children and adolescents with frequent and engaging occasions for them to acquire the attitudes associated with rewarding adulthood. As a result, suburban youths are increasingly prone to engage in antisocial and self-destructive conduct, since prolonged childhood or adolescence is inherently an alienating status. During such prolongation, one is *alien* to being a child, since that time is over, and one is *alien* to being an adult, since one does not feel or act like an adult. The data revealing this proposed connection between post-industrial suburbs and increasing youth alienation have not yet been definitely presented—though we have seen many data demonstrating generally increasing youth alienation. But, before the data are finally developed, sensitive analysis of the suburban environment may enable us to know what to look for, and how to begin corrective action. Without such advance planning and action, we may get ourselves inextricably committed to massive and destructive child-rearing environments.

Unquestionably, some of the factors frustrating the healthy articulation between childhood and adulthood in post-industrial suburbs also generate alienation and disorder among youths in other contemporary environments. And many of the remedies proposed later in this book may be of help to youths living in urban or rural environments which have been affected by post-industrial forces. However, some of the environmental and educational factors of post-industrial suburbs are unique. Those factors create a special concentration of problems for youths from such communities. As a result, we do not perform a service to clear analysis or to the youths themselves if we simply say that all youths from all kinds of environments face the same kinds of problems to the same degree and should be treated to the same kinds and quantities of remedies. A better approach is to recognize that different environments—and we have already demonstrated ways in which post-industrial environments are different—do create different problems that require different emphases in correction.

Some of the rhetoric of contemporary educational reform—open education, busing, career education, back to basics—relates to the issues underlying the alienation of youth. Unfortunately, the analyses supporting such reforms often fail to connect them to the realities underlying the issues. For instance, reformers often neglect to recognize the essential continuity, for many suburban youths, of high school and college education; this continuity means that frequently high school and college reforms must be thoughtfully coordinated if we wish to produce a constructive effect. Again, "back to basics" implies a return to earlier patterns of education, but a supposed focus on "basics" is only one of the many differences between traditional and modern schools. These "other differences"—greater teacher-student intimacy, a variety of student responsibilities—may have had as much to do with the "virtues" of traditional schools as did their emphasis on drill. Some of the other reforms proposed (e.g., changing systems of school financing) fail to deal with the essential challenges; for instance, in the case of financing, alienation and poor articulation are related more to what money is spent for than to the amount of expenditures. Members of very poor communities may sometimes have a high sense of integration.

To set the stage for the body of the book, let us identify an example of a problem confronting education in post-industrial environments that relates to alienation and articulation with adulthood. We can then analyze the interrelationships among this issue, the suburban community, and existing educational practices. The analytical technique demonstrated in this example will introduce some of the essential methods employed elsewhere in the book.

Affective Learning

One major learning chore of the young is to acquire the skills and attitudes possessed by competent adults. These skills and attitudes do not inevitably occur in adults, in the sense that all healthy humans inevitably can feel cold or taste pepper. Skills and attitudes leading to maturity are *learned*. Some adults learn them better than others; some learn them poorly; and some learn them not at all. The learning of such skills and attitudes is critical to good articulation between youth and adulthood.

As a result of the learning, informed youths become genuine adults. They are able to support themselves, get married and raise families, and be satisfied and constructive members of society. Some knowledge possessed by most adults is of the type usually learned in school: mathematics, reading, history. Such knowledge is termed "cognitive knowledge." However, most of the knowledge or skills possessed by adults are not usually thought of as being taught in school. This body of adult knowledge and attitudes goes under several names. For instance, it might be called "common sense" or "coping skills." John Dewey described it as "incidental learning."[43] And, in some sense it is akin to socialization to adulthood. However, since this knowledge particularly relates to the control or understanding of the emotions of ourselves or others, we will call it "affective knowledge."

"Affective knowledge" is a more neutral phrase than "coping skills" or "common sense," and such semantic neutrality is appropriate. We can learn to control or direct our emotions to attain either good or bad ends: we can learn to hate our children, to want and use harmful drugs, or to dislike work. The neutrality implicit in the phrase "affective knowledge" stimulates us to recognize that, whenever we develop emotional responses (i.e., attitudes or values), we are learning, regardless of whether the responses are "good" or "bad." And, as will be demonstrated, children and adolescents are practically always learning emotional responses, even if those responses do not constitute common sense or coping skills. Thus, in

analyzing affective learning environments, we must persistently
ask, What emotional responses are being learned and taught? Sometimes this question will enable us to perceive not only that common
sense is not being taught, but also that very harmful affective
knowledge is being transmitted.

Of course, affective knowledge is taught in schools. But the role
of the school in transmitting such knowledge can be counterproductive, since youths may be taught affective knowledge that is
not conducive to commonsensical conduct. In the past, it seems that
schools taught more useful affective, or commonsensical, knowledge than they do today. However, we can increase the quality of
affective learning in suburban schools, as will be generally discussed
elsewhere in this book. At this point, let us take one typical instance
of useful affective knowledge and

1. consider its significance in adult life;
2. see how the knowledge is ideally learned;
3. see how the knowledge is, or is not, taught in post-industrial environments; and
4. discuss the policy implications for society of a trend toward a situation where large numbers of youths lack that knowledge.

Skill at Negotiating
Consider the concept of skill at negotiating. This skill is composed
of many elements needed in life situations not directly related to
negotiating: skilled negotiators are good judges of human nature;
they must often be tactful, persuasive, and persistent, and sometimes determined and bold. In other words, negotiating skill can be
an indicator of many other important affective skills. A person unskilled at negotiation would be very likely to lack other important
interpersonal skills. But, for the moment, let us keep this broad perspective in the back of our minds and focus solely on negotiating.

Most adults should know something about negotiation. If one
wants to buy a good used car cheaply, one has to know general principles of negotiation, as well as particular points about used cars.
Negotiation can be learned. But, to become skillful, one must learn
how to ask questions and not be put off by vague answers, reject
high-pressure techniques, size up the plausibility and reliability of
sellers, have the courage to make timely and wise commitments, be
persuasive with sellers to get their price down, and live with the
results of an imperfect decision. Much modern shopping does not
require negotiation, since prices for small items are usually inflexi-
ble. However, adult life is replete with explicit and implicit nego-

tiating situations: renting and buying houses and apartments; taking jobs and getting raises; buying cars, boats, and audio equipment; and participating in law, sales, politics, and administration. For example, over 90 percent of all legal disputes are settled without judicial decisions. This means that the settlements are negotiated, and negotiating settlements is far more than simply understanding the underlying legal issues. So we can assume that a lawyer who has learned a good deal about law, but nothing about negotiating, will not be particularly competent.

In some situations, it is not evident that negotiation is possible: the potential buyer is told that there is one set price; the job seeker or employee is told that there is a fixed wage scale. However, the skillful negotiator tries to devise ways of getting around such anti-negotiating statements; thus, part of negotiating involves transforming something that appears settled into a negotiable issue.

Adults who have not learned how to negotiate will face many frustrations as they proceed through life. They will usually pay the highest price, come out on the short end of many deals, or do poorly in important jobs. They may keep feeling that people are out to get them; they may not realize that they simply have not been well trained, and that the adults around them are more skilled than they are. The frustrations arising from the lack of this skill are similar to the disappointments generated by the lack of other affective skills, for example, persuasive ability, leadership, cooperative planning, followership, creativity, knowing how and when to persist, a sense of humor. In general, these frustrations are caused by the inability of the unskilled person to cope with the demands of social life. All too often, unskilled persons conceal their lack of skill with the charge that society, or the citizens around them, are insensitive, selfish, or cruel. Instead of trying to correct their own shortcomings, they may sink into a form of paranoia, where each successive personal failure is increased proof of the malevolence of other persons or institutions.

The environment around youths in post-industrial suburbs is more deficient in resources to assist them in learning such affective skills as negotiating than are most other American environments. We can perceive this deficiency if we consider the characteristics of a model, or ideal, process for teaching youths how to negotiate.

Such a model should put youths into an environment where simple, realistic negotiations are taking place between people with significant negotiating skills—an environment such as an open-air market, a small-town general store, or maybe a one-man repair shop.

The sellers and buyers typically would be adults. In a place like this, children could see how the negotiators differ, protect their own interests, and usually stay on friendly terms. Eventually, the children could begin to buy (or sell) some things themselves. If they were slow in acquiring skills, they would lose money or goods, and so they would work hard at learning. The traditional children's summer lemonade stand—or the farm produce stand by the road—are elementary examples of this approach.

In our model, as the children grew, they could learn and apply more complex negotiation skills, as they bargained about starting wages or raises in jobs (in unbureaucratic environments), engaged in more ambitious selling or buying ventures, or participated in politically active clubs or groups where coalitions were formed, votes traded, and compromises negotiated. Because the environment would include skilled adults and less skilled youths, the beginning negotiators could improve their skills by observing and dealing with more experienced practitioners. Through the whole process, learning would be stimulated by the money and visible prestige which go to better learners, and the losses and embarrassments of poor negotiators. At the same time, the environment would not put such severe demands on young learners that they might be unduly injured by occasional failures. No failure should be so severe that the damage would discourage a reasonably resilient youth from trying again.

The ideal learning environments for negotiation that we have sketched formerly existed in many American small towns, and still exist in a few city neighborhoods, but are rarely found in modern suburban neighborhoods. In such communities, because stores and businesses are remote from homes, children rarely go to the store alone and thus are not left on their own to make buying decisions. Furthermore, stores in shopping centers usually are parts of large corporations, managed by bureaucratic, remote enterprises. Prices are fixed and not subject to negotiation. Employees are paid by centrally determined wage scales. The suburban emphasis on cleanliness and precision, and the affluent environment, discourages small, marginal enterprises that compete by offering lower or bargainable prices for services or goods. Suburban politics, as reported in the media, tends to center on intellectual or conceptual issues, as compared to the pragmatic bargaining or the deals between voting blocs associated with big-city politics.

The comparatively high incomes of many suburban families also affect the negotiating environment. When such families shop for food, or minor services, they may well buy the first quality product available, regardless of cost; the parents' per hour earnings can be so high that it is more rational for them to spend ten dollars after a twenty-minute search than to get an equivalent product for seven dollars after forty-five minutes of shopping. As a result, there is little incentive to shop or bargain for simple, visible purchases made in the presence of the young.

None of this means that there is no negotiating in the suburbs. Real estate developers negotiate. Shopping center leases are negotiated. Unions and management negotiate. Residents negotiate when they buy or sell their homes. Elaborate high-level political negotiations occur. Many suburban parents spend long hours at their remote jobs, essentially engaging in sophisticated negotiations. However, suburban negotiations are largely invisible to the children or are so elaborate, prolonged, and abstract as to be boring to all but the trained and initiated.

Of course, there are also in-the-family negotiations about children's responsibilities and rights. These exchanges have learning potential. But the potential can be greater in poorer families where parents may refuse a child's request, not because of some abstract principle, but simply because they do not believe they can afford the item being requested. When such rejections occur for the latter reason, children may still try to change their parents' mind, or work with the parents to devise some compromise. In such cases, the shortage of funds puts the problem in a bounded, tangible framework which fosters disciplined, reasonable exchanges. There is no great incentive for the child to try to stimulate guilt in the parents. The essential cause for the denial is beyond the parents' control. In a more prosperous family, many of the children's requests can be afforded, and either the request is granted and there is less to negotiate about or the parents must refuse the request "for the child's own good." The problem is that the child's "good" is a highly subjective concept. Therefore, it becomes an awkward framework for negotiation: it stimulates many children to pester, and probably many parents to finally yield, because of the problem of drawing definable lines. Of course, persistence and even stimulating guilt can be useful negotiating tactics, but only when the other party will always be available to listen and to accept guilt. In adult life, there is not infinite negotiating time, and healthy and effective adults— who tend to attain and retain power—have only a limited capability for being stimulated by guilt. Consequently, persistence in negotiation must be coupled with tact and persuasion, and guilt stimulation is valuable only as a short-run tactic.

Another flaw to in-the-family negotiating is that the children are typically only dealing with two parents. Presumably, these two people possess only a limited part of the total spectrum of negotiating skills and attitudes; indeed, we can assume that, despite the inevitable differences of temperament that married partners demonstrate, the parents will have far more in common than any other two randomly chosen adults. Thus, because of the size of the family, and its inherent homogeneity, the children are not provoked to learn a variety of ways to negotiate. In-the-family negotiating is also carried on with the understanding that all parties have love and concern for each other—the children will not be grossly cheated, and disputes are often open to reconsideration. But this very openness militates against the parents teaching their children the skills needed when they are dealing outside the family, when each negotiator wants the best deal he can get for himself or the interests he represents.

Schools and Negotiating Skills

As is evident in the contrast between the model and the modern suburban environment, many suburban youths have a special need for acquiring such affective skills as negotiation. We may hopefully imagine that this lack can be filled by the suburban educational system. Unfortunately, post-industrial schools and colleges are extremely poor environments for teaching such skills.

Many elements of school programs are mandatory: there is no choice, and skill at weighing choices is the *sine qua non* of a negotiator. Where there are program choices in school, they are often so simple as to be innocuous: should a bright student take the college preparatory program, the general program, or the distributive education program? Furthermore, course and program choices are not usually about matters with simple, direct consequences, such as How much should I charge for lemonade, or pay for a second-hand bike? Instead, school choices are about matters with vague and remote aftereffects, such as the choice between taking French or biology. Choices about such remote issues frustrate learning about negotiations, since the learners do not see clear, timely results indicating whether they were right or wrong. Also, in making their choices, the students rarely have to persuade someone else, such as a faculty member, that they should be permitted to do what they want. And persuasion is a key element of negotiating.

Furthermore, in choosing, or in engaging in their limited in-school negotiating, the students are surrounded by other students their own age; in comparison, in away-from-school negotiations, young people are usually surrounded by experienced adults or, at least, older children. Suburban students are additionally hampered in learning about negotiating from their fellow students because most suburban students come from equivalent home backgrounds and will tend to have common attitudes about what is fair and appropriate. This commonality prevents them from seeing different (and sometimes more effective) ways of looking at things or of dealing with disagreements. The development of sophisticated attitudes about choice is also handicapped when most students come from affluent homes: such students are unable to transmit useful affective perceptions to their peers. Some of the problems implicit in the preceding analysis of youth attitudes about negotiation and choice are exemplified in the following anecdote, extracted from an essay by a sixteen-year-old student.

The adolescent has to handle what's inside of himself as well as what is happening around him. Sometimes the inside feelings are so strong that he must struggle to deal rationally with his reactions. He must learn not to overreact to situations despite strong emotions, and he must watch that he doesn't hurt other people's feelings.

The emotions which demand the most energy, thought, and figuring out are ambiguous and present themselves in indirect ways. They threaten because of their obscurity. For me, anger has been one of the most demanding emotions. . . .

This same pattern of feelings can occur with peers—for example, when smoking grass in a large group, George, the typical fifteen-year-old of the 1970's, goes off from a party to smoke his dope with a couple of friends. On the way, four more friends latch on. They are not George's closest friends, but he likes them and would like to be thought well of by them. When they decide to smoke, George finds that these friends have no dope, and are expecting him to be hip, cosmic, and peaceful, and give them some of his. George may feel that they are "using" him, but he wants them to like him and think he's cool. Although George feels that they are using him in a selfish way, he also feels helpless in terms of their position (they could tease him and spread ugly rumors about him if he wasn't gen-

*erous—why not?), so he gives them some of his dope. George is
angry that he has been used and forced into a helpless position, but
he must watch out for his anger. He doesn't want an angry word or
motion of his to prove him "uncool" in front of his peers.*[44]

While the text talks about the management of anger, the anger
actually arises because of George's failure to effectively protect his
rights. His task was to firmly and tactfully protect his possessions
against his peers' incursion. He failed. His environment did not
teach him how to deal with such challenges. But not only did George
fail, his fellows—who used guilt to coerce him—are also learning
affective styles with only short-run values. When they deal with
adolescents or adults from other statuses or environments, they
may receive a rude and painful shock.

Even the teachers, the adults that children see in school, are, by
definition, deficient in bargaining experience. Schoolteaching does
not stimulate individual teachers to practice negotiating: they are
generally paid uniform wages, set by rules or a union contract; their
raises are established by set formulas; and they usually do not
negotiate about their work responsibilities.

Continuity of human relations is another element that affects
negotiating situations. When relationships between parties are
transient (e.g., many pupil-faculty and student-student situations
in large schools), effective negotiation techniques often involve dis-
honesty, overt pressure, or other immature behavior. These techniques are effective in transient situations, since the other party
may not go to the trouble to rebuke or correct occasional incidents
of mendacity or other forms of immaturity. In more permanent relationships, immature negotiating is self-defeating, for the other
party eventually retaliates. Consequently, young people trying to
learn about negotiating in large schools can be handicapped. The
youths may assume that trickery and evasion are the most important elements of negotiations, while, actually, responsibility and
accuracy are probably far more crucial because the most important
negotiations usually take place in continuing relationships (e.g.,
work, politics, business dealings).

School grading systems can also shape learning about negotiations.[45] Each student grade is, in effect, a sale-and-purchase situation between student and teacher—a negotiation. That is, the teacher asks the student to do some task and offers a grade as a reward.
Since the task or appropriate grade is often not clearly defined in
advance, part of the student's responsibility is to understand what

the teacher really wants, and/or persuade the teacher that the student's product deserves a high grade. These responsibilities for analysis and persuasion are important elements of negotiation. However, many modern schools strive to eliminate these "subjective" elements from the learning situations. The striving takes several forms. Grading systems are softened (e.g., pass/fail), so that students need not try hard to get satisfactory grades. Teachers attempt to make assignments more precise (objectives are clearly specified), so that the students' responsibilities in interpretation and persuasion are diminished. Increased reliance is given to objective, short-answer exams, so that negotiating over grades is less important. These modern grading arrangements increase the predictability of the students' in-school world; they also diminish the need for persuasion and interpersonal analysis. However, one cannot say that perfectly predictable worlds are satisfying or interesting. Furthermore, it is evident that the adult world toward which the students are moving is far from predictable. It is true that the more precise grading arrangements we have described may increase learning of cognitive skills, since students will learn these skills better if precise performance goals are specified. But the irony is that the schools seem to be increasing their systems for teaching what the students do not need to know, and to be lessening their systems for teaching affective skills that students need to know more than ever.

One other aspect of learning about negotiation in school warrants discussion. It may be suggested that an appropriate solution for the lack of student negotiating skills would be to develop a course called "How to Negotiate." Such a course would include books, lectures, pen-and-paper tests, and academic grades—that's what school courses are about. Presumably, it would be taught by a teacher who had had little real-life negotiating experience. It is likely that *some* negotiating skills could be learned through such a technique—but not many. The essential skills in negotiating relate to the negotiator's understanding of human nature—the ability to press and persuade others, to resist their blandishments in personal discussions, and to live with ambiguity. Lectures, books, tests, and grades do not stimulate us to learn these affective skills.

Undesirable Affective Learning
From the preceding outline, we can develop a model of some of the affective styles which children and adolescents from post-industrial environments may display in negotiating. They may feel particular-

ly uncomfortable in situations where they are asked to negotiate with strangers over important matters. They will approach the negotiations in a rigid fashion and expect either far too little or too much. Insufficient attention will be given to collecting information in advance or to carefully listening to the "other side." The youths may miss the chance to collect allies or to reshape the issue so as to produce a result of possible benefit to both participants. They will not display persistence in the face of strong resistance. Excessive emphasis will be given to the stimulation of guilt, and youths will be prone to practice bad faith or to attribute it to others (in inappropriate situations). And when the issue is eventually settled—by a deal being either made or rejected—the youths will tend to have a great deal of uncertainty as to whether things were handled correctly. This discomfort will lessen the savor of even a "successful" negotiation. While one may say that the affective learnings I have just outlined are the "natural" concomitants of youth, I disagree. They are the natural outcomes of certain learning environments. Some modern young people are placed in such learning environments, and others are not. When we recognize that many youths may "grow out of" affective styles that do not assist competent negotiations, we mean that, as they grow older, they may move into more heterogeneous environments than those they lived in when they were young. As a result, they may be stimulated to abandon one set of learned attitudes and to learn another set that may help them more in negotiating. Unfortunately, the old attitudes may be held too long, and serious and destructive bargains made, or other injurious commitments launched. And the longer any pattern of learning is maintained, the more it is integrated into the patterns of our life and the harder it is to abandon.

This analysis of the nature of negotiating skills has direct relevance to recent history. During the last half of the 1960's, America witnessed a dramatic series of student and youth strikes and demonstrations. Despite the vigor of the activities, they had only a transient effect on the schools, political parties, and other institutions they criticized. In comparison, during the 1930's, there was a widespread outburst of sit-down strikes and other forms of labor unrest. As a result of this adult unrest, a number of major industrial unions were formed, new and constructive labor laws were passed, and important industrial practices were changed. More recently, unrest by black adults has produced changes in the laws relating to voting rights and discrimination in employment, housing, public accommodation, and education. The real income of many groups of blacks has increased. Between 1965 and 1973, the number of black elected officials in the South increased from 110 to 1,144. In other words, adult unrest in America has often produced noteworthy change.

It is true that the youthful protestors of the sixties are no longer young, and they occupied a transient status. However, during their youth they were unable to develop persisting institutions to be of service to future youth cohorts who are presumably—if the rhetoric of the protesters was correct—still faced with many of the same challenges of unresponsive institutions. In contrast, most of the labor militants of the thirties have retired, died, or gone to other jobs, but the unions they founded are still engaging their successors.

Perhaps one reason for the inconsequence and transience of youth activism was the negotiating ineptitude of the youths involved. They lacked the skills to shape dissent into concrete, negotiable grievances, to design implementable programs, and to persuade others of the justice of their cause.[46] Furthermore, their techniques relied a great deal on guilt stimulation, and they displayed little insight or tolerance of their opponents. This ineptitude at negotiating is only one of the affective, or common sense, skills lacking in many suburban youths.

Conclusion

The preceding analysis suggests to us many ways in which post-industrial communities, and their schools, neglect or even undermine the learning of the important affective skill of negotiation. Furthermore, we can see that the forces generating this ignorance are also diminishing the learning of other related affective skills. We can derive, from such an analysis, recommendations for changes in suburban schools and communities which will assist students to learn negotiating skills. For instance, within schools, changes can be made in grading systems, student responsibilities and assignments, teacher responsibilities and reward structures, the kinds of persons who are hired as teachers, the responsibilities and selection of administrators, the way programs are structured and evaluated, and the socioeconomic and age mixture of pupils in schools and classrooms. In suburban communities, changes can be made in zoning and housing arrangements to promote greater community heterogeneity, in the retailing systems in communities to facilitate increased contact by youths with bargaining, in organizations that foster youth activities, and in community employment arrangements so that youths may be able to get more employment experience at younger ages. Individual families, themselves, can revise their child-rearing patterns. Details about the character of such changes, and a frank discussion of the time span involved, will be presented later in the book. However, at this stage, it is evident that the analysis has revealed to us new ways of looking at the problems of many suburban youths, their communities, and their education systems.

But the individual does not usually see a conspiracy by society to coerce him into certain roles. The beauty of heroes as a character-building force is that the individual, daydreaming, chooses for himself, within the opportunities the available models provide—which, fortunately for the social order, usually "just happen to be" more supporting than erosive or subversive.
—Orrin E. Klapp[1]

CHAPTER 2
How We Attain Adulthood

The preceding discussion proposed that attaining successful adult-hood meant acquiring the skills and attitudes that helped one to earn a living, enjoy work, conduct a successful courtship and mar-riage, rear healthy children, make and keep friends, and participate in community life. Of course, some chronological adults have al-ways existed who have fallen far short of attaining these ideal goals. However, we should not assume that the proportion of such adults— reared by families, communities, and societies—has remained con-stant. Indeed, a basic proposition of this book is that the proportion varies, and that modern suburbs may produce disturbingly high proportions of such immature adults.

If a social system, such as a modern suburb, produces a high pro-portion of immature adults, this outcome may cause disturbing secondary effects that can have profound social implications. Ex-ploration of those implications can establish a framework for a more extended analysis of suburban child rearing and social policy.

The Consequences of Unsuccessful Adulthood

Assume that we evaluate the significance of immature adults from an individual perspective. We would conclude that they are, by defi-nition, likely to be alienated, or apart from, the central activities and values of their society. After all, the central activities of any society that persists must always revolve around work, marriage, friends, and community life. We presume that these alienated adults are quite unhappy, although they may seek to defend or justify their status. But, regardless of the philosophical justifications, or ration-alizations, such persons may offer, we are understandably suspi-cious of the rationalizations proffered by relatively friendless people who do not like their work and who contend that their unhappiness is caused by the shortcomings of the world. Sometimes we charac-terize such attitudes as paranoia or megalomania. However, we can-not assume that all alienated adults are entirely incompetent or in-effectual. Human talents represent a complex mélange of learning and innate capacity. Thus, innately talented persons who have not learned how to integrate their talents with the values of the com-monwealth may be unhappy and angry but still influence the course of events. Artists and political demagogues represent two forms of roles sometimes adopted by such talented and alienated persons.[2] Naturally, such mischievous and gifted creators have their maxi-mum effect when high proportions of alienated persons are found throughout the community. A typical example of the alienated, but still effective, intellectual creator is Jean Jacques Rousseau. Some of the spirit of his influential and prolific writing is suggested by the following excerpt, in which he sketches an outline of an idealized totalitarian state:

He who possesses the courage to give a people institutions, must be ready to change human nature, to transform every individual, who by himself is a complete and separate whole, into a part of a greater whole from which this individual in a certain sense receives his life and character; to change the constitution of man in order to strengthen it, and to substitute for the corporeal and independent existence which we all have received from nature a merely partial and moral existence. In short, he must take from man his native individual powers and equip him with others foreign to his nature, which he cannot understand or use without the assistance of others. The more completely these natural powers are annihilated and destroyed and the greater and more enduring are the ones acquired, the more secure and more perfect is also the constitution.[3]

Even unsuccessful adults who do not try to affect public policy can still seriously corrupt community life. In any community, individual failure is never solely a personal matter. After all, much of the cost of child rearing is not paid by parents, but by taxpayers: the social collective. Some of these taxpayers are parents, others are not; even when taxpayers are parents, many taxpaying parents pay large parts of the tax share of other parents. And it is the community—not individual families—that supports schools, sanitary services, and other protective and social systems that make the infant death rate in industrial countries half that in underdeveloped nations. Thus, half the American children and adolescents now alive are surviving through the economic and social sacrifices of the polity. But if the community has helped to make life, learning, and even affluence possible for its members, it can be expected to ask the matured children—who benefited from the community sacrifices that produced these outcomes—to make equivalent contributions on behalf of other community members.

Unfortunately, unhappy and unsuccessful adults are not too likely to "repay" the contributions of the community, and, because of their failure to meet these implicit obligations, the vitality of society is sapped. In the end, many of the persons whose sacrifices and commitments rendered such great benefits to children and adolescents may be deprived of the social order and support they feel they deserve. The failure of unhappy adults to repay the communal debts they began to accrue in their childhood can be predicted with some assurance. For instance, adults who are not materially productive may go on welfare or fail to support their parents in their old age (and pass that personal obligation on to the community). Or their income may be so low that they pay meager taxes to help the community assist others. If such adults are unable to find satisfying work (partly through their lack of coping skills), their sense of personal frustration may pollute the work environment of others. And if they father or bear children whom they cannot responsibly raise, they increase the burden on other members of society.

But, suppose we agree that we wish to foster in children and adolescents the affective knowledge necessary for a satisfying adulthood. Our motives may be altruistic (incompetent adults are unhappy) or "selfish" (incompetent adults are a threat and drain to the community), but the problem is still essentially the same. The first step toward its solution is to evolve a method for analyzing environments in which children grow and learn, in order to see if they develop such skills in children. This method should be particularly aimed to analyze extrafamily environments, which in modern suburbs are historically unique and should be subject to careful analysis.

Analyzing Learning Environments

One can create a generalized model of environments that foster the learning that is necessary for a successful adulthood. It will not be important whether such environments—if they are considered at an abstract level—are composed largely of intense human interactions, such as hugs or beatings, or impersonal events, such as might be brought about by traffic light systems, school report cards, or the physical arrangements found in large supermarkets. As we will eventually see, all these systems, whether their climate is personal or abstract, can have significant learning influences.

Reinforcers

Our generalized model will first focus on the positive and aversive reinforcers that exist to foster learning in the system. Edward L. Thorndike, one of the early researchers in behaviorism, put the matter very directly: "The essentials of training of the emotional and appetitive activities is then to induce the person to make the desired response and to reward it."[4]

If these activities are taking place in a social, political, or productive system, the reinforcement process must be integrated into the system. In other words, all members of any system must be taught the norms applied throughout the system, that is, what forms of conduct are rewarded and punished. The reinforcers used are not always obvious or tangible. Still, wherever we see predictable and uniform patterns of human action, we can assume that some significant reward system is in operation.[5] In the case of traffic systems, for example, citizens gradually learn that ignoring traffic lights can subject them to serious danger or arrest. As for report cards, such communication devices—if the parents are interested in their children's schooling—can stimulate the parents to give their children serious praise or punishment for school conduct. The last example, supermarkets, requires a more extended discussion as to what may be learned by young patrons. They will learn that, while they may shop among various items offered, they cannot try to change the posted price through explicit negotiation. They do not expect the checkout clerks to cheat them (since there is no incentive for them to overcharge), nor can they persuade the clerks to lower the price. While the supermarket can be filled with employees and customers, it is not typically a place for even casual human interactions. The constant transiency of its inhabitants, the large number of persons involved, and the fact that customers are walking around aisles and sales clerks are busy checking them out mean that social exchanges are not initiated in the supermarket unless prior social relationships exist between the parties. Supermarket customers and employees learn that shopping is not an occasion for asking someone about the weather, their health, last night's television show, or the score of the ball game. In contrast to a supermarket environment, one can consider a smaller (neighborhood) store, where routine contacts over time among the smaller pool of customers and employees are relatively predictable. Thus, reinforcers exist to foster sociability. In some city neighborhoods, stores even advance personal credit to families. Such advances require the proprietor to develop insight into the customers. Conversely, if the customers want to attain the advantages associated with such credit buying, they must be able to win and keep the proprietor's confidence.

The conduct we see occurring in different environments is partly the outcome of the reinforcements in that environment. And newcomers to such environments will be stimulated to acquire the affective knowledge appropriate to that environment, in order to attain the prevailing rewards and avoid discomfort. When persons educated in one environment shift to another, they will have difficulty detecting, or responding to, the reinforcement system in the new environment. The degree of difficulty will be determined by the innate adaptability of the individual involved and the instructional effectiveness of both the old and new environments.

One of the most important reinforcers in all societies has been valuable goods and services, which individuals and institutions have distributed to persons who have displayed constructive affective skills. Thus, the goods and services stimulated the pursuit of such learning. In industrial societies, money typically serves as the substitute for these goods and services. In other words, we learn affective skills to make money to buy goods.

But the power of money (or goods and services) to act as a reinforcer is dependent on scarcity. Obtaining money to buy candy, ice cream cones, bicycles, books, and baseball gloves can motivate only if children and adolescents cannot otherwise get these goods. In comparatively affluent suburbs, money may have lost some of its value as a reinforcer. It is not that children and adolescents do not want any money, but the modest sums that they can easily earn cannot buy them the things they might fantasize about, and their simpler needs have already been satisfied by the relative generosity of their parents. Of course, some adolescents, even from affluent families, still do work for money and use the money to run an auto or to save for some ambitious project. But, unquestionably, the growth of affluence has made money a less effective reinforcer for provoking affective learning in the young, and/or compelling parents to act more deliberately in shaping a money management policy vis-à-vis their children. Deliberate policies of maintaining tight allowances for children are hard to adhere to when the children know that the money is really available for their needs, and that other families in their homogeneous neighborhood do not follow planned scarcity arrangements.

Some idea of the learning complexities generated by prosperity is suggested by a longitudinal study of the adult mental health of a small sample of Americans born during the late 1920's and raised during the depression of the 1930's. The outcome is presented in table 5. As one can see, the adults who had been raised as deprived middle-class children received the highest mental health scores.

Role Models
In addition to reinforcement, learners need constructive role models:

Table 5.
*Clinical Ratings of Men and Women on Psychological Functioning,
by Economic Deprivation and Class Origin, in Mean Scores*

Clinical ratings	Middle class		Working class	
	Nondeprived (N=25)	Deprived (N=30)	Nondeprived (N=11)	Deprived (N=26)
Ego strength	3.24	3.82	3.32	3.06
Ego integration	2.84	3.43	2.86	2.33
Utilization of endowment	2.73	3.40	3.59	2.71
Capacity for growth	2.54	3.27	2.50	2.40
Acceptance and realistic handling of impulses	2.46	3.22	2.32	2.27

Source: Glen H. Elder, *Children of the Great Depression* (Chicago: University of Chicago Press, 1974), p. 248.
Note: The difference between group means (nondeprived vs. deprived) is statistically significant ($p < .05$) on all five ratings for the middle-class subjects. Only "utilization of endowment" varied significantly by deprivation among the working-class subjects.

persons who display significant coping skills in the environment.[6] The models must be proximate, or at least accessible to the learners, and they must suggest ways in which the learners can move through a series of intermediate steps to attain the satisfactions enjoyed by the model. Obviously, prominent, successful people are not automatically useful as models. For example, in Arthur Miller's play *Death of a Salesman*, Willy Loman, the marginally successful salesman, has a fantasy dialogue with his extremely wealthy brother. Willy asks his brother, "How did you make it?" The fantasy figure replies, "When I was 21, I went out, alone, into the jungle. Two years later, when I returned, I was rich!" But the figure gives no idea of what operational steps the brother took to attain wealth.

Willy is obviously incapable of imagining and attempting the necessary intermediate steps to attaining eventual wealth. Of course, the play is partly about Willy's personal inadequacies. Still the anecdote also suggests our need to be provided with role models that point us somewhere and show us how we get there. In Mason Locke "Parson" Weems' "fabulous" biography of George Washington, we are told that Washington attained greatness partly due to his honesty as a boy. The role model presented by Weems focuses on a remote and heroic figure. Still, unlike Willy's brother, Weems' image of Washington offers children concrete steps (e.g., tell the truth) they can take at the ages of six, seven, and eight to become more like a hero. Of course, one does not become a great hero just by telling the truth, but it probably is a good first step. Although not all young people will become great persons, if they have learned to tell the truth even when it hurts, they have learned an important affective skill. Gradually, they may also learn to be both truthful and tactful, and, still later, they may learn to plan their conduct so that they do not commit actions that they will be embarrassed to describe later in a truthful fashion. All these learnings can have a great deal to do with successful adulthood.

The discussion about role models has been directed at literary figures. But the same principles apply to parents, adult friends, and relatives of children and adolescents, and to public and entertainment figures. The model must represent a desirable status to the learner, and the conduct of the model must instruct the learner how to proceed through a series of incremental steps that plausibly relate to the eventual outcome. It is not crucial that the learner eventually attain the exalted status reached by the model. George Washington was a useful model to many youths who never became president. Youths start off copying one model and shift to others, as circumstances and their own self-knowledge change. Still, all models that have general application can be subjected to the question, Are the incremental steps they promote helpful?

The role models available in any learning environment can be identified. We can estimate their degree of attraction to children and adolescents. We can look carefully to see if there are plausible, constructive, and rewarding intermediate steps to lead followers from immaturity toward growth. And we can also ask if the conduct displayed by the models ultimately fosters adult attitudes and skills in the young.

Obviously, suburban environments have many shortcomings apropos of role models. Children are usually raised remote from locations, such as work sites, where adults are usually seen displaying skills. Because they are especially remote from their parents' work sites, they cannot observe the intermediate steps related to successfully practicing the parents' work role. And, when parents are in managerial, professional, or white-collar work, those subskills are often difficult for children to even identify. For instance, how does a doctor actually practice the art of screening patients' requests for emergency help? Who should come first, or second, or who can be ignored, and why? Applying such priorities is often a central work skill, but only prolonged and close observation can instruct any observer in that skill. Without such observation, the observer may only see a chaotic and arbitrary environment that discourages emulation. Actually, the one class of adults that children routinely see at their jobs is teachers. It is thus not surprising that a 1974 study showed that 23 percent of American college students planned to go into teaching—at a time when there was a widely recognized oversupply in the field.[7] Obviously, many of these students have unrealistic aspirations. However, since the range of career role models they are close to is highly limited, their choice is understandable. What other alternatives have they been given a chance to observe? Unfortunately, the pursuit of teaching and social service related roles—so ideologically popular with students—also tends to reinforce them to seek further formal education, typically a prerequisite to these professions. By prolonging their education, the students are further isolated from contacts with noneducator role models—though such different role models may actually offer to them the kind of examples they need.

But adult role models need not be engaged in paid work to offer rewarding instruction to the young. Anytime the young are able to observe adults in serious social interaction, they can acquire powerful images of the nature of adult conduct. For example, a Kikuyu tribesman from Kenya, who eventually attained a formal education, offered this description of his youth: "Father would let me go to sleep in the men's house even though the men were still discussing. Some of the other boys' fathers made them stay awake until all the male guests had left. . . . We learned much in the men's house—of stories and legends of the Kikuyu, of riddles, and of men's affairs. That was where we learned how to be men when we grew up."[8] In modern suburbs, much of the out-of-the-home adult social interaction occurs either on the job or at some site beyond walking distance from the home. Naturally, children are usually absent from such occasions.

The age homogeneity typical of suburbs also deprives children of easy contacts with another important class of role models: young adults—in their twenties—who have passed through school and are moving into careers and marriage. Such models might present useful incremental alternatives to suburban youths, since by the time such youths are old enough to be seriously interested in careers and marriage their parents—perhaps in their mid-thirties—are already well established. In the eyes of the children, there is an enormous experiential gap between their perspective and that of their parents. Encouraging young adults to act as role models for adolescents might also provide these adults with a valuable and maturing experience. Helping to shape someone else's character is a demanding and rewarding responsibility; fostering such experiences might encourage some young adults to be more concerned about their own conduct and values.

Community
Acquiring an understanding of, and commitment to, community is also a critical adult affective skill. Work, marriage, and community engagement are all important adult responsibilities. To successfully carry them out, an adult needs to be able to make judicious commitments and accept a sense of collective responsibility for the progress of some group enterprise. At the very least, we should hope that adults see such collective enterprises as important and rewarding. Of course, it is notorious that not all jobs, marriages, or communities are important and rewarding. But it is also true that many workers, spouses, and community members fail to take effective steps that could significantly enrich their own communal lives. Sometimes such steps require adults to have the courage to refuse to join or to quit, sometimes they need the insight to change themselves, and sometimes they can bring about significant change in their microcommunity. But regardless of the step that is appropriate, it is never correct to place all the blame for a sterile community on the community as an entity or concept, as compared to finding fault with the affective skills of many of its individual members.

While living in a community, to a degree, requires an amalgam of skills—tact, persistence, discretion—we may also hypothesize the existence of an overriding affective skill: the ability and desire to satisfyingly participate in corporate life. This skill will stimulate the development of other related skills and may enable us to persevere in efforts to help others learn similar skills. Thus, the inculcation of a procommunity attitude in citizens can be a precondition to the creation of any social environments in which people learn constructive affective skills.

The family provides children with the basic unit for community experience. It asks its members to share sacrifices and pleasures and offers emotional and material rewards that may be greater than the sum of the individual contributions. However, the family can only be the children's first step in learning about community. The number of persons participating in a nuclear family is typically small, the range of responsibilities it accepts are limited, and the children have not deliberately chosen to associate with their family (and thus have not practiced making and keeping conscious collective commitments).

Living, working, or playing in any communal environment is not easy. The problem is compounded when the participants must make a deliberate decision of whether to join the community. Frequently, such decisions carry with them some element of commitment: if you join, you have to stay for a long period of time or be subject to a severe penalty for leaving early.[9] The commitment requirement typically exists to protect other community members, who perceive that their community environment will be eroded if it is filled with transient, uninformed, and uncommitted persons. There are many examples of this connection between commitment and community: marriage, military service, certain kinds of training programs, or fraternal organizations with demanding initiation processes. At a national level, when we maintain tax policies that foster home-ownership—as opposed to tenancy—one motive for the policies is presumably our desire to encourage the family's geographic stability: buying a home is a form of commitment to a neighborhood, and a neighborhood of homeowners may be more of a community than a neighborhood of tenants.

Children learn about commitment and community (beyond their family experiences) by being in environments where they are required to make commitments, where breaches of commitments are costly, and where the common ties created by the making and keeping of commitments are ultimately seen as rewarding. The creation and maintenance of such communities for children and adolescents take a high level of affective skill: the creators and maintainers must judiciously use rewards and punishments that reach both individuals and groups; there must be incentives for the young to take the risk of making commitments; adequate information must be given to potential committors, so they learn to look (somewhat) before they leap; breaches of commitment must be subject to appropriate penalties; and symbols must be used—uniforms, badges, songs, ceremonies—to enhance the postcommitment sense of collective identity. Sports and adult-managed youth groups exemplify the ways such systems reach the young. Because of the complexity of the process, effective systems to promote community and commitment require ultimate adult management. In other words, although many elements of the enterprise may be under adolescent control, the basic structure should be designed and maintained by adults: for example, adults set aside and create the playing field, provide for the meeting place, pay the salary of the supervisor, teach newcomers the rules of the game, or finance the uniforms that identify the boundaries of the community.[10]

Work, church, school, sports, ethnic group, and neighborhood are the typical communal systems that have affected American youths. They are systems that have had traditions and are largely adult structured. Many of these systems, such as work, have lost some salience for all American youths. Some of the systems have especially lost salience in modern suburbs.

Churches, for instance, are rarely within walking distance of the modern suburban home. Furthermore, research has suggested that more affluent and better educated persons, though they may maintain church affiliation, focus on the rational, cognitive, and social service elements of religious activities—as opposed to the affective, ceremonial, and expressive.[11] This focus should lessen the appeal of churches to the young as community building forces, since community building requires intensity, expressive elements, and powerful symbols: as it were, a certain degree of parochialism. We should not expect modern suburban churches to usually provide such elements.

School spirit—the essence of the school as a community—is undermined by a focus on cognition and individualism. Many current trends in modern education, especially in schools emphasizing college preparation, have focused on cognition and individualism. College admission is essentially determined by scores on cognitive tests, and service in school activities is often given little or no weight in the application review process. The school is thus stimulated to give first consideration to improving students' scores. This stimulates the evolution of an environment in which school spirit is not rewarded and is looked down upon as unsophisticated.[12] Suburban schools, especially those in more affluent suburbs, give high emphasis to college preparation.

The growth of compulsory education, and the evolution of "compulsory college" for youths from certain classes, has also undermined the tradition of school and college spirit. In late adolescence, there is a high symbolic and (genuine) learning value attached to being able to choose commitments—or to choose not to make them. When high school attendance is mandatory, and the real degree of choice around college attendance for many youths is nil, adolescents may try to define themselves by rejecting the community they have been "drafted" into. This is not to say that all communities must be voluntary. However, earlier school and college traditions were founded on an assumption of voluntarism, and that voluntarism has now disappeared; community will be hard to maintain unless this discrepancy is frankly confronted and the system redesigned.

In the case of ethnicity, its more vital elements relate to people's generational proximity to a foreign country. The farther back persons can trace their family's emigration to America, the less likely they will speak a foreign language learned at home, or English with an accent; know relatives born in the Old Country; or feel strong ties with an ethnically oriented religion. And, between 1920 and 1970, the percentage of white Americans having one or both parents foreign-born declined from 39 percent to 6 percent.[13] Evidently, some ethnic sense persists, even after these ties have declined, and some suburbs—because of their homogeneous character—actually have strong traditional ethnic elements. However, while third-generation ethnicity may serve some symbolic character, it will lack much of the force associated with first-generation ethnicity. After all, ethnicity is not an idea but a way of life; and when the critical elements of that way of life are not routinely practiced, the community identification generated by such traditions is less tangible. The decline of ethnic practices in the home can have a twofold effect: children will have a less tangible sense of their own communal identity, and children from nonethnic families (who may, in other American environments, at least have known practicing "ethnics") will not have a contrasting norm against which to define their own community. Homogeneous, comparatively affluent suburbs are less likely to bring children in contact with the vital traditions of ethnicity.

Sports are still an important community-building element for many suburban youngsters, and many suburban parents and schools actively assist in maintaining such systems. Still, criticisms are sometimes proffered as to whether the programs engage the medium skilled as well as the highly skilled youth. When there are very large high schools, *the* school team can only use a small fraction of the students, while smaller schools provide an athletic role for all but the most incompetent.[14] Of course, most suburban high schools are very large. Furthermore, the low population density of many suburbs—as compared to central cities—means that many children do not live within easy walking distance of a site for organized recreation, for example, a ball field, a youth center. Thus, many sports activities require a high degree of parental involvement, since parents often must drive children to the site. Then, they stay to watch or to help run the game. Under these circumstances, children represent not only their teams, or their communities, but also their individual parents. And the parents are not always oriented toward the whole team, but toward the performance of their individual child. These elements create complicated individualizing tensions in an essentially collective activity.

The quality of neighborhood life in modern suburbs is mottled. When the community is defined by automobile travel, the neighborhood of the children may be significantly different than that of the adults. Also, some suburban areas are not physically defined in an apparent sense: there is often no point of demarcation where one community ends, and another begins. This is what is referred to as urban sprawl. But this lack of definition makes it harder to sense whether one belongs one place or another, or whether one really lives in any neighborhood at all.[15] The prolific political subdivisions of typical suburbs—school districts, county lines, communities that share common police services—also handicap the development of any strong sense of place.[16] Someone who lives in three or four jurisdictions actually lives in none. The persistent subdividing of the school to foster more rational operation—preschool, elementary school, junior high, and senior high—further diminishes the forces promoting a sense of locational identity. And when a family has several children at different school levels, more complications are generated. At some point, most parents abandon serious efforts of trying to stay in touch with these institutions and resign themselves to staying away unless disaster occurs. But such understandable patterns of withdrawal do not enable the children to see that communities are systems to be enjoyed, that they generate tangible obligations to be met, and that their priorities can be reshaped by their members.

Diversity
Diversity is another significant factor in environments that foster healthy affective learning. There is a great deal of experimental and field work on the learning consequences of diversity, but the data present a somewhat clouded picture.[17] Sometimes people learn tolerance and affection from prolonged, and even forced, intimacy with persons having different backgrounds and values—and sometimes such contacts breed increased hostility. The ambiguous data invite a broader and more theoretical construction.

Diversity fosters constructive affective learning, if it does not seriously threaten the identity and self-esteem of the learners involved.

On the other hand, only trivial learning will occur if the diversity is so modest or of such low intensity that no significant emotional demands are made on learners. The passage between this Scylla and Charybdis is not easy. If the diversity is excessive, the participants will be excited to fear and anger and will either flee from, or hate, or suspect the intrusive persons or experiences. If the diversity is too modest—and all that occurs is tokenism—people will continue their old ways and treat the diversity as a form of quaintness or novelty.

The inherent human need to limit and control diversity means that people (particularly suburban children and adolescents) cannot be surrounded by large, powerful, persisting doses of diversity. It will just become unmanageable. But without some diversity, children "learn" to routinely expect sameness, a dangerous expectation that is not consonant with adult reality. Diversity must be introduced in manageable amounts. This inevitably raises the question of priorities. If we cannot bring an infinite number of different things and persons into a learning environment, what few kinds of diversifying contacts will we choose to foster?

Perhaps a useful rule is to first consider the kinds of adults and children that contemporary suburban adolescents will probably come in touch with when they are between the ages of (let us say) 20–35. What age cohorts and socioeconomic statuses will such persons represent? They may include infants—the children of these former adolescents; elderly people—the aged parents of former adolescents; and very effective and wealthy people and poor people— their bosses and varied subordinates. Unquestionably, for most adolescents in modern suburbs these persons represent a far greater diversity than they will come close to in their schools or communities.

Some of the themes raised in the discussion of community have relevance to the analysis of manageable diversity. For instance, when commitment is coupled with the development and maintenance of community, the promotion of diversity is subject to moderating forces: new members are careful about joining communities that demand commitment, and we cannot hope to easily foster accelerated diversity. But if we can encourage any degree of diversity within powerful communities, we can accrue valuable benefits: when people are committed, and diversity appears, they are prone to try to work things out, as compared to running away. But we have to be careful. If diversity creates excessive stress in a powerful community, the bonds of commitment may drive community members to intense resentment toward the alien body from which they cannot flee. And so the element of legitimacy—which fosters the deliberated, moderated promotion of diversity—is important when we strive to increase diversity.

But diversity is more than a matter of contrasting persons: it can also mean contrasting forms of social interaction. Presumably, the same rule of moderation applies to such situational contrasts as applies to personal contrasts: some diverse situations are good, but too many are too much. To evoke rules for evaluation, we must first consider the kinds of social interactions that will eventually be thrust on contemporary adolescents when they are between the ages of 20–35. In one sense, these interactions will be characterized by an increased variety of personal contacts; increasing the personal diversity around modern suburban youths will thus simultaneously increase their ability to constructively deal with more varied kinds of social interaction. But increasing interpersonal variety will not be enough. For example, assume that we greatly increased the variety of persons who became teachers, but they all still had traditional teaching responsibilities. That is, they oversaw groups of children and adolescents who talked, wrote, and read about events and received grades for their conduct. While diversifying the personalities of these teachers might be constructive, it would not satisfy the students' needs to move from talking, writing, and reading to doing and seeing tangible consequences from their actions. Youth environments can be analyzed to discover the variety of interactive demands now thrust on their inhabitants, as compared to those they will face as adults. Among suburban youths, presumably, we would discover that they have inadequate experiences in intergenerational communal activities, involving either small (one-to-one) or large groups, especially groups dedicated to attaining some important common goal; protecting themselves from persons who seek to take advantage of them; teaching others; accepting responsibility when their personal failure can generate significant consequences for others; receiving orders or advice from persons who are not teachers but bosses, peers, or subordinates; and so on.[18]

The Fallacy of Natural Learning

The model that has just been sketched has analyzed the learning of affective skills in a highly formalistic fashion. It assumes we can and should deliberately manipulate the environments around children and adolescents to move them in directions we deem desirable, either for their individual benefit or for broader social purposes. From this presentation, one might assume that learning always requires deliberate manipulation and planning. This is incorrect. Much human learning is the incidental product of typical human interaction. For instance, children usually learn to talk by being maintained in an environment which contains many persons who talk and pay some attention to them. Gradually, the children perceive that, if they acquire speech, they will attain increased control over this environment, and growing satisfaction. From this combination of models and reinforcement, children "naturally" learn speech. But if such models and reinforcement were not available—as has occurred to some few children raised away from routine human contact—the children "naturally" do not learn speech.

Or, to put the matter on a larger plane, what we characterize as "natural" is essentially the predictable outcome of an environment. However, it is not inevitable that environments that generate such "natural" outcomes must surround children or other learners. For instance, it is technologically possible to design an environment in which a child would be raised to physical maturity without significant human contact. Or, at other levels, we can—and have—created environments that surround children with different experiences than those that typically reinforced them in the past. And what will they "naturally" learn in these environments?

While this analysis appears to have philosophical implications, the fact of the matter is that such manipulative conduct on our part is inevitable. We can no more seriously debate the rightness of shaping children than we can debate the rightness of continuing to breathe—and thus possibly using up some of the oxygen in the air. It is true that some philosophers and ontologists have debated such issues as continuing to breathe, too, but when we overhear such discussions, we do not expect any of the participants to actually decide to stop breathing as a result of their conclusions. Similarly, no one who now disputes the rightness of "shaping" children is going to refuse to shape them, if and when they attain positions of authority— as parents, teachers, community planners, or political leaders. They may shift the modes of shaping they apply, or the ends they attain, but we could only absolutely stop shaping children if we let them die—and we will not choose to have that happen.

Readers may also wonder how other societies have succeeded in raising children into healthy childhood without recourse to such formalistic analysis. The bald fact is that post-industrial society does not operationally use—or perhaps even "know"—all the knowledge that has been acquired by our ancestors and by other cultures. In discovering new values, we have sometimes obscured old learning.

The contradictions that underlie post-industrial society have made it hard for us to perceive some public issues in a realistic, effective framework. Our individualism and materialism (and perhaps our hedonism) have handicapped us from using authority and judicious deprivation to instruct our young. Our focus on cognition has gotten in the way of applying common sense when it is not buttressed by elaborate and difficult-to-develop data, and the same focus has made us ill at ease in frankly aiming to shape the values in addition to the I.Q.'s of our young. To put the issue starkly, the statistics already presented about alienation among youth demonstrate the steady increase of self-destructive and other-destructive conduct among our young. This increase has occurred despite the concurrent increases in medical knowledge, affluence, and formal education. Evidently, adults and their institutions in more "ignorant," poorer, and less educated societies (or in earlier periods of our history) "knew" and were doing some correct things with their children that we are not now doing. Perhaps the folk wisdom of such earlier societies can give us a clue to what we have forgotten.

Most of such wisdom is highly prescriptive in its approach. For instance, many popular traditional concepts, such as "bad companions," and proverbs, such as "a rolling stone gathers no moss," vividly articulate basic behavioralistic themes—"bad companions" refers to appropriate models, and a "rolling stone" is someone who will not make a commitment. The following exchange, overheard by a Westerner, between two contemporary young African teachers and their tribal chief expresses some of these traditional social concerns with affective learning in an eloquent fashion.

The teachers bent one knee as they gave him the customary greeting, waiting in silence until he spoke.
"How is your school?"
"The classes are full and the children are learning well, O Chief."
"How do they behave?"
"Like Ngoni children, O Chief."
"What do they learn?"
"They learn reading, writing, arithmetic, scripture, geography and drill, O Chief."
"Is that education?"
"It is education, O Chief."
"No! No! No! Education is very broad, very deep. It is not only in the books, it is learning how to live. I am an old man now. When I was a boy I went with the Ngoni army against the Bemba. Then the

mission came and I went to school. I became a teacher. Then I was chief. Then the government came. I have seen our country change, and now there are many schools and many young men go away to work to find money. I tell you that Ngoni children must learn how to live and how to build up our land, not only to work and earn money. Do you hear?"

"Yes, O Chief."[19]

We should also recognize that we are looking at history from the perspective of the current "winners," the societies and social systems that are now existing. Many cultures and social groups have "lost"; they are extinct. Either all their members and descendants have died or their descendants have so changed their values—like the Huguenots that emigrated to America in the eighteenth century—that their ancestors would not recognize them. One cause for the extermination or radical transformation of cultures is their failure to produce successive cohorts dedicated to the perpetuation of the culture. Oftentimes, the failure is the product of dramatic technological or social change, or outside intervention. Thus, the decline of the buffalo herds undermined the core of the Plains Indians' culture and made it difficult for them to transmit their traditions to their descendants, and the introduction of compulsory formal education (which must take place away from the tribe) among the Point Barrow Eskimos of Alaska is eroding the substance of their hunting culture.[20] Sometimes the adults in these affected cultures have welcomed the changes, for their benefits—the introduction of modern medicine into many primitive cultures has rendered important benefits to many adults, but concurrently enormously increased the rate of population growth and the socialization problems of the youth of the society. However, in the long run, the decline in the process of cultural transmission can be both psychically and physically dangerous to all persons who are alive when the inadequate adults attain physical and chronological maturity.

Of course, one might assume that a new and better culture will be formed by the cohorts disaffiliated from their parents' culture. But that is not necessarily the case. The information we have about alcoholism, suicide, and crime rates among American Indians indicates that sometimes the extinction of one culture can lead to the creation of an alienated underclass that is so angry and rootless it cannot belong to the future or the past. Dramatic changes around the young can be either good or bad. Change, per se, is not progress, unless we are willing to say that the word *progress* itself is a neutral term. Furthermore, the value of any change is partly dependent on its relationship to the total culture of the environment. Western society has had hundreds of years to develop a modus vivendi with formal schooling: but when the hunting culture of the Alaskan Eskimos had to adapt to the same system in twenty-five years, it is not surprising that the effects have been disastrous. Again, Westerners have dealt with alcohol for two thousand years and have developed moderately successful ways of integrating it into their culture. But this partial success is no guarantee that American Indians will have equivalent success when they must make an equivalent adaptation in two hundred years.

Thus, formalistic approaches to policies to encourage useful affective learning are necessary when societies are faced with events that change basic existing procedures. The development of modern suburbs represents a change of that scope. On such occasions, systems that have been taken for granted must be deliberately analyzed. Sometimes, the outcome may be a strong affirmation of things that were simply assumed in the past. Sometimes, it may lead to the reversal of recent changes that were injudiciously adopted. And, sometimes, gradual and even dramatic changes may be accepted and encouraged. But, regardless of the outcomes, the proposition is that, unlike the American Indians, we may have some choices: our intruders are not powerful military invaders but technologies which enable us to fulfill many of our fantasized desires. And, just like the Indians, we may be wise to refuse—if we can—the gratifications that have been proffered. The choice is ours.

Learning Hurts

Another premise underlying the model warrants explicit discussion: that most learning is painful. Learning often hurts. The proposition flies in the face of a great deal of popular cant about the joy of learning, the pleasures of discovery, and so on.

Unquestionably, there is some human satisfaction obtained from perceiving or experiencing novelty.[21] And experiencing novelty is a form of learning. However, the word *novelty* also implies a new occurrence of only modest importance. And the more significant the new information, the more likely it is to be resisted by the learner. When we talk about the resistance to innovation, and reflect on the controversy that has often surrounded the announcement of now accepted scientific discoveries, we are simply considering instances of human resistance to avoid the pain of learning. If we contend that the new information is wrong, we can ignore it, not learn, and escape pain.

Resistance to serious learning is an essentially healthy posture. It means that we examine important new ideas and propositions with care before integrating them into our lives. And since important ideas, by definition, are those that should compel us to reorganize our life patterns, it also means that our life patterns (due to this tendency of resistance) will be relatively predictable. From that predictability flows certitude in human relations, which lends consistency to social life. Without that consistency, human cohesion might be impossible, and the species could cease to exist.

Operationally, the preceding discussion means that, if we want to impart significant, and perhaps novel, ideas to children and adolescents, we must be prepared to design pervasive, persistent, and highly reinforcing learning systems. When the environment of modern suburbs reinforces highly individualistic and withdrawn attitudes, and we wish to counter these trends, words alone, or discussion about the pleasures of group support and commitment, will have only modest impact. Of course, it is possible that we may win a degree of intellectual support among some students who are intrigued by the appeal of community. But as the operational implications of these proposals appear, the students will discover that they are not simply being asked to write papers about the joys of community, but to learn how to actually live and work within a group. At that point, they are being asked to move from observing novelty to absorbing serious new affective learning. The process must be carefully and powerfully designed to deal with the resistance that will arise. Substantial reinforcers must be provided. They must reach a level of deep emotional appeal and rely on symbols; physical touchings; ceremonies; persistent, proximate personal relations; and the entire panoply that has been used by other societies—and earlier American educational systems—to overcome the inherent and healthy resistance to significant affective learning.

But after we have confronted the pain of serious learning, we should also recognize the "pain" of nonlearning, or constant sameness. Typically, we call such sameness boredom. And just as organisms will strive to avoid deep learning, so will they strive to avoid boredom, or the absence of stimulation. Occasional boredom is part of the stuff of life; but persistent, prolonged boredom creates intense anxiety and frustration. And so boredom may be a more dangerous status than ignorance. To escape boredom, individuals may attempt many dangerous outlets: drugs, alcohol, reckless sexual experimentation, or the dramatic and brutal release of aggression. Sometimes the aggression is directed at others and sometimes at the self in the form of suicide and other modes of deep self-injury. Of course, persons seeking an outlet from boredom do not always recognize their basic disability; they may simply feel a deep sense of dis-ease and a latent yearning for an emotional outlet. But boredom can often be diagnosed as the root cause, if we carefully analyze the day-to-day activities of the actors and seek to see if they have regular structures for the focus and release of their emotions, for example, human aggression or affection.

The limited research that has been done on adolescents in modern suburbs has demonstrated one palpable fact: they are very bored.[22] This is not surprising. Their environments have high levels of rationality and they are not engaged in activities that stimulate significant emotional engagement or reward. Furthermore, their contacts with diversity, significant role models, and constructive affective learning demands are all quite limited. In many ways, these youths see themselves as emotionally "marking time." Finally, the young in modern suburbs lack the affective skills that might enable them to find constructive stimulation even in such an environment, or move (all or part of the time) to more stimulating environments.

We thus have a highly unstable situation, in which people are bored and are given few directions or resources to do anything productive about it. To quote one traditional proverb, "Idle hands do the devil's work."

What about Values Education?

At the moment of this writing, "values education" is an innovation of widespread interest to educators. It might be appropriate here to discuss its relevance to the approaches proposed in this book. Like many new educational developments, one of the appeals of values education is its very ambiguity. In one sense, as we will see, schools must always engage in values education, and so one simple definition of the approach—teaching students about right and wrong— is so obvious as to render the concept of "innovation" meaningless. Therefore, I will, somewhat arbitrarily, present and justify a definition which I believe characterizes the spirit of the current movement, and will follow it with a critical discussion of its implications.

Pedagogically, values education is contemporarily used to describe curricula (or lessons) which invite students to analyze, discuss, and assess the value implications of various acts—in other words, to talk about values as compared to doing good. In such classes, teachers are expected to refrain from interjecting their own values and merely to present a challenging, value-laden problem. They are further expected to ensure that the discussion adequately explores the various alternative resolutions and their value implications. Supposedly, the teachers' self-restraint is required so that they do not impose their personal values upon the young students—such intrusion would be an act of disregard for the students' personal uniqueness.

An example of this approach is demonstrated in the following typical review which appeared in a periodical that assesses curriculum materials for teachers.[23] First, the review describes how the particular values curriculum—prepared for students from the fourth to the seventh grade—presents, through filmstrips and texts, a number of value-relevant incidents: shoplifting, pranks, and cheating in school. These materials are designed to provoke class discussions which are supervised by the teacher. The reviewer notes that the materials ideally should be accompanied by a guide for teachers which would describe "methods for teaching moral issues to clarify rather than impose them." The review, with its own implicit value position, is meant to help teachers in their selection and use of values education materials.

The literal language of the review suggests that teachers should not impose their views about shoplifting or cheating, but merely help students "clarify" their own values. After all, the reviewer implies, there are pros as well as cons on these issues: for example, most cheaters and shoplifters are not caught; their actions save them time and money; the first time one is caught, he or she will usually be given only a warning. But this is all preposterous. One cannot seriously imagine any teacher suggesting to students that the pros for shoplifting deserve consideration. (Or can one?) The giving of such consideration in discussion implies that the breaking of the law deserves the same respect given to its observance. This is hardly a message to give to a ten-year-old. If adults do not understand this, the issue is beyond discussion with them.

In other writings about values education, it is suggested that students can be taught to make independent, deductive value judgments that will enable them to attain gradually increasingly higher levels of "morality." The stress on independent judgments—supposedly free from pressures toward conformity—is part of the rationale underlying the above remarks about "clarifying rather than imposing" values. Were teachers so to impose, they would be directing the students toward conformity rather than growth in self-actualized values.[24]

It is obvious that these proposals about values education are pervaded with value-laden words: *impose, conformity,* and *self-actualized.* In one sense, this is proper, for values are emotional subjects. Unfortunately, the proponents of values education often fail to realize that such words do not stimulate analysis but polarization. Perhaps the provocative words are used because the proposals would not stand up well to analysis. For instance, we can engage in some mind-stretching word substitution. For "impose," we can say "make people obey the law"; for "conformity," we can substitute "willingness to see the wisdom in someone else's position"; and for "self-actualize," we can talk about "receiving gratification from doing what we enjoy."

As suggested earlier, schools must always engage in values education if, by the term, we mean making children conscious of the values essential to collective life. This responsibility is inescapable. A number of people cannot work simultaneously in the same school building without a unanimous acceptance of certain common values. If students frequently cheat, exams are meaningless. If students vandalize the restrooms, the rooms become filthy. If students break into each other's lockers, or sell drugs, the environment becomes chaotic and dehumanizing. Of course, teachers and other students must compel potentially disruptive students to conform to certain basic principles. People must be indoctrinated, if you will, to obey the law. One hopes that they will see its wisdom and understand how such obedience is in their interest. However, regardless of the rational unacceptability of such inhibitions to some few deviants, the overwhelming majority of students, teachers, and parents are entitled to demand lawful conduct from others. Now it is true that some values issues are unquestionably more complicated than others, and that sometimes the external guidance we receive is neither clear nor prompt. Thus, as children grow up, they should acquire increasing ability to resolve complex values issues with wisdom. Most societies have had a common means of dealing with this problem. Essentially, they assume that when individuals are faced with temptation there is a danger that they will yield and then discover some "out" or excuse to rationalize their selfish behavior. To avoid this outcome, societies try to diminish the ambiguity in value conflict situations: they increase the number of generally accepted and disseminated social norms and so lessen the areas of individual discretion in tempting situations. Finally, when individuals are confronted with inescapable and relatively original temptations, societies typically strive to identify role models whose conduct they hope the tempted persons will emulate. But the thought that persons who are tempted to take some improper action to their own advantage should typically govern their decisions by vague, undefined, highly personalized standards—and by the desire to escape "conformity"—would be anathema. The expectation would be that persons acting according to such premises might often do what is most gratifying to them and invent some theory to explain why their conduct was right. But the contemporary approach to values education does invite such self-justifying conduct. Perhaps one might say that it reflects a rather noble—or utopian or naïve—perspective of human nature. In any event, there is no significant body of research that suggests that students who do "well" in values education are any more likely to transform such abstract, verbal talents into concrete, good conduct.[25] All that the available research shows, thus far, is that students with higher I.Q.'s tend to do better in analyzing values questions.

In addition, while there is no research on them, the following propositions may be worthy of consideration here. Many adults want schools to "improve" students' values, but they are rather vague about what they positively want to be done. Many publishers of curriculum materials like to produce new texts, especially if they are likely to have a high rate of obsolescence. Many students, in the short run, prefer teachers who say, "Whatever you think is as good and valuable as whatever anyone else thinks." Some teachers feel more at ease when they are not responsible for holding students to certain standards of conduct.

The reader may correctly infer that this book is about the values students reveal through conduct rather than through their verbal analyses; that is, are they, in their day-to-day behavior, kind, polite, generous, and truthful. Furthermore, the book assumes that parents and adults in general must accept authority and responsibility for determining much of the "shape" of any child's mind and values. This role is inescapable. Before children have attained the age of discretion—let us say, sixteen—we have already decided for them their native language, most of their cultural attitudes and values, much of their sense of right and wrong (e.g., stealing, cheating, engaging in arson are bad), their attitudes toward work, and so on. These critical elements of human character have been "decided" because the children have been given little or no choice over them; they have simply accepted—or been reinforced to accept—what was put before them. After such acceptance, there is little chance that most children, at the age of discretion, will choose to become exiles, thieves, or drifters. Putting unrealistic romanticism aside, the obvious fact is that "the choices" available to persons at the age of sixteen have been dramatically inhibited by their place of birth, their family, and their community. This is inevitable and unlamentable. The most serious "wrongs" relating to such inhibitions occur only when adults deny that they engage in these proxy choices, or when they fail to analyze the full implications of such situations. When such irresponsible denials are made, children can be tempted to test boundaries that should not be tested, often to their own injury and sometimes to the injury of others.

Of course, not all constraints that adults place around children are wise or good.[26] Societies, therefore, also generally develop various protective devices to shield children from parental excesses and to assist them over the handicaps generated from excessive childhood deprivation. But such interventionist techniques must be used with discretion. Society will never possess the resources to intervene in the lives of most children and their families. Thus, educational approaches that imply wholesale disregard for the values and attitudes of the parents of minors—as is sometimes suggested by values education—can usually only stir up confusion and mischief. These approaches can rarely present to minors realistic alternatives to the fact that they are the children of their parents—with all the strengths and limitations that implies. None of this is said to preclude adaptation and incremental change from one generation to the next. But successive generations can no more escape being powerfully influenced by their predecessors than they can seriously weigh the repeal of the law of gravity. The task of the school is to take this base of parental values as a given and to work with it to help students to adapt to social life. This means that they must learn to resist the inevitable siren song of temptation, whether its guise is "You know better than they do" or "All values, whether generous or selfish, are equally acceptable and to be respected."

Applying the Model to Different Environments

The proposed analytic model contained several elements: reinforcement, role models, community, and diversity. It will be instructive to apply these elements to summarily analyze the affective learning implications of two environments found in contemporary America: rural areas and central cities. This analysis will both test the model and give us a perspective to understand the affective learning problems arising in modern suburbs.

Many nonacademic activities of rural children are observed and reinforced by adults or older children. Smaller schools, farm work, and small-town intimacy all serve to promote increased adult observation of the conduct of children and youths, and to stimulate adults to try and encourage such activities into socially productive channels.[27] Earlier generations of American novelists—Sherwood Anderson, Sinclair Lewis—bitterly satirized some of these tendencies. But other novelists, such as William Faulkner, Thomas Wolfe, and Samuel Clemens, have described small-town and rural life in more affectionate terms. These different approaches probably represent personality, and philosophical differences between the authors; they may even distill down to the contrasts between individualism and communalism. In any event, observation (and the consequent reinforcement) can lead to either approval or criticism. While observation is a two-edged sword, it is still a more desirable alternative than is indifference. Reinforcement also is stimulated by the availability of adult and adolescent role models. For instance, role models are available because of the character of much rural work: most of it relates to farming, food processing, and extractive operations. The products are usually tangible, and the workers' activities are often physically visible to children. Even if children do not reside on farms, the activities are still proximate. Within smaller rural towns shopping often occurs in owner-operated stores. The owner sets credit policy, determines the prices of articles, makes his own personnel decisions, and decides which customers to court and which to discourage. His commercial relationships are obviously connected to the social life of the town: he fishes with the banker, goes to church picnics, sends his children to the school. Thus, not only is he readily available as a model, but also the observers can see, within the microcosm of his world, a highly complex body of integrated relationships. Actually, this microcosm may not be qualitatively different than that which involves the Rockefeller brothers and their vast family enterprises, or the subtle, interpersonal networks which manage great corporations or state universities. However, within the small town, the elements are all conceptually manageable even to relatively young persons. And so, highly instructive institutional and personal models are available for the young.

The small town or family farm represents community epitomized.[28] The town is often a physically delimited area, and so is the farm. The community has more than purely economic ties: many activities—church picnics, dealing with floods or other weather crises, helping at harvesting—require exchanges of help and shared self-interest. Even the comparative poverty and lack of social services in many rural areas foster further interdependence. The limited population of the rural community means that it is feasible for residents to know each other, and this possibility offers them an incentive to maintain such a norm. The limited diversity of economic activities in the area means that all community members can hope to understand all the productive activities underway in the area and to have an appreciation of each other's activities.

But despite these elements of homogeneity in rural areas, there are significant elements of diversity—especially as far as children and adolescents are concerned. Diversity exists because each community is, to some degree, a microcosm: it contains babies, children, adolescents, adults, and old persons. It also contains very poor and comfortably well-off persons, farmers, merchants, service people, and perhaps a few professionals. Very possibly it also contains ill and mentally disturbed persons. While these varied types do not cover as broad a range as can be found in a large city, they are often easily visible to all children and adolescents. Thus, the actual contacts between the young and diversity in many rural communities is probably greater than in most other environments.[29] We should not look only at interpersonal diversity. Diverse activities are often also easily visible: buying and selling, servicing machinery, managing a farm (which can include bookkeeping), politics, law, banking, teaching, and the ministry. These activities have the same microcosmic elements that are so useful to the young in interpersonal relationships.

Of course, we are familiar with the shock of discovery many country persons have reported when faced with the diversity of a large city. It is sometimes contended that such shocks reveal the shortcomings of rural life and the advantages of urban child rearing. However, we should distinguish between the dramatic and confusing diversity of the city and the diversity which should accompany any healthy learning experience. Premature or excessive urban diversity (as suggested earlier) does not necessarily lead to increased learning, but may simply promote withdrawal. One might hypothesize that the ideal learning mix is to be raised in a small town and to move to an urban area at some later appropriate time. The models imprinted by childhood in a small town may be important tools for interpreting the confusion of urban diversity: perhaps without such early and simple models, urban confusion is hard to interpret. Some interesting insights along these lines can be drawn from the auto-biographies of important persons who were raised in small towns and later went on to urban success.[30] One can often sense the high degree of assurance (and perception) with which they approached complex urban activities and institutions.

Obviously, urban areas have many more learning possibilities for the young than do rural areas. However, they present these possibilities in a far less orderly form than does a rural environment. The city proffers an enormous diversity of models, but many of them are transitory, remote, or engaged in abstract or intangible work—exactly what does an advertising account executive, trust officer, or city planner do? And how can some observer tell whether they do their work well or poorly? Still, within the city there have often been microcommunities that served to provide children and adolescents with proximate, manageable personal and institutional models: ethnic neighborhoods or youth clubs within walking distance of the home. In the past, there were also smaller, less bureaucratic schools and a great variety of jobs for the young, which supplied powerful reinforcing systems and made proximate role models available. The public transportation system also assisted youths to travel to other city environments where more useful models and reinforcers were available: to appropriate jobs, to distant relatives, and (as the home neighborhood began to have limitations for an older child) to more diverse areas of the city.

We must also recognize that the learning possibilities in the ethnic neighborhood are partly dependent on the degree of cohesion in the neighborhood. In other words, we cannot simply assume that a neighborhood peopled with persons of *apparently* the same status will necessarily be coherent.[31] The apparently common status may mask far more diversity than is easily perceived. Indeed, the diversity may be so extraordinary as to be destructive. Or the ethnic group may have undergone such tension as a result of its transition from rural to urban life that its cohesion has significantly disintegrated. The literature of immigrant life in big cities reveals a variety of collective reactions to this transition, and perhaps all that can be concluded is that, for some ethnic groups, in some neighborhoods, in some cities, when certain social classes are involved, ethnic neighborhoods provide stability and cohesion and that, on other occasions, neighborhood environments have even been destructive to the health of their young inhabitants.

Now, we have been given a general outline of the principles that foster desirable affective learning. Our next task will be to apply these principles to the analysis and redesign of varied modern suburban learning environments, including families, schools, and communities.

Intelligence is quickness to apprehend as distinct from ability, which is capacity to act wisely on the thing apprehended. You get the best ability from children reared in an economic status without luxury, which admits them at an early age to the society of people responsible for a community. The community may be a big one, but needn't be, merely responsible persons doing public work.
—Alfred North Whitehead[1]

CHAPTER 3
Administering Suburban Schools - I

The chief responsibility of the school administrator is to help design and manage a learning environment in which students grow toward a satisfying and effective adulthood. Modern suburban society, in many ways, requires a learning environment that differs from that typically found in American schools. The following two chapters will explicate the principles which should govern the design and management of schools in a modern suburb. The principles may also be of interest to nonsuburban administrators managing schools in other post-industrial environments. The "school" involved may be any formal educational institution, from an elementary school to a college.

A designed learning environment is an *artificial* entity. It is necessarily simplified, abstracted, and symbolic. Thus, the task of designing a school is not simply an effort to replicate the external world within the school: just because America is governed by an elected president, we do not assume that the school should be governed by an elected principal; just because adult thieves may be prosecuted or jailed, we are not compelled to apply equivalent adjudication procedures or penalties to misbehaving students.

The word *artificial* and its noun, *artifice*, are rooted in the word *art*, which implied conscious selection, design, and management of materials into an integral composed entity. By calling a school environment "artificial," we suggest a process of just such selection, design, and management—all to ensure that the environment ultimately educates youths to function in the adult world where presidents are elected and where both success and failure can have dramatic consequences. The design process must steer a careful course. On the one hand, it must avoid simple, naïve replication of the complex and confusing adult world. On the other hand, it cannot ignore the implications of the progression of the young from school to adulthood. Thus, the design must present the student with a series of stages of increasing complexity. In a dynamic society, the process of design is really a perpetual process of redesign, as the learning environment is continuously revised to make it more congruent with the shifting society. The design process is not always conscious, and it is never the work of a small group. Innumerable persons are engaged in continuing experiments aimed at making the design more adaptive. Many experimenters are administrators, teachers, and school board members who simply engage in trying to improve their conduct on jobs. This book represents another element in this continuous process of social adaptation and design.

The word *environment*, in the phrase "artificial environment," means the totality of experiences surrounding the students. Clearly, this includes the textbooks, the lectures offered by the teachers, the academic standards set by the school, and the attitudes and skills of the teachers. But these elements are only part of the forces that shape the students' learning within the school. Other important forces relate to the types of contacts that occur among students, and between students and teachers; the nature of the demands that are made (and not made) on students by the school; the forms of rewards and punishments offered to stimulate learning; and the way that students are grouped, scheduled, and directed as they progress through their school years.

Some writers have described these factors as the "hidden curriculum" of the school, but it may be more accurate to call them "almost forgotten curriculum." The distinction suggests that the total learning implications of the school are more forgotten than deliberately concealed. One study touching on this matter examined the effect on student attitudes of participation in a production of the musical *The King and I*. The students, under the general direction of the faculty, provided the cast; designed and manufactured the scenery; managed the lighting, costumes, music, and rehearsals; and so on. The plot of the play gave great emphasis to the theme of intergroup tolerance. The researchers observed that the organization of the production "required students to practice mutual dependence on others, reinforced tolerant behavior and rewarded commitment to the common task. For example, when actors had memorized lines, the rehearsals flowed smoothly and brought satisfaction and praise from peers and the director. A well-executed prop, an appropriate costume completed in time, was visible and complimented. Conversely, all else being equal, an unrehearsed dance, an unlearned speech or song, an incomplete set, were evidence of a lack of commitment and attention to an assigned task necessary to the production. . . . if this deliberate failure was frequently repeated, expulsion from the group and activity was imposed."[2]

Projective tests were administered to participating students and a sample of nonparticipating students both before and after the experience. The tests measured the students' attitude toward cooperative efforts through answers to such items as "Family tasks should be arranged so individual members can do as many things as possible on their own with a minimum of joint cooperation" and "In most cases, I would rather do something as part of a group than do it by myself."

The researchers found that the students participating in the production of the play, compared to the nonparticipants, displayed significant positive shifts in their attitudes toward cooperation. Furthermore, the shifts were unrelated to whether the participants had actually acted in the play or had handled nonacting responsibilities. This lack of contrast between actors and other participants was revealing, since the researchers had theorized that the actors—especially those assuming roles that required them to portray tolerant attitudes on stage—might be more stimulated to adopt tolerant attitudes in life situations. But they found, instead, that all participants in the production were influenced more by their day-to-day cooperating responsibilities within the group than by their formal roles in the play.

One may say that the hidden curriculum of the play—the cooperative responsibilities associated with the production—was far more influential than its formal theme. Thus, a well-produced pro-anarchistic play might instill cooperative attitudes among the production group; an individualistically oriented class on "how to cooperate" might actually make students less able to cooperate.

Instruction by Artificial Environments

Artificial environments instruct by offering models of conduct and by establishing systems of demands, rewards, and punishments, all of which stimulate the learner to acquire new skills and attitudes. For instance, the production of *The King and I* required the students to voluntarily dedicate themselves to a group project and to practice and to learn interactive skills. The structure of the project rewarded them if they succeeded, expelled them if they persistently failed, and gave them examples of and instruction on how to improve. The production was a successful environment for teaching affective skills because it was a community in a school. As a community it offered the stimuli of group approbation and disapproval, the satisfactions of collective achievement, and the final sanction of banishment. But despite its potency, it was simply an artifice: a conscious microcosm. The community was defined by the task set before it: the production of a successful play. From that definition, the learning characteristics and reward system of the community naturally emerged.

Understandably, the learning community I am about to describe can also be a model or revised school; sometimes, in this text, those terms will be used interchangeably with "learning community." The concept of the school as a learning community is not an unusual one. In 1916, John Dewey proposed that, "in place of a school set apart from life as a place for learning lessons, we have a miniature

social group in which study and growth are incidents of present
shared experience. Playgrounds, shops, workrooms, laboratories not
only direct the natural active tendencies of youth, but they involve
intercourse, communication, and cooperation."[3] Many other educators—from Plato and Ignatius of Loyola to Bruno Bettelheim and
George Richmond—have made equivalent proposals.[4]

Dewey's proposal was not unheeded; it played an important part
in setting the goals of the Progressive Education Movement; however, the deeper implications of his proposal may have been disregarded. The fact is that, despite the widespread support of the movement and its principles among educators, there has been a steady
diminishment of the forces making the school an intergenerational
learning community. One cause of this diminishment was the failure of many Progressive spokesmen to adequately recognize the role
that school administration and environment play in determining the
nature of the learning community. They placed greatest emphasis
not on the responsibility of the school administrator, but on the task
of the individual teacher in creating the learning community. This
emphasis suggested that the individual class, and its teacher, was
the essential learning unit in the school. It implied that such units
could maintain learning communities regardless of the goals and
procedures prevailing throughout the total school. In a sense, many
of the Progressive educators apparently applied essentially individualistic attitudes to the implementation of Dewey's communally oriented theories.[5] In his later writings, Dewey leveled criticisms to this
effect against many Progressives.[6]

Another cause of the Progressive's failure was the essentially
naïve psychology applied by Dewey and many of his followers. They
seemed unable to perceive that students (like most other human beings) were persons with innate needs to laugh, cry, and feel the pas-
sions of sex, anger, patriotism, and poetry, and were susceptible to
both selfishness and deep generosity.[7] This insensitivity to students'
complex emotional needs led them to conceive of school as an essentially rationalistic community: even when the school strove to foster
affective learning, such learning was seen as the outcome of intellectual application. Perhaps this misperception was part of the cause
of Dewey's ultimate disappointment with many of his followers: he
failed to foresee the many emotional (and irrational) needs that reformers hoped to satisfy through promoting his ideas. Inferentially,
this failure also related to his inability to perceive the students' affective needs that his proposals did not satisfy.

Part of the teacher focus of Progressive Education was caused by the timing of the movement. The movement began at a time when the concept of the one-room schoolhouse still had a certain viability, even though that tradition was speedily expiring. The one-room schoolhouse naturally justified the concept of the teacher-centered learning community.[8] Indeed, some of the successful learning communities cited by the first Progressives occurred in one-room schools.[9] But the growth of the movement coincided with the tendency to enlarge individual schools and school districts. These enlargements were motivated by a desire to increase efficiency and rationality in the system and by increasing urbanization.[10] As a result, individual teachers were required to closely coordinate their efforts with the policies of both the school and the system. These enlarged and comparatively bureaucratic schools have become increasingly isolated from their surrounding communities and have attempted to win support by generating demonstrable increases in student cognitive learning, as evidenced by increases in college admissions, test scores, and new courses and curricula. These patterns of cognitive emphasis are probably intensified in suburban schools, where comparatively sophisticated parents often ask that schools produce demonstrable results. But the overall effect of such developments has been to continuously lessen the learning community elements in the school.

The personnel practices applied to teachers are a typical example of the way modern schools diminish learning community values. In hiring teachers, little consideration is given to the teacher's experience or abilities in working cooperatively with other teachers; the overriding concern is how the teacher will act alone in a classroom with students. Salary increases for teachers are largely unrelated to the teachers' acquisition or display of cooperative skills. Under these circumstances, it is unlikely that teachers will possess a high level of cooperative skills or that they will be able or willing to engage in relatively complex cooperative activities with other teachers. But the creation of a learning community in a multiteacher school (as opposed to a one-room schoolhouse) will require close cooperation among teachers—since communities are based on cooperation, as opposed to isolation.

Larger enrollments per school, another product of enlargement, have diminished the intensity of student-teacher and student-student contacts, as a result of the depersonalization that is naturally created by numerical growth. But relatively intense relationships are important to a community. The larger schools have emphasized elaborate student time schedules that have discouraged the development of communal activities among the students, since the schedules give first priority to formal classroom subjects. There also apparently has been a tendency to lessen the frequency and intensity of school extracurricular activities—such as sports, extramural activities, ceremonies—although such activities may generate a sense of community among students and faculty.

Other school changes have also undermined the learning community concept. College attendance has become a major objective of many students (and their families). This has had important effects on precollege conduct. For instance, college entrance criteria (as a result of improvements in testing) have increasingly focused on individualistic, cognitive-oriented skills, as opposed to character and interpersonal skills; thus, college-bound students are rewarded for individualistic test-taking and information-acquiring skills, as opposed to rewards for displaying leadership or loyalty. Compulsory high school attendance, and the anticipated prolongation of school through college, has discouraged adolescent identification with their schools—in striving to establish adulthood, adolescents are provoked to become rebellious about school, since school attendance is associated with continuing immaturity and dependence. The desire of teachers to establish themselves as a profession has stimulated the appearance of specializations and academic disciplines within schools; this lessens the likelihood that students will see themselves and the faculty as a finite, identifiable group, focused on a recognizable common purpose.

The essential task confronting contemporary suburban administrators and their staffs is to conceive ways to structure their schools into intergenerational learning communities, to gradually put their concepts into operation, and to maintain the integrity of their efforts by relating day-to-day operation of the school to the maintenance of that community. In effect, to carry out many of the unfulfilled aspirations of Dewey. The community should provide a reward structure that assists the learning of important affective skills. Such learning will be possible because communities are the natural environments that permit the learning of these complex skills. Without a community, students may have neither an adequate occasion nor stimuli for undertaking this difficult—and sometimes painful—learning.

It is relevant that the theme of community for the young was stressed in the final report of the National Commission on Marijuana and Drug Abuse:

All people, especially the young, need to be wanted and loved and to participate fully in the social system of which they are a part. The most fundamental values of this nation promise all our citizens an equal opportunity to share in the "American dream": to experience something of value; to be assured that their existence matters; to assume some responsibility for the ongoing activities of the community; and to enjoy the rewards which responsible participation can yield . . . But unfortunately, education is the career which this nation has designated for its young. For some of them, though, it is a meaningless one: a largely barren period of waiting until the community is ready to permit them to assume an adult role.[11]

As long as the nation does designate education as the "career of the young," we cannot expect our youths to assume full adult roles; however, we can reorganize the school to create meaningful preadult roles; such roles will result in new structures, new demands, and new responsibilities and rewards. To some extent, this procommunity emphasis conflicts with important Western philosophical themes. David W. Minar pointed out that "English liberalism and in good part the liberalism of the French enlightenment tended to be anticommunity in bias. That is to say, they viewed the individual as the integral element in social life and the more inclusive units as his artificial creations. Thus, community was not a thing in itself but an aggregate without independent existence and will, at best an instrument to individual welfare."[12]

These individualist themes have had their effect on school structures. Thus, many educators have stressed the allegedly voluntary elements of learning. Voluntary learning implies that the individual, and not the collective, should be the sole judge of what should be learned. This stress is inconsistent with the frank proposal to organize schools to stimulate, and even compel, students to learn important cooperative skills. But the individual can be exalted to the detriment of the community; if too great an emphasis is given to individual values, there will be no possibility of sustaining the community upon which society rests. Indeed, the data recited earlier suggest that the isolation of youths from intergenerational communities has already reached the level of serious dysfunctionality.

Furthermore, the concept of voluntary learning by children is solecistic. "Voluntary" would imply that the learners have a choice of whether or not they want to learn, and about what they learn. But children do not know how to be self-supporting and socially effective, and parents and society can not be indifferent to whether these skills are learned. Thus, school attendance is usually compulsory for children. Even when it is not legally compelled, there are strong parental and social pressures motivating attendance, and often there are no other viable ways for children to spend their time than to attend school or college. Under these circumstances, it is not surprising that children "choose" to learn materials put before them in the classroom by adult authority figures. The trouble with calling this process voluntary is that we may fool ourselves and actually forget that adults, by deliberation or drift, are deciding what children should learn. If we admit that the learning is directed and compelled by adults, we may diminish the amount of drift.

The proposed stress on constructive affective objectives in the learning community may seem to challenge the role of cognitive learning, particularly programed instruction and other forms of individualized teaching which are the products of behavioral psychology. This discipline has led to the production of carefully organized packages of cognitive learning materials in such fields as mathematics, science, and reading. While the learning community will be concerned with cognitive learning, it will relate this learning to the students' responsibility to learn how to participate in communal activities. The learning community approach does not reject the perspectives of behavioral psychology, since such behaviorists as B. F. Skinner and Edward L. Thorndike have done significant research relating to affective learning.[13] However, adoption of the community approach will mean that the narrower objectives of behaviorism (i.e., cognitive behavior) will be subordinated to the essentially emotional bases of human life. The community will strive to help students instruct and satisfy these emotions. One early critic of overindividualistic schooling made some pertinent remarks about this issue when discussing his differences with John Maynard Hutchins about learning priorities:

Hutchins, in what seems to me a modern example of medieval scholasticism, says, "An education which is liberal should free man from the mammal within." And again, "The noblest achievements of mankind, the highest aspirations of the human spirit, these are the essence of our education, designed to suppress the mammal, or the earthworm, within us and make us truly human." But the development of the intellect is surely a capstone held up by the physical and emotional foundations of human life and not a substitute for everything which went before us in the long history of evolution. Surely educated men do not desire to give up the joys and sorrows and the

personal and social ties which depend mainly on these foundations.
To me the ideal he expresses is inhuman. Is not one of our primary
tasks to understand and learn how to guide, so far as we can, the
elementary emotional forces which so largely dominate our interests
and our behavior and lend significance to life even if they compli-
cate it?[14]

If one wants to form communities, it is appropriate to ask, "How
are communities made?" Communities are born and continue
through a combination of coincidence and artifice.[15] The coincidence
may be rooted in geography, circumstances of birth, climate, or
technology; any of these forces may stimulate a group of people to
develop a continuing, purposeful relationship. Thus, the English
people are a community, partly because England is an island; a family is a community, because of marriage, the shared responsibilities
of child rearing, housekeeping, and emotional and physical suste-
nance; and a group of people living around a railroad station in a
wilderness will tend to become a community due to their shared concern with the operation of the railroad. Artifice can be recognized in
communal groups formed through the conscious development of
Little League teams and Boy Scout troops and the planning of new
suburban developments.

But viable, persisting communities rest on both artifice and coincidence. When community members are brought together through
coincidence, they must develop systems of symbols and communication to assist their natural tendency to cooperate. For instance, a
friend organized an experimental residential school, which, he
hoped, would generate a sense of community among students. There
were coincidental factors fostering their community: their shared
residence within the same building, and the many common elements
among their day-to-day responsibilities. However, the organizer,
early in the experiment, made it a rule that all the students (who
were away on varied tasks throughout the day) had to have their
evening meals together four times a week in the residential building.
At a verbal level, the students were all in favor of having a community; that was one of the reasons they went to the residential school.
Still, the students resisted the eating-together rule or asked for the
power to create exceptions for themselves.

Such a rule ensured that the students would be routinely brought
together in an environment which stimulated them all to exchange
information, jokes, and adventures with one another. The rule "arti-
ficially" fostered the sense of community already inherent in the pro-

gram. When asked what caused him to see that the rule was appropriate or wise, the organizer answered: "I was committed to the group working together, and sensed that the evening meal was tending to become a segmented and uncongenial occasion. People all went different directions during the day, returning at different times, eating in dribs-and-drabs in the evening, and going off to watch TV, read, talk with their intimates, and finally to their rooms to sleep. And the more this happened, the more likely it was to continue, since co-incidental residence and dispersed but parallel day-to-day experience obviously were not creating the community I envisioned. Since we had to eat anyway, I just decided we'd do it all at the same time."

The story suggests the medley of circumstances, leadership, and intuitive artifice underlying the development of successful communities. The artifice may be at a relatively simple level, such as requiring students to eat together, or it may extend to elaborate mechanisms, such as the first moon shot which generated a sense of sharing among many Americans.

There is a great diversity of artifices used to create and direct human communities. Indeed, these artifices form many of the most significant products of man, including music, ceremony, popular institutions, visual art, widely understood symbols, uniform patterns of dress, common bodies of belief (e.g., myths, folklore, history, religion, and law), shared jokes, oaths, and other forms of mutual commitment to attain important goals. In sum, community-building artifices encompass the most noble and creative feats of man, as well as symbols and systems that have stimulated communities to commit atrocious wrongs.

But the design of a communal learning environment is more than an exercise in emotion-generating artistry. The process requires us to relate the community activities to the attainment of affective learning. Therefore, the artifices used to maintain such a community have a special purpose. They must stimulate participants to learn affective skills; in exchange for this learning, the participants should receive the benefits that arise from community membership. This poses a special challenge. For example, communities do exist in many suburban high schools, but they often frustrate constructive affective learning. These communities consist of the disparate communities of youth and faculty. As long as the youth communities do not become especially disorderly, they persist without exciting the engagement or attention of the faculty communities. The members of the youth communities and subcommunities share patterns of dress, attitudes, speech, and conduct.[16] Often, they read the same kinds of magazines, listen to the same music, and watch the same TV shows. Through coincidence and artifice a student community thus exists. However, that community does not assist the learning of important affective skills, nor do its values and goal systems help students to become satisfied adults. Indeed, student communities may even teach counterproductive skills and attitudes, for example, drug use and egocentrism.

Thus, as we consider designs for student-faculty communities, we must restrain from using artifices that, while creating community, frustrate healthy affective learning. An instance of such a dysfunctional design can be seen in the occasional attempt of administrators, teachers, and intellectuals to create bonds between faculty and students by portraying the out-of-school community as rapacious, shallow, and materialistic.[17] Unfortunately, this presentation inevitably diminishes comfortable interchange between the school (and students) and the out-of-school sources that can greatly assist the learning of affective skills; and the out-of-school world is the great arena for the practice and development of those skills. Thus, although such an intense intraschool community may seem simple to design, in the long run it will frustrate the learning of adult-type skills.

Furthermore, we must be concerned with the integrity of any learning community we design. "Integrity" means that there must be an inherently plausible relationship between the learning community and the natural life goals of its participants. Without such integrity, or plausibility, the community may enjoy a brief, spirited life, but eventually its transient participants will develop an attitude of frustrated disillusionment toward its precepts. Many recent attempts at building learning communities (e.g., free schools and communes) were undoubtedly handicapped by this lack of integrity. The community participants gradually realized that this community life was irrelevant to the life patterns of the larger society, and that they would someday have to live in that society. Probably one of the major frustrations confronting many modern adolescents who participate in the youth culture is their perception that the youth culture is irrelevant to adult life. And so the satisfactions of the youth culture are ephemeral. On the other hand, many modern schools do teach skills quite relevant to adulthood; unfortunately, the instructional process generally disregards the communal needs of the students. And so we must merge artifice and purpose.

An "Ideal" Revised Suburban School

An "ideal" restructured suburban school should strive to be a true learning community. If it is a public school, the school board members and parents in the community will presumably be in sympathy with the proposed changes. Or the school may be a subschool within a large educational unit, tolerated by the overall enterprise and satisfying the aspirations of a minority of parents and students. Here and in the next chapter, I will sketch the new responsibilities that such a school will place on administrators and the benefits it may generate. Many suburban administrators are already applying some elements of this outline, as a result of their own adaptations and inventions, to meet the challenge of suburban education. However, the purpose here is to present a revised school *in toto*, so that readers can see the relationship between existing and proposed improvements. The presentation will articulate much of the theoretical rationale for the changes, so that administrators may revise specific proposals to meet local needs and changed circumstances.

To create a strong sense of school community among suburban students and faculty, administrators must become sensitive to many issues that often have low priority in contemporary schools. Furthermore, these administrators, and their teachers, will need authorities and skills they do not now have. Students, too, will acquire new authorities and responsibilities; acquiescence maintained only by raw coercion, as opposed to participation, is a poor cement for community. In sum, all community members will assume active, engaged roles in making the community work. We can expect that both educators and students will have mixed responses to these developments. People usually want new authority, but resist the responsibility that is concomitant with it.

Much student conduct in revised schools will continue to be determined by the attitudes of the students' peers. This has always been the case and will not change as long as students learn in "schools," that is, in environments that are overwhelmingly populated by students of about the same age. The sheer preponderance of numbers, in addition to the shared identification of individual students, will compel these intrapeer pressures. The learning community administrator will be concerned with how to mobilize and direct these pressures to assure affective learning. In effect, he or she will manipulate youth group conduct so that it serves constructive, adult-determined ends. This does not mean that these youths will not find their activities satisfying, or that they will be deprived of all room for initiative; however, their satisfactions and initiatives will be within parameters settled by adults and will tend in constructive directions. The manipulations will be largely conducted by reshaping the school so that it becomes a more fulfilling community for students and faculty.

These changes will proceed slowly and tentatively. The immediately following portion of the text will present a catalogue of desirable measures, without discussing their order of possible appearance or priority. The rate and sequence of change, in individual schools or school districts, will be decided by tactical contingencies beyond the scope of these sections. However, there will be some discussion about the timing of change later in the book. The final appropriate mix of the proposed elements for any individual school or area will depend on innumerable variables, such as the values of the area; the styles and perceptions of the administrators, faculty, parents, and students; and the experience garnered and the precedents set by previous developments.

As the presentation proceeds, it will be evident that some of the proposed changes will excite resistance from some faculty, parents, or students. One may question whether it is realistic to attempt serious change in the face of such resistance. However, incrementalism, subschools, and voluntary-but-binding commitments are key principles in dealing with this serious stratagematic question. Incrementalism means that one should have a general plan, carry it out bit-by-bit, and learn and refine as one proceeds. Through subschools changes that are unpopular with the larger entity are carried out among smaller groups of the students, faculty, and parents. Voluntary-but-binding commitments are fulfilled by inviting persons who sympathize with the proposed—and clearly stated—goals of the subschools to enroll (as parents, staff, or students) in such schools; such enrollment should be for at least some predetermined substantial period of time; and during that period, the enrollee is bound by a signed document to follow the voluntarily accepted plan of the school. The principle of commitment also means that the school will have some publicly stated penalty system (e.g., refusal to facilitate the transfer of credits of those who inappropriately withdraw) to discourage breaches of such commitments.

It should also be directly remarked that graduates of the proposed new school will be peculiarly prepared to accept leadership positions in society. This may seem an anomaly, since it also will become evident that many elements of the school's operation are not mirror replications of post-industrial society. Instead, they harken back to earlier forms of social interaction. However, it should not seem strange to Americans living in the late 1970's to consider that small-town life and perspectives seem to provide the best training for modern leadership: consider Plains, Georgia; Whittier, California; Stonewall, Texas; Abilene, Kansas; and Independence, Missouri—the home towns of five recent presidents. The one exception, John F. Kennedy, had a carefully managed upbringing. And, of course, the upper and upper-middle classes in England, which have provided much of the leadership in English society—including many leaders of the egalitarian Labor party—have traditionally sent their children to "artificial" schools. As will be seen later, the proposed school will produce leaders because it will teach students to work with others. Conversely, perhaps many existing post-industrial schools fail to produce leaders because their graduates do not know how to be active followers.

The new school designs and administrative responsibilities will generally relate to:
• Creating and managing school spirit
• Organizing new kinds of interaction within the school
• Forming new and varied subdivisions within the student body
• Planning and managing new kinds of buildings and grounds

Creating School Spirit

School spirit is critical to a sense of community. It is the by-product of coincidence and artifice, which work together to produce faculty-student community. The major coincidental force is the fact that students and faculty spend a great deal of time in the same building together and share a major common concern: the development and graduation of able students. The role of artifice is to take the basic given of coincidence and manipulate it so as to attain the maximum constructive community-building effect.

Ceremonies
Ceremonies are one of the most important forms of community-building artifice, for at these periodic public occasions groups reassert their sense of communal dedication. Even when the ceremonies center about the status of some individual (e.g., the awarding of an honor), the transaction involves interaction between the group and the individual and so integrates the individual and the group. Furthermore, the periodicity of ceremonies—for example, the annual

commencement—ties the particular ceremonial occasion to the persistence of the community and generates perceptions relating the present community to communities of the past and future.

But while a ceremony has certain routine elements, it must be marked off from the routine activities of the day or year and thus encompass both repetition and demarcation. The demarcation can be achieved by innumerable techniques: the assumption of special postures by the participants (raising hands, taking a step forward), the wearing of prescribed costumes, the recitation of symbolic words, the recognition of a unique moment of time, the gathering of the group at a significant place, the appearance of particular persons, or the recognition of important symbols.

A number of developments have handicapped the presentation of well-artificed ceremonies in suburban schools. Large student bodies, and segmented student schedules, make it difficult to provide for regular occasions on which identifiable groups of students gather together for ceremonies. Sometimes architectural design is also a handicap; there may be a reluctance to spend money on space which is largely set aside for ceremonial occasions.

However, the integrity of the ceremony is as important as its artifice. In other words, despite sensitive artifice, a ceremony may be seriously flawed—and lose its community-maintaining potential— if the participants do not feel there is an essentially rational pattern underlying the occasion. Modern high school commencements are examples of ceremonies that lack integrity: often students do not feel that the ceremony actually demarcates the moment of transition from studenthood to a significantly new status. And the students are largely correct. The commencement only marks a long-recognized *fait accompli* and is thus anticlimactic.

Students realize that their scores on objective tests administered two and three years before are excellent predictors of the likelihood of their graduation, and that often colleges have already admitted them months in advance of graduation. Therefore, the students see the ceremony as a belated recognition of something they took for granted long before.

Furthermore, life after high school commencement for college-bound students will not be much different than life as high school students. The college-bound graduates have friends and relatives in college and understand that college studenthood is in many ways similar to high school—the life that is "commenced" is not unique.

This lack of integrity in high school commencements is the product of a long and significant chain of developments that have eroded the integrity of many school ceremonies. The developments have been caused by systemic and technological changes that have been adopted to improve the functioning of the school, reduce costs, make operations more rational, and diminish the tensions and frustrations of students, faculty, and families. One typical systemic change has been the revision in college entrance procedures, so that students apply in the January preceding high school commencement and receive a decision on their application by April. This process assists the planning of both colleges and students and gives students broader college choices by permitting, and even encouraging, them to apply to a number of colleges simultaneously. The process of early and numerous applications is fostered by the technology of objective testing (e.g., scoring machines, computer print-outs), which allows colleges to sort and evaluate large numbers of applications expeditiously. Such early admissions, which assume the certainty of graduation, diminish the tensions on all concerned, since there is less uncertainty as to whether a student will graduate or get into college. There may still be tension about what particular college will admit a student, but test scores are good indicators of the level of prestige of the college that will admit the student, and even this tension is settled long before commencement.

The fact that most adequate contemporary high school students will go on to college, and thus not undergo a dramatic transition from school to work, is another development affecting the integrity of the commencement ceremony. This pattern is the product of changing social expectations, plus a level of national affluence that permits society to support prolonged attendance by high proportions of young persons in institutions that do not directly produce material wealth. Equivalent changes have diminished the integrity of other school community-building ceremonies.

One of these other changes has been the increasing emphasis on "objectivity" and rationality in the curriculum of the modern school. Thus, Talcott Parsons observed that the thrust of schooling is that "who states a proposition is as such irrelevant to the question of its . . . value."[18] This statement implies that students should be trained to "objectively" analyze acts and words, independent of the status of the actor. Unfortunately, this simple statement leads to outcomes that have problematic benefits for children and adolescents. Translated into classroom conduct, this approach means that students must remember that George Washington may have padded his expense account, that the pioneers countermassacred the Indians, or that America, like every other major nation, has engaged in colonial wars. One writer, in a collection of writings on the social science curriculum, proposed that "it is indefensible to exclude even groups under the age of 9 from serious discussions of the role of the citizen."[19] Another article explained what the term "serious discussions" meant. It included the consideration of such matters as "the realities of the political system, not the constitutional or 'rule book' maxims. . . . The students of today and tomorrow must know how the political elites in nations function, how they got to be elites, and how any new group or individual who wants to influence the system must operate. . . . Lay bare the real conflicts, hates, and frustrations of groups and individuals in the society. . . . The venality as well as the noble elements of technological, political, and social man must be treated from the perspective of the individual."[20]

The teachers and the texts proffering this angry and disturbing curriculum can demonstrate that they are merely mirroring the materials presented in college courses or various public media, and that the information and arguments are factually correct, or at least arguably justifiable. Essentially similar patterns of social criticism are also found in many materials presented to students in literature courses. These curricula are consonant with the themes of objectivity and rationality: that is, some elements of the "realistic" curricula are factually true, even if their significance is problematic, while in other parts of those curricula, where controversial opinions are presented to students, the proponents can demonstrate that those opinions are at least supported by some authorities. If the sum picture presented to students by these curricula is confusing, or disturbing, to them, "even groups under the age of 9" supposedly have the power to weigh the alternatives and make up their own minds. These contentions about student powers of judgment assume a special unreality when applied to many suburban students, whose environment naturally shields them from immediate contact with any first-hand experiences or responsibilities to assist them in the weighing process.

This form of rationality undermines the integrity of much of the ceremonial life in school, since a major proportion of this ceremonial life centers around pride in the American community. Through this pride, the in-school community is bound to the larger society. The achievements and structure of the larger society also provide students with a model of an admirable and holistic community; they may use this model to provide a guide for the development of a healthy in-school community. But without pride in the society, the school community becomes in-bred, egocentric, and corrupted. However, it is difficult for children to maintain and display pride in their country when their respected social science teachers and the curriculum they teach strive to cultivate a negatively critical attitude in the students toward the symbols of this pride: national heroes and honored traditions.

In sum, a major anomaly confronts any effort to form a learning community in the school. This anomaly is rooted in the fabric of modern intellectual life. The school, theoretically, aims to teach both cognitive and affective knowledge. The cognitive material, it is hoped, will help in seeing things dispassionately and objectively. However, affective knowledge is dependent on students developing a sense of commitment to the whole faculty-student community and, ultimately, to the local and national community surrounding the school. This cannot be entirely an objective and dispassionate process. One student of comparative education put the problem in the following terms:

It is difficult to think of any educational system which has lasted over time, that has based morals mainly on reason and enquiry, and done it effectively. Moral education, in other words, is largely a matter of developing faith. The enlightened liberal educator will, it is true, seek to broaden the choice offered by his moral principles; he will suggest to his students that faith can be served by different courses of action and that reason can help to select the course to be taken. But this is a far cry from saying that reason itself can establish the basic ethical assumptions by which man acts. In fact, once reason is accepted as the arbiter of faith, it will be more likely to destroy than to affirm. The philosopher may indeed be able to build abiding moral precepts on the wings of intellect—but few of us are philosophers.[21]

As the preceding text has implied, first priority should be given to the development of emotionally healthy personalities, committed to the general traditions of their society. Probably this molding process should extend at least through high school—and perhaps through college. At some later stage of growth, the matured adult should strive to engage in the process of integrating intellectual objectivity with appropriate affective understanding. Of course, the integration will be less than perfect. But imperfection in such integration is inevitable. Still, the shortcomings of such an effort will be less than those that occur when persons are deprived of comfortable roots in their society, due to a premature exposure to "objectivity." Persons without roots will be driven to misperceive the essence of their society, since the phenomenon of alienation generates a high level of anger and anxiety: these effects seriously warp the ability of observers to make accurate judgments about major issues. The problem is that alienation makes observers too committed to justifying their anger and loneliness by blaming the actions of others.

Up to this point, the discussion on ceremonies has not talked about how to develop particular ceremonies. Instead, it has concerned itself with the general issues of ceremonial integrity and the effects of rationalism. However, without an appreciation of these basic issues, ceremonial design is a sterile process. Conversely, if we direct ourselves toward the maintenance of procedures in the school that permit ceremonial integrity, and if we strive to control the reflexive application of rationalism, the design of effective community-building ceremonies will proceed rather easily.

A number of occasions for ceremonies already exist in schools, and in some cases the ceremonies are being conducted effectively; however, we need more ceremonial occasions, and their quality can be improved. But the improvements must be concerned with increasing integrity and controlling rationalism. Take the instance of high school commencement. Integrity would be greatly increased if students did not know whether they would actually graduate until a week or so before commencement. This means that the students must be subject to some form of test shortly before graduation. If they failed the test they would receive a certificate of completion of school, a different document than a diploma; that certificate would indicate that they had attended school for a certain number of years, and completed certain work, but had not been eligible for graduation. The diploma test would ask students to display both cognitive and affective skills. Perhaps it would include an interview by a panel including adults outside the school faculty. There must be some genuine (but perhaps remote) possibility that the students might fail the test—even if they are cognitively adept. If they apply to college before graduation, their acceptance must not be taken to mean they will graduate. And if they fail to graduate, that failure must be meaningful—for instance, it must postpone their college entrance for a year.

Of course, this process would be tension producing, and the commencement would be correspondingly tension releasing. That is why such a commencement would "work," that is, produce a sense of excitement and community for graduates, other students, family, and faculty. At this point, I will not analyze in detail endless arguments that may revolve around this proposal. The basic facts are that the high school and much of suburban adolescent life is boring and without challenge for many able students; that such students are not challenged to learn important skills, or stimulated to care about the group they are in; and that the tensions generated by the proposed alternate process may be the inevitable price we pay to attain learning and satisfaction.

As for meliorating the impact of rationalism, it is unrealistic to propose that suburban grade and high schools substitute a collection of explicit legends and myths for much of their current curriculum. However, a continuation of current curriculum and instructional patterns may create growing numbers of articulate, but emotionally incompetent, students. Perhaps we should recognize that children are especially subject to conceptual overload, and that a school curriculum is more than a collection of disparate facts and arguable theories. At the college or graduate school level, one may contend that professors are dealing with mature adults, and that the facts and theories can be set out like a menu from which the students can pick and choose. However, at the high school level, this approach may leave us with students who can complain about the world but not have the skills needed to change it. School curricula should be judiciously screened at appropriate levels and reorganized where necessary. The new curriculum should present the child and adolescent with a model of society that contains certain complexities and contradictions. Still, the model should proffer an image that satisfies the students' basic need for a tangible and plausible series of concentric communities (e.g., the family, school, township, and nation) that invite and deserve their loyalties. Without such a curriculum, it will be difficult to establish a school-based learning community that stimulates the attainment of affective competence. These gradual and cumulative curricular revisions may do much to improve the operation of society, by developing a growing pool of able adults capable of dealing with the tensions generated by our complex and dynamic world. But this pool of ability first needs calm and stable communities in which to mature.

Unquestionably, this screening proposal touches on sensitive issues. But the issues must be approached both frankly and temperately. All school curricula involve elements of deliberate selection based on diverse theories. One theory is that the school world should be a balanced mathematical sample of all the ideas and information relating to human society. Presumably, this theory would mean that any attempt to give greater weight to one part of the "sample" than another would constitute censorship. But the theory is always qualified in its application. For instance, we do not ask that a child's family proportionately mirror the indifference and hostility that the child may find as an adult in the world. There will be some indifference and hostility in the family, but the natural expectation is that the family should be an especially sustaining community. That is what young children need. And so it is for the school. The confusion and conflict inherent in adult political and organizational life must be strained and reorganized for the school, if we wish the suburban school to serve the important functions it should fulfill.

With further reference to the matter of censorship, we cannot ignore the fact that many of the proponents of the "whole truth" approach sometimes display questionable consistency in applying the approach. There are few pro–Ku Klux Klan materials in modern textbooks, and sophisticated readers are aware that many "whole truthers" evince strong commitments to particular partisan political groups. Under these circumstances, one may wonder about the degree of objectivity they display in developing reading assignments and class projects. It may be that we are sometimes asked to accept one mythology as a substitute for another. However, if this is the case, the "new" mythology must face the test of integrity: does it plausibly relate the foreseeable life patterns of suburban students? And, against this test, the "old" mythology, even today, may well have more integrity than the "new" one. Most suburban students will mature, and live, as middle- and upper-middle-class Americans. The only integral mythology that can be put before them is one that helps them to admire the society, country, and class in which they will live their lives. Perhaps, over time, America will evolve more creators of symbols and myths (i.e., artists) who want their creations to live and who will strive to create symbols and myths that fulfill the persisting needs of our society—as opposed to producing faddish, trivial, and angry products. But, meanwhile, the schools must accept a screening function.

There are many occasions apart from graduation for ceremonial enrichment—though commencement should be a crucial occasion. Ceremonies can include homecoming days, pep rallies, patriotic occasions, religious celebrations (if communally acceptable), or convocations to recognize the beginning of a new school year. Important feats by individual students or groups of students can be collectively honored. Classes of students can make presentations to the school of materials they have bought or made. Schools can begin with daily in-class ceremonies, such as singing the national anthem or saluting the flag. Cohorts of new students should be welcomed by the whole school. Diverse intraclass and subgroup ceremonies can be developed.

This pattern of enriched ceremonial life will assist administrators in reshaping the value structure of the school. For instance, elsewhere in this book we discuss the need to involve students more deeply in caring for the maintenance of the school building. If the groups of students who do this job are recognized on appropriate ceremonial occasions, they will find their responsibility more enjoyable. Compared to such public approbation, a report card with grades is only a very mild stimulus. Where possible, ceremonies should involve alumni, parents, and representatives of the public community, for example, members of civic groups, political figures, students or faculty from other schools.

The ceremonies should include the many traditional elements: special words, songs, garments, and locations; artistic or traditional symbols; music; prescribed forms of touching (like shaking the hand of graduates) and ritual postures and gestures. The central elements and themes of the ceremony should be determined by adults, and these elements should be continuously followed (to provide continuity and tradition). However, arrangements can be made to encourage judicious student involvement. Speaking time can be allowed for a student representative, the ceremony can honor a student gift to the school, or students can participate in the selection of a speaker.

The enlargement of ceremonies will also enrich the symbolic life of the school. Ceremonies will provide occasions for the creation of new symbols and give recognition to existing symbols. These symbols can increase the sense of in-school community (e.g., gifts from previous classes) and help to tie the school closer to the larger community (e.g., gifts from outsiders, such as an American flag). Furthermore, the symbols, as well as the ceremonies, can help reshape the value system of the school. Groups or individuals who have performed noteworthy acts can be symbolically recognized: their names inscribed on the honor roll, their trophies placed in the hall, their gifts designated by a plaque. These recognitions reward the actors, stimulate other students to emulate their actions, and remind all students and faculty that commendable conduct creates persisting mementos.

This enlargement of ceremonial life may diminish the time available for cognitive instruction. The effects of such a loss, however, can be moderated by the overall decrease of student boredom and frustration within the revised school; and this decrease may actually increase student learning per unit of time devoted to cognitive learning. But even if the overall effect of the lost time were to somewhat diminish the cognitive learning by students, the lost learning would be fully justified. We understand that many parts of the current school curriculum are only indirectly related to the day-to-day life of many adults (e.g., algebra, poetry, physics, foreign languages) and that the basic justification for the current curriculum is that it represents a series of calculated guesses about what information taught to children or adolescents will be of most significance to them ten or twenty years hence. The guess is always partly right, and partly wrong. If we enlarge ceremonial life at the expense of other school curricula, we are "guessing" that this enlargement will be of more use to the students than some other subject matter. Of course, that guess, too, may be wrong. However, ceremonial enlargement represents a deliberate effort to develop a pattern of schooling consciously related to the needs of suburban students; any existing discipline or specialty in the curriculum that claims its materials rate preference over ceremonial time must justify that claim against the long-range needs of such students and, in particular, against their apparent deficiencies in affective skills.

The matter of voluntary or involuntary participation in ceremonies should also be considered. At this time, the lack of ceremonial integrity and the rationalism in the school curriculum have diminished much of the satisfaction of school ceremonies. Thus, there is resistance to participation in ceremonies. This resistance probably can be corrected, not so much by compulsion, but by making the environment more supportive of ceremony. For instance, there would probably be widespread student support for commencement if it had integrity; then, compulsion might be unnecessary. There still may be pockets of resistance, but if these pockets are small, compulsion is appropriate (especially in the case of faculty—if they do not like it, they do not need to work there). In the case of students, overt compulsion is more complicated, since most students have little choice among public schools. The lack of choice may stimulate adolescents to express their aspirations for maturity by rebelling against the school itself. We will later discuss steps to deal with this lack of choice. However, with reference to ceremonies, a sense of community requires, in part, putting the interests of the whole over those of specified individuals; since widely attended and well-structured ceremonies make the community possible, the school must be prepared to discipline students who egocentrically assert their will over the interests of the whole. In determining responsibility and imposing discipline, administrators may be able to share their authority with students, since the discipline is invoked to protect the spirit of the student-faculty community.

This discussion of compulsion and ceremonies provides an excellent example of the learning community as a tool for affective teaching. The ceremonies help make the school a community and give the students and faculty a rewarding sense of identity. But the ceremonies only work for the whole, and for each "citizen," as long as everyone attends and works in the planning and production. Therefore, the "citizens" must learn how to contribute time and energy. Most of the contributions will be voluntary and usually will generate pleasure and satisfaction. Sometimes the "citizens" may have conflicting aspirations, but they will be helped to sublimate their immediate aims to the good of the group, and to their own long-range interest in the community. Some very few irresponsible "citizens" must be required to do their share, and the group will exercise compulsion on them to protect the whole. This process offers the students profound instruction in tact, persistence, and cooperation and provides powerful rewards in exchange for such learning.

We have been discussing a proposal to somewhat lessen the diffusion, cynicism, and rationalism in the school curriculum, and to use ceremony to help make it a richer learning community for children, adolescents, and faculty. Clearly, this proposal is at variance with some currents in the larger society. Debunking history is now a popular theme. Drugstores and public libraries are filled with books proclaiming the imminence of social desolation. Cynicism toward tradition and authority is stock fare for TV personalities. Our periodic political campaigns subject all citizens to endless disastrous forebodings.

However, despite these obstacles, we should not underestimate the powerful community-building forces within the school. The potential is rooted in the nature of a group with shared concerns using a common building. Because of this potential, the presentations of teachers and the curriculum of the school, if organized into a coherent whole and related to an artful and more integral ceremonial life, may well create an in-school community that reaches out, with affection and confidence, to the society that supports the school. And from this posture, the students can learn the skills and attitudes that will ultimately help them participate in, and direct, that society.

Postcommencement Expectations

The postcommencement expectations of students have a great impact on their affective learning at all levels in school. We have already discussed the assurance of college entrance long before commencement, and the resulting view that commencement is a moment neither to look forward to nor to look back on. In this way, student postcommencement expectations have deprived the high school of a vital community-building tool.

There are also other relevant postcommencement expectations. Graduates of grade schools, high schools, and colleges usually do not expect to return to their schools to offer assistance to the students, to visit former teachers, or to provide counsel to the learning community. Graduates usually do not expect that the next educational level to which they apply will ask their former teachers whether the applicants, while below, displayed characteristics evincing maturity (e.g., persistence, leadership, loyalty), in addition to their achievement of good test scores. Furthermore, high school and college students in academic programs do not generally expect employers to consider offering them reasonably significant jobs on the basis of the maturity they have displayed in school. All these student expectations inevitably color their day-to-day conduct. If we wish to revise this student conduct, and increase affective learning, we must reshape the students' expectations. In part, this will require school administrators to try to reshape the existing attitudes of external institutions; in part, it will mean reshaping the styles of the school itself.

The external institutions can have their attitudes affected by the conduct of school administrators. For example, as schools develop programs which ask students to display affective skills, the administrators can inform employers and colleges that their diploma means more than demonstrating a modest tolerance for boredom. Teachers and administrators can give colleges and employers references for former students that discuss their character strengths and weaknesses in plausible detail. The references will be based on student performance in challenging and realistic situations. As external institutions discover that such data are available, they will be stimulated to ask for it. It is even possible that, over time, some external institutions may discover that informed character references are better predictors of later performance than are cognitive test scores, and that some students with attractive scores are actually lower achievers as college students or employees than lower-scoring students who have demonstrated affective skills, such as persistence and persuasive ability. These changes in external expectations can be provoked by changes in internal school administration.

Some readers may feel that this emphasis on references to satisfy employers or college entrance requirements may unduly penalize students for "improper conduct" before school graduation. It is true that one aim of the proposal is to give greater significance to student conduct in school; in sum, better conduct will be eligible for greater rewards than at present, and poor conduct will be subject to greater penalties. This is not to say that every mischievous youthful act should scar a student for life. However, student conduct in the eyes of students is either relevant *or* irrelevant to adult life. At present, displaying leadership, tact, or loyalty is evidently irrelevant. That is, good conduct often is not recognized or is rewarded in delayed and indirect fashions; poor conduct is also comparatively disregarded. Under these circumstances, students have few incentives to learn good conduct—why bother to learn such difficult things; it does not seem to pay. The effect of the current situation is to discourage students from learning important skills—and even, in the short run, to penalize students who do trouble to learn them, since they are using up time that could be better spent in acquiring recognized and rewarded cognitive skills. The fact is that whatever we do with students penalizes certain conduct and rewards other kinds; it is impossible for any person with authority over others to avoid shaping their learning. About the worst way such authority can be managed is to deny its inherent effect, for then we determine the learning of others without even seeing what we are doing. The current system excessively rewards cognitive skills and thus penalizes affective skills. An attempt to make postgraduation status relate to affective skills will help overcome this imbalanced reward structure. It might even assist students to lead fuller and richer lives.

Another important desirable change in expectations will be to cause more suburban high school students to abandon the present expectation of attending college immediately after graduation. That abandonment will require many changes in attitudes among students and other persons and institutions. As the change occurs, the affective learning thrust of high school will become increasingly relevant. Students will see that high school references carry weight if they seek work, and that affective learning can make them more capable in coping with out-of-school challenges. Commencement will also acquire greater integrity, since it will demarcate the transition from school to nonschool: from adolescence to obvious adulthood. In such circumstances, the commencement would become a dramatic and satisfying puberty ritual. After such a ritual, the students might comfortably see themselves as adults and be prepared to assume adult responsibilities in work, marriage, and community affairs.

Admittance to School
We have already discussed the need of adolescents to learn about commitment. The discussion emphasized that suburban environments are especially lacking in occasions for such learning.

This lack of commitment opportunities in suburban environments can create a twofold drawback: suburban children may suffer a deprivation of important affective learning experiences, and they also can develop hostility toward an environment that frustrates their natural exploratory needs. This sense of hostility, directed toward their school, may simply represent their desire for commitment, transformed into unconstructive resentment. The learning community must be prepared to deal with the need for commitment.

One step may be to permit graduating grade school students and their families to choose between attending the learning community as compared to some other public high school or subschool. The choice implies some degree of student responsibility, authority, and commitment. It signals to the students that the learning community offers more freedom to them than the traditional high school, and that it asks more of them. The choice legitimizes many of the unique demands the community may make on its students. Before making the choice, the students and their families should be given information about the community, through literature and meetings with faculty, students, and alumni. The choice should require the students and their families to submit a written application.

The mechanics of such a potential choice are not insurmountable. Today, most grade school graduates can only go on to the high school that their grade school "feeds." The proposed change means that there must be at least two high schools available to graduates of each grade school. These same two schools might be available to graduates of several grade schools, so the proposal does not necessarily mean a great increase in the number of high schools (though there may be other good reasons for increasing that number). The choice can be created by (*a*) designating two or more existing high schools as alternative choices, (*b*) subdividing an existing high school into two or more separate institutions in the same building (see the discussion about student grouping in Chapter 3), or (*c*) creating additional high schools and buildings. In any case, at least one of the new units will be a school conducted on learning-community principles. Acceptance of applicants into the learning community should not be automatic. Part of learning about commitment consists of discovering how to want and strive for something without the assurance that whatever you want you can get. Acceptance can depend on the apparent commitment of the students and their parents to the principles of the community. What was the character of the student's grade school conduct? Perhaps an excessively individualistic student, or one with excessively individualistic parents, should not be admitted to a cooperatively oriented school. Or, if such children are admitted, they should enter with full knowledge that new demands will be made on them.

This concept of student and family choice will give the learning community a unique sense of identity—which is one element of community. Such uniqueness may seem anomalous since most American schools tend to have relatively common curricula; probably such commonalities will continue to persist, even in the learning community. However, school identity is not necessarily dependent on radically different and unique curricula. Common curricula and unique identity may both be maintained, if attention is given to such matters as codes of student conduct, ceremonies, and other symbolic factors. Rupert Wilkinson made the following remarks about the development of school identities among public schools in Victorian England:

the device of tacitly accepted etiquette among students was closely connected with a process which economists of the American automobile industry today call "marginal product differentiation." Although the Victorian period saw a basic standardization of public school institutions, it was also a time when each school strove to make itself a unique object of loyalty by elaborating its own language, folklore, and customs, and—for such schools as Eton and Winchester—making compulsory its own special variants of football. At several schools, the "new boy" had to take an examination

testing his knowledge of the school and its unique-seeming tradi-
tions. The effect of the exam was to crown the newcomer's period
of orientation with an initiation.[22]

Acceptance of applicants may also be conditioned on the community maintaining an appropriate mix of students. If some serious
imbalance arises in the mix of students, extra consideration should
be given to applicants who can help to correct this imbalance and
thus assist the progress of the whole community. It is not easy to
say what is an imbalance. Presumably, the community needs both
natural cooperators and members who need help and prodding. The
"naturals" make the community go, and the less skilled students
provide occasions for the naturals to refine their skills; at the same
time the less skilled acquire, through experience and interaction,
the skills they lack. Undoubtedly, too many of either group may
handicap the school in doing its job.

Admittance also raises the issue of transferring out and in. Transferring out, especially to a nearby school, should be severely discouraged. The students and their families make an informed commitment, and it promotes poor learning to treat such commitments
as acts revocable at convenience. In adult life, all important commitments look different in the middle than they did at the beginning; the person with affective skills is the one who is able to deal
with such challenges and benefits. In addition, there is the matter
of responsibility to others; for instance, when the student was admitted, it is likely that some other student was denied admission, in
preference to the student now seeking to transfer out. But, ultimately, transferring out must be permissible. Transfers into the
community should be discouraged for the obvious reason that such
transfers lessen the evolution of a sense of community.

The question of the relationship between transfers and family
moves to new homes or jobs will naturally arise. Such moves obviously handicap the development of the learning community by
necessitating student transfers. At the same time, the fragmented
and undifferentiated nature of many modern school programs gives
parents little incentive to assist healthy maturation of their children
by avoiding frequent moves. However, if school programs begin to
emerge that foster identity and community, parents may be more
willing to forego moving because of the clear learning benefits that
stability can create for their child. Furthermore, if enrollment in a
learning community becomes a deliberate act (rather than just the
next step in schooling), parents and children who apply for admit-

tance will be advised, when they apply, of the school's desire to have the students attend through the whole program. Then parents are saying, by the act of enrollment, that they are tentatively making a commitment to keep their child in the school through the program. In instances where a parent's job is obviously subject to routine transfers, the parents may be explicitly asked their views about the transfer situation. After all, the potentially transferring parents are asking the school to accept their child in preference to another. If the school must make such a choice, it can ask for plausible signs of family commitment.

In the longer run, this policy of designing schools that are communities, and of asking for parental commitments, may have constructive effects on social policy. Today, many parents unselfishly decide to accept certain drawbacks to live in communities which they believe offer the best school opportunities for their children. If learning communities apply an antimove policy, they may convince parents that the tax level of the community, or the size of its lawns, is far less important to learning than the parents' willingness to accept diminished geographic mobility. As this parental attitude becomes more widespread, employers and communities may adopt policies about community "turnover" that are more congruent with actual social needs.

Bringing Back Alumni
A close relationship between the school and its alumni can make the school community a more relevant microcosm. The alumni can be involved in many school activities: tutoring, coaching, managing dramatic activities, and participating in other extracurricular affairs. Useful activities can be accomplished in pre-schools by some grade schoolers. High school alumni can assist in college advisement and job seeking. In these activities, the alumni may simultaneously be engaged in self-learning, for example, learning as grade school students through their responsibilities in assisting in their former nursery school.

But the return of alumni does far more than create new teaching resources. It demonstrates to present students the validity and coherence of their community: even former students, who are not under the control of the school, still choose to return and participate in the teaching process under which they were educated. This demonstration can convince students to strive to meet the affective learning tests posed by the school. At the same time, the aim of attracting back alumni is a constructive challenge to the learning

community. Return is likely only if the graduates have commitment
to the school; in other words, if the school was a community when
they attended. So one measure of the effectiveness of the school's
community is its ability to generate loyalty. Information from the
alumni about the relevance or irrelevance of their former school
experiences to the next level they attended will also provide the
school with useful information about the quality of its learning
processes.

The alumni can prepare students for their next level of experience and offer counsel about any choices they may have to make.
Furthermore, they can be of assistance to the students when they
graduate and attend the alumni's school. These activities will help
present students to understand that their school creates commitments among and between present and past students. As a result,
individual incidents of human interaction in the school will be seen
as forming part of a pattern of relationships. This understanding
will encourage the students to temper their current actions with an
appreciation of their long-range implications; such habits stimulate
the development of foresight, sensitivity, and persistence.

Unquestionably, the alumni can also obtain significant satisfaction in returning to their former school in a different and constructive role. Put simply, it is pleasant to return to an area where one
was subordinate and fulfill a more superior role. The present students may find their subordinate school roles made more tolerable
by their own perception that more authoritative and responsible
roles lie before them.

Reorganizing Interstudent Responsibilities
More occasions must be created for students to be responsible for
the conduct of each other. These patterns of shared responsibility—
and authority—are essential characteristics of a community, in
which members perceive there are networks of shared obligations.
The responsibilities can include tutoring, participation in sports
and clubs, maintenance of buildings and grounds, performance of
community service chores by groups of students, and going on
camping trips. Some activities, such as tutoring other students, will
be a natural extension of existing school programs. Other activities,
such as expecting groups of students to work on community service
chores away from the school building, may require sharp revisions
in current school patterns. In later sections of this chapter we will
discuss more carefully the development of these new patterns. But
all activities of this sort have one important common element that

will present students with a novel and constructive challenge: the activities will require students to give and receive directions and advice from each other, as well as from overseeing adults.

The significance of this challenge is suggested by a remark made by a high school teacher. The thrust of the remark was that one could not expect marginal high school students to accept tutoring from better students: this would involve too much loss of face. The remark was made before a group of teachers. The members of the group gave the remark a mixed response; some said that the proposition was absolutely correct, while others said that the resistance could be overcome.

The remark points out some of the difficulties involved in many student-to-student responsibilities. Modern students do not feel at ease giving and taking help or orders from each other: because they do not see their schools as communities, and they do not expect to receive academic help from most other students or to render such help to them. This pattern forms an interesting contrast with past traditions—when youth-to-youth help in learning was viewed as natural. For instance, in their autobiographies both Benjamin Franklin and Andrew Carnegie described how they and their young friends organized groups to learn through reading and discussing books among themselves.[23] Apparently one of the effects of the individualistic focus of modern schools has been to diminish the ability of the young to help each other learn.

This ineptitude of modern youths is simply another sign of their lack of affective knowledge. Giving and taking orders or advice is a skill. That is, it is not too difficult to teach someone to utter orders in an articulate style or to compel someone to mechanically respond, "Yes, I will do that." However, such formalistic conduct will rarely do the job. When an able supervisor gives orders or advice, he or she perceives the relationships among the task at hand, the resources available, and the skills, attitude, and work load of the subordinate receiving orders. The subordinate must also engage in a nearly equivalent analysis. These assessments require affective skills in the supervisor and the subordinate. In a particular instance, any of the foregoing items, such as the attitude of the subordinate, could be studied in an intensive and subtle fashion.

It is not surprising that high school students can have difficulty giving or receiving orders or help from their peers; it is a complex skill that they have not practiced. However, these difficulties are largely of adult manufacture and can be corrected by new adult policies. The new policies must make it clear to students that they are expected to give and receive orders and tutoring from each other. Time must be set aside for such activities. Assignments must be made. Teachers must be prepared to oversee the activities, to prevent gross incompetence and to tactfully intervene in appropriate situations. Performance-oriented criteria must be established, so that students can see what goals to aim for. What levels of attainment do tutees currently have, or what should they attain? What kind of chores should student groups undertake, how long should they take, and how shall attainment of the task be defined? Students who show skill at giving or receiving orders or advice, or at related skills, such as planning or persuasion, should be recognized and rewarded. Students who conspicuously lack such skills should be given help and be stimulated to improve.

This process will be facilitated by the evolution of the school into a learning community. Community members expect to receive help from one another and are solicitous when giving orders. If the students are gratified at being in a respected community, they must do their part to deserve their membership.

Interstudent responsibility, focused on group tasks, will also make it harder for students to hide from maturity. Such concealment is all too frequent today. One study discussed and analyzed the concealment possibilities in modern colleges. The discussion is equally applicable to many suburban schools. The study noted that society has "postponed for many years the stabilizing influence of earning one's own living. In the sheltered atmosphere of the college campus, the risks of the student of experimental and recreational drug use are minimal compared with the potential consequences of such behavior for a jobholder. The student who gets drunk or 'stoned' five nights in a row and misses his morning classes may still get a passing grade in the course. The jobholder, on the other hand, is likely to find himself unemployed the second morning he fails to show up for work."[24]

But the demands of other members of the school community who are burdened by lax "citizens" can stimulate slack students to display stability. In the same manner, team members in competitive sports encourage and goad teammates to improve.

Selecting and Training Appropriately Qualified Teachers
If the school aims to become a community, the teachers will have to accept some new responsibilities and abandon some old ones. The new responsibilities will require them to be more concerned with the affective conduct of students: to see that the students dis-

play responsible attitudes toward teachers, fellow students, and the community in which they learn. This will require the teachers to assume similar responsibilities: to attend and participate in the ceremonies, to honor the school symbols, and to develop a greater measure of interpersonal skills than many teachers now possess. These interpersonal skills will include cooperative planning with other teachers and students; the ability to delegate important responsibilities to students and to sensitively oversee their completion; the willingness to demand and receive intraschool and intragroup loyalty from students, other teachers, and alumni; and the flexibility to work easily with out-of-school adults who will assist students in learning and applying affective skills. A later chapter will analyze these new demands from the perspective of the individual teacher, but this subsection will consider the demands from the perspective of administrators who will hire, train, and supervise such teachers.

Many teachers will have difficulty in acquiring these skills, for they are not usually developed by modern teacher-education programs. Indeed, such programs probably tend to have a high degree of individualistic emphasis. Almost all college classrooms are self-contained, college assignments are usually given and graded individually, and ceremony is a dying college tradition. Another complication is that many schoolteachers have probably selected their profession because it is a craft that removes them from many interadult demands. Finally, at the high school level, many teachers have become accustomed to presenting carefully defined materials to large numbers of students throughout the school year; this pattern conflicts with the thrust of the learning community, which envisions teachers relating to smaller numbers of students, over broader areas of the curriculum, and over longer periods of time.

Selecting and training teachers will be difficult, although there will be important forces supporting the effort. The support will arise from the innate desire of almost all human beings to work within a community. The problem will be that teachers, despite this desire to enjoy community, may very often be unable to appreciate the mix of voluntarism, compulsion, rationality, and ceremony that makes community work. In other words, the staff may resist the steps that produce the very ends they desire. The resistance may take several forms: the rejection of compulsory ceremony as irrational and anti-individualistic; the refusal to accept authority over students performing nonacademic chores as part of their school work on the grounds that such chores are anti-intellectual or exploitative; the denial of the principle of collective responsibility; or an unwillingness to become concerned with the governance of student conduct out of a belief that administering discipline is demeaning.

Unquestionably, reshaping these attitudes will take time and understanding. Visits by faculty to schools successfully practicing these patterns may be helpful. Some faculty members (perhaps physical education teachers because they typically work with students in teams) may show greater understanding of the objectives; others may gradually be brought along through staff training and discussions. However, administrators will be most successful in their efforts if they rely on affect-oriented techniques, for example, ceremonies for the staff alone or group meetings at unique sites under unique circumstances.

Staff selection is also important. The deficiencies in present teacher training and experience suggest the kinds of training and preparation that can be most relevant in evaluating job applicants. The training should be in schools, colleges, and programs that aim to inculcate cooperative skills in their students, by having them engage in cooperative efforts and by creating a community spirit within the group. The faculties in these programs should engage in similar cooperation. Special consideration should be given to applicants who have held cooperative responsibilities—in business, government, or community affairs. This experience is so desirable that administrators should attempt to revise hiring and certification criteria to give special emphasis to such qualifications, even to preferring persons so qualified, but without teacher training, over applicants who have merely had traditional teacher training.

Supervising Teachers
Teachers in the community-oriented school will have greater discretion and more diversified responsibilities than they generally exercise. Consequently, they must be given more occasions for supervision and support. It should be possible to find the time for such supervision and support, since many traditional teacher responsibilities will have been shifted to students; as a result of these shifts, teachers will have time away from class supervision to participate in meetings. These discussions between teachers and supervisors will focus on the progress of groups of students and individual students, as well as the kinds of intergroup coordination that should be undertaken.

The faculty may examine whether particular groups of students are effectively doing their community service chores, or if a group has planned an appropriate drama for the school festival, or how students can help organize a welcoming ceremony for the incoming freshman class. In other words, how well is the community working? Inevitably, such discussions will raise questions about the competencies and interests of the students. The talk will be about how well students are doing at affective learning: are they assuming responsibilities, displaying leadership, planning realistically. These matters are not subject to definitive conclusions; however, sensitive professionals can obtain constructive insights through exchanges of opinion with experienced colleagues. The discussants can develop plans to restructure the demands and supports offered to students. Some students may need further recognition and reward, either from the teacher or from other students supervising their conduct. Perhaps greater demands or responsibilities should be placed on a student who is avoiding responsibility. Again, recognition can be given to a group of students in tribute to their performance, or students may find their responsibilities diminished as a result of inadequate performance. The by-product of these discussions should be better learning for the students. There will be routine occasions during the day for such discussions, and the school will have private areas for such meetings.

Supervision will also be related to teacher evaluation and rewards. At this time, teacher hiring in many school districts is a relatively careful process. However, the probationary process, after which the teacher receives tenure, is often a pro forma matter. And once tenure is received, teacher salary increases are usually dependent on seniority and acquiring college credits through taking graduate courses. This pattern means that, once a candidate is selected, the supervisor's role in reviewing conduct is only modest. The supervisor can do little to increase or lessen the teacher's pay for displaying conspicuous competence or incompetence. This powerlessness diminishes the incentive for either the supervisor or the teacher to engage in productive retraining or demanding cooperation. This process of routine salary increases and ritualistic supervision is allegedly justified on the grounds that seniority and completed courses are reasonable measures of teacher competency, and that supervisors do not have the time for more careful reviews. In fact, the research demonstrates that there is only (at best) a modest relationship between seniority and courses, on the one hand, and teacher competency (as measured by increased pupil learning), on the other. It is true that, in some school systems, the supervisors are spread far too thin to enable them to effectively supervise or evaluate teachers. However, the learning-community proposal assumes the existence of smaller schools or subschool units within the school. Such arrangements should provide for the creation of adequate supervisory staff. The staff may be financed by enlarging the basic pupil-teacher ratios and giving greater responsibilities to groups of students. It is more important that teachers be well supervised, trained, and coordinated than that good ratios of poorly coordinated teachers be maintained.

Giving supervisors real authority over teacher raises and their day-to-day conduct will radically revise the character of the school. Supervisors and teachers will become a great deal more concerned with what each other is doing. They will be stimulated to consider what the objectives of individual teachers and groups of teachers are and how things can be managed to achieve them. It is likely that, over time, the process of supervision and salary increases will develop certain regularities. However, unless union patterns make for intensive rigidities, the supervisor's salary-assessment responsibilities should make for a cooperative and sensitive relationship among the staff. People will be stimulated to ask what they should be doing and why. This will provide students with a constructive example of adult cooperative activity.

The proportion of students who participated in district music festi-
vals and dramatic, journalistic, and student government competi-
tions reached a peak in high schools with enrollments between 61
and 150. The proportion of participants was 3 to 20 times as great
in small schools as in the largest school. . . . The findings indicate
that the small school students lived under greater day-by-day at-
traction, obligation, and external pressure to take active part in the
various behavior settings of their schools.
—Roger G. Barker and Paul V. Gump[1]

CHAPTER 4
Administering Suburban Schools - II

New Kinds of Interaction between Students and between Students and Adults

If students are to learn important affective skills, they must be put in touch with persons who possess those skills, and they must see the skills being exercised. Important affective skills are possessed by able adults, and they are exercised in situations where adults are asked to accept diverse responsibilities. Students, therefore, during their school years, must be brought in contact with a number and variety of adults in diverse situations. These occasions will enable students to discover more about affective skills and will stimulate them to practice the skills themselves in their contacts with these adults and eventually with each other.

Parents and Outsiders in the School Program
Parents and other adult outsiders should be given greater roles in in-school activities. These roles can easily arise out of the reshaped responsibilities of the students. If the students are responsible for the maintenance of the school or grounds, the production of plays, or the performing of out-of-school services to the community, occasions will naturally arise when the students will need forms of counsel that the teachers may not be able to offer: how menus are planned, budgets developed, gardens maintained, community service agencies contacted, or costumes designed and made. Adults may be invited to the school to talk with students, or committees of students may be directed to go out, find, and interview these adults on their jobs or at their homes. From these meetings it should be quite possible for the adults and students in many instances to develop continuing relationships.

Sometimes these adults may be discovered by the teacher, or perhaps the teacher may develop a list of qualified adults and ask the students to contact the persons on the list to see which ones are available for the task at hand. The students themselves may also be asked to develop such a list.

The matter of soliciting parental help can be assisted by the school adopting a parental "time tithing" policy, which would require each parent, or family, to periodically contribute a predetermined number of hours to personally assisting the school program. Money could not substitute for personal time. Acceptance of this policy by parents could be one condition for a student's admittance to the learning community. While such a program would unquestionably need community support, it would provide a simple mechanism for creating a pool of out-of-school adult help. Naturally, not all the parents may have temperaments that let them easily fit into the school program; but this is one of the valuable challenges of such tithing. In life, we are often forced to work with persons with whom we are not easily congenial. Then, we are stimulated to change our expectations, grit our teeth, and see it through, or discover unexpected virtues in our companions. This requires ingenuity and flexibility; tithing ensures that the students and teachers will be faced with such challenges, which will give them occasions for affective learning.

When adults come into the school to meet with students, the teachers will strive to stay in touch with the resulting developments, for the teachers have the ultimate responsibility for the children's school-related development. They cannot adequately exercise that responsibility unless they are informed of all important relationships that arise from the children's school work. Further, the external adults may be unable to be of full help to the students unless they know something about the children's other activities in the school. In other words, the teachers, in order to establish a cooperative and supportive relationship with adults who regularly come in contact with students through their school work, must be accessible to these adults.

Another constructive way to use the counsel of external adults is to send students out to collect information: how are budgets developed in organizations (economics); the adventures of immigrants, travelers, and war veterans (geography, social science); the responsibilities of computer programmers (mathematics); how surveyors operate (mathematics); what advertising copywriters do (writing). Or each student (or group of students) can be held responsible for finding and bringing one guest who is not a parent into the school to discuss an appropriate topic. Teachers can help students develop lists of questions to guide their interviews.

These occasions will help students see how adults act in different jobs and professions, and such assignments as interviewing or finding people to invite will provoke the students to strive to emulate the behavior that will be more likely to win the cooperation of outsiders. That behavior involves a series of important affective skills.

The learning community, in its efforts to enlarge its pool of instructors, will naturally also use the experience of older and retired members of the community. Such efforts will supply the community with a precious pool of former gardeners, accountants, salesmen, carpenters, housewives and mothers, politicians, and doctors, who will immeasurably enrich the formal instructional skills of the faculty. The presence of older people will require the learning community to view them as a natural part of its society. Such a view will only make the community's practices congruent with those of most human societies, as can be seen in one study of the role of the aged in primitive societies:

aged men and women have been generally regarded as repositories of knowledge and the imparters of valuable information. . . . They have been esteemed as experts in solving the problems of life. They have supervised and instructed in the arts and crafts, and have initiated hazardous and important undertakings, such as house-building, boat construction, the planting and harvesting of crops, and warfare. They have been in constant demand for treating diseases, exorcizing spirits. . . . They might shop for the household. They might concentrate on the lighter tasks and, whenever possible, utilize their long experience and greater knowledge in the more complicated skills, rituals, and ceremonies of daily life.[2]

The integration of the community of the aged into the school will demonstrate to the students the rich progression that lies before them and will help them understand that old age does not mean isolation, but rather an occasion to be of service and to possess authority. This proposal may seem to fail to recognize the dynamic character of modern society and to give excessive weight to experience. However, modern schools probably overemphasize the learning of new, cognitive information that is only modestly relevant to the immediate life of their students. Older persons will bring into the school rich experience in planning, cooperation, and communication—all highly relevant and valuable skills that do not change radically.

Out-of-School Responsibilities for Students
Almost none of the economic costs of suburban schools are borne by the students themselves. Schools are supported by the taxes of parents, other adults, and businesses. The taxes contributed by students who pay taxes on incomes they have earned are very slight. This arrangement places students in an essentially unsatisfying role: under current arrangements the only service they can render to society is to be patient and to learn. This is a demeaning position. It implies that, despite all that society is doing for the students, there is nothing worthwhile a student can do in exchange

at the age of twelve, fifteen, or seventeen. Adults may see the lack of demands as a favor to the students, but to live on the largess of others for many years is not flattering. Perhaps many students do not express obvious gratitude for these benefits, but it even takes maturity to continuously accept gifts with style and gratitude. The matter is further complicated by the content of modern school curricula and the media. These sources try to stimulate interest by emphasizing that we are in the midst of a series of social crises. The children's natural response is to desire to do something to help, especially since they are clearly being supported by the society. But they are told to wait. Under these circumstances, one can imagine that students may be possessed by dramatically conflicting views on their roles in society: one, an overwhelming sense of ineffectuality, powerlessness, and despair, and, two, a resentful and exaggerated sense of their suppressed potency. Neither of these views constitutes healthy adaptation.

To correct this situation, students should be expected to carry out constructive community chores as part of their school responsibilities. The chores will be a recognition of their responsibility to the community that is supporting their learning and an occasion for the students to acquire, in a small but vital way, a sense of impact and potency. The students should not be paid for the chores, since they represent the students' repayment of the implicit social debt provoked by their subsidized school attendance. The chores also are a mode of recognizing the students' active participation in the extraschool community, and, naturally, they will also be an occasion for the learning and exercise of affective skills. The chores can involve such activities as the maintenance of gardens, parks, and playgrounds; the rendering of services for shut-ins, the hospitalized, and the aged; or working at child-care centers. The tasks accomplished should be clearly attributed to the students and school, through flags, plaques, diverse ceremonies, or students wearing clearly identifiable badges or uniforms. These attributions will give the students pride and will win them well-deserved respect.

Most of the chores will be done during the school year but not necessarily during school time. Some chores may be especially adapted to group summer assignments. In almost all cases the chores should be organized so that students accept both individual and group responsibility for successful completion.

The organizing of such chores will be a time-consuming task, even when significant responsibilities can be delegated to students, alumni, or upper classmen. However, in the long run, the chores represent a significant increment to the wealth of the community. This may arguably justify an additional budgetary appropriation. Parental time (via tithing) can also be helpful in the organizing process. In the final analysis, the school's faculty will be responsible for seeing that the chores are properly performed. However, this should not require the faculty to routinely engage in on-the-scene supervision. But the faculty members must stay in touch with these activities, through visits and interviews, so that they can maintain the knowledge and contacts that permit them to work with the whole child.

The great significance of work contributions toward developing community-oriented attitudes among students should also be recognized. The derivation of the word *liturgy* gives us some understanding of this significance: "In ancient Athens, the man whose wealth exceeded a certain sum had, in a yearly rota, to perform certain 'liturgies'—literally, 'folk-works.' He had to keep a warship in commission for one year (with the privilege of commanding it, if he chose), or finance the production of plays at the Festival, or equip a religious procession. It was a heavy burden, and no doubt unwelcome, but at least some fun could be got out of it and some pride taken in it. There was satisfaction and honor to be gained from producing a trilogy worthily before one's fellow-citizens."[3]

Reorganizing Student Social Activities
Student social activities are a vital part of modern student life. Unfortunately, the activities often fail to provide the students with the types of interactive demands that facilitate important affective learning. This failure is due to the lack of important affective learning opportunities in suburban environments and the comparatively low degree of adult interest and control over many student social activities.

An example of the lack of affective learning arrangements is the frequent absence of important physical challenges in the secure suburbs to inspire more intense group engagement. Such challenges stimulate youths to make cooperative demands on each other—and to grow through these demands. Because of the lack of adult interest and control, youth interaction is not directed at assisting the young to develop adult attitudes and skills. Furthermore, without adult direction, the modes of interaction may take a rather sterile and unsatisfying form, for example, the development of transitory rock groups. "Adult direction" does not mean constant adult presence or adult approval of individual actions. It does mean that adult-established parameters determine the general form of youth conduct. For instance, it means youth dances and entertainment where adults can also comfortably participate. But, in addition, it means that adults ensure that there are situations where youth can comfortably go dancing. It also may mean that high schools have fraternities, sororities, and other student social clubs, under general adult direction—and that the faculty ensures that such groups are formed and continued.

These adult-designed activities stimulate the young to engage in rewarding social exchanges and provide a framework that assists these exchanges. The framework stimulates the young to think in terms of planning parties, service activities, camping trips, and expeditions; making arrangements to provide tutoring for other members of the group; or designing and conducting group ceremonies. At the same time, the engagement of adults provides the young with mature role models and helps them to see the tie-in between the youthful activities and their eventual adulthood.

The Role of Humor
A viable community must provide its members with occasions to enjoy themselves in simple, direct fashions: practical jokes, foolishness, parties, funny stories. The operational structure of the modern school lacks many characteristics that encourage humor among students and faculty. Humor is fostered by situations where people have prolonged and intense contacts which have built shared understandings to joke about and which create dramatic tensions that invite the release of humor. A flexible time division also helps, since rigid schedules restrict the play of imagination that leads to laughter. Large, relatively crowded buildings also dampen humor, since discipline must be maintained in such environments to prevent disorder.

Many of the changes already proposed will encourage the release of humor among students and faculty in the learning community. These changes include students' being directed to work in small continuing groups with somewhat flexible schedules, generally under the supervision of faculty members who have persisting responsibilities for these students. Such patterns will provide many occasions for the development and release of humor. However, the learning community should also deliberately set aside formal occasions for fun. This would be a simple recognition of the Latin proverb, "Semel in anno licet insemenire"—once a year it is lawful to be insane. Of course, Halloween has been one traditional American occasion for such license, but suburban environments often lack the materials for spontaneous play. Through the exploration of different strategies the learning community can help fill this lack.

The humor—which is a form of subliminated release of aggression—may be directed against another learning community or school, through practical jokes or other forms of pranks at a traditional time. Perhaps a periodic festival of satires and farces, filled with loud and noisy jokes and costumes, poking fun at members of the community, could be held. Or every subgroup might present a humorous skit to the whole group of which it is a part. A school joke book could be produced annually by the students. Masks and funny costumes are important, too; different initiation ceremonies can evolve that provide occasions for their use.

But the release of humor in school is both a satisfaction and a vital area of affective education. There is a subtle, but critical, line between humor and sadism. That line can be learned. In the short run, if the line is not understood, jokesters can cause deep pain. In the longer run, if the line is not understood, the system will arrange to outlaw humor (which is what happens in many existing schools). In the longest run, an environment without humor becomes arid and overcast with apathy; such environments are inherently unstable.

Humor, then, must be an integral part of the learning community so that the students and faculty can learn how to work with it: to sense the skills that transform harsh-sounding words into a spirited joke and to give students and faculty occasions to be both the maker and the butt of jokes—so that both tolerance and tact are learned. Because the community will create strong mutual obligations among its members, the jokesters and the butts will also realize that they share important responsibilities; this sharing gives them strong incentives to temper both their humor and their resentment at provocative humor. Furthermore, the community members will begin to discover how humor, as a release for frustration and anger, may be a vital solvent for groups facing challenging responsibilities.

Different Subdivisions within the Student Body

Students in the schools are divided into various subgroups, some of which are structured into cohorts, for example, second grade, freshmen. Other groups are formed within cohorts, for example, a particular class or one of several home-room groups in the freshman class. Still others are intercohort, for example, the school chorus or football team. In some modern schools, the total student body is also subdivided into vertical subgroups, for instance, there are three subschools of 700 students each in a school with a total enrollment of 2,100.

These grouping patterns are affected by several factors. In some schools, students take academic programs that are not strictly shaped by cohort: a sophomore may enroll in a particular class typically taken by freshmen, or vice versa. Accumulation of credits is thus substituted for passage through years. Where there are subschools, the total student body of the major school may still use some common work areas and take shared classes. When students have home rooms or are grouped in continuing classes in elementary schools, these home rooms or classes may have varying degrees of continuity: they may be restructured each year or even persist over several years.

All these modes of grouping or regrouping students have significant implications for the nature of student learning, since the existence of communities depends on the development of identifiable boundaries which demarcate groups with persisting, important, shared interests. In many cases, the current forms of division lessen the possibility for in-school community. Constructive changes in these forms are possible and necessary.

Dividing Student Progress through School
The traditional basic boundaries in most schools are formed by the existence of identifiable cohorts of freshmen, sophomores, juniors, and seniors. It is desirable to make strenuous efforts to maintain the annual class as a significant entity in the school—even at the expense of affecting some students' rate of progress through school. This maintenance would cause members of such a group to generally take the same subjects at about the same point in their school career. As a result, each student's relationships with students in his or her cohort would assume a relatively persisting character. Such relationships would strongly affect the nature of interstudent relations, since continuous relationships—as compared to transitory contacts—provide occasions for more intense emotional engagement, which should tend to train the students in the direction and management of their more profound emotions. In contrast, transitory contacts simply stimulate us to conceal our emotions, and the persisting concealment of powerful emotions can provoke alienation and apathy. Furthermore, the development of identifiable cohorts will provide students in all cohorts with predictable patterns

for structuring intercohort relations. This should foster intercohort engagement—in contrast to the current situation, where the comparative lack of patterns fosters general withdrawal.

It is true that the principle of division by cohorts—like all other modes of establishing identity—poses problems. It does not easily allow for students who may be able to cover the basic program at an accelerated rate. Furthermore, some especially slow students may not be able to keep up with the learning rate of the class. However, the learning community will attempt to deal with these problems by providing a variety of affective responsibilities (e.g., tutoring or community project planning) to enrich the affective learning of students who have satisfied the cognitive standards and by using the cognitively skilled students to assist the slow learners. The members of the cohort will thus be striving to help each other through school, rather than expecting the fast ones to run ahead, while the slow ones fall farther behind. Students who fall decisively behind should be shifted back to an earlier cohort, but this should be infrequent. Needs currently met by the use of electives, and other modes of allowing for cognitive or affective diversity, should be satisfied by extracurricular or other noncredit activities. In other words, if some students have a special capability in, say, language or mathematics, the school's posture is that the students should enjoy themselves through intensely practicing that skill, but they should not receive formal credit for it. This pattern would imply that all students should have a basic body of common responsibilities, some common free-time activities, and some divergent ones.

Another device to protect the integrity of the cohort can be the precommencement exam referred to in the previous chapter. If students fail that exam and still want a diploma, they should be permitted to stay behind for one year, fully participate as students, and take the test the next year. This preserves the logic of the test and commencement—commencement is not simply attained by putting in time: the test must be passed. But there can also be alternatives open to the student about to take the senior exam. The student can ask for a postponement of the exam, stay in school for one more year, and then take the examination. The logic is that taking the test should represent a decision—a step toward maturity—on the part of the student. A deliberate decision to postpone that step, if the student accepts the consequences of persisting studenthood (e.g., continued service activities), can be another form of maturity and should not be criticized. In sum, the suggested test option arrangement permits the school to keep students in their class group and ensures that they meet a meaningful final standard, without excessively penalizing them.

Planning and Dividing the School Day
In the majority of elementary schools, the school day is planned around the work of the self-contained individual class and teacher. This creates some flexibility in working out the day to suit the needs of the class and its subunits and allows for spontaneous shifts in plans. After grade school, the student in any cohort is taught by a variety of specialized teachers, who are sometimes also responsible for teaching students in other cohorts. To use teachers' time efficiently, the practice is to devise schedules so that different teachers will be available to particular groups of students and/or individual students. This involves an elaborate planning process, through which each student's activities are coordinated with the available time of each teacher, so that students will not have to wait to see an already busy teacher and a teacher will not be left with free time and no students. The aim of the process is to avoid "down time," that is, occasions when the machinery is shut down and workers are paid but have no work to do because of poor planning of the production process (e.g., the nondelivery of raw materials). In the school, down time might occur if teachers or students had blocks of unscheduled school time, which they might not purposefully use in teaching or attending class. However, this scheduling system has other important learning consequences.

Undoubtedly, it teaches students and teachers to think of their school day in terms of clearly defined time blocks, or periods. Teachers lecture and conduct classroom discussions with this constraint in mind. And, very likely, students listen and participate in class discussions with a similar perspective. Learning about such constraints has some obvious values, for much of adult life is carefully bound by time and schedules. Being regimented by periods teaches students to keep in mind what the time is and how much is left for the discussion of lecture work in each period. But, the modern school probably overdoes the matter.

An important negative effect of being tightly bound by time is that students learn that the schedule can only permit very limited spontaneity: the end of the period is always looming ahead. No matter how profound or funny the topic under discussion, the students understand that it must be finished within a comparatively limited time. It is practically impossible to let things run on, because down time will then be created for other classes. The likely effect of this process is that students and many teachers may unconsciously restrain their emotions to ensure that they do not get too excited by any topic under discussion, for, if they do, they may be left high and dry at the end of the class and be compelled to move on to some entirely different issue. It is probably highly frustrating to leave a discussion on the significance of *Romeo and Juliet* to go to trigonometry class, and then to a history class on the slave trade.

Of course, as with other aspects of time management, adults often have to coordinate their emotions and their schedules. President Lyndon B. Johnson once said that the hardest part of his job was the distribution of posthumous Medals of Honor to the families of servicemen; presumably, the president, after the distribution, had to go on to other, remotely connected, duties. The students' responsibilities for emotional management have some parallels to those of the president, or other adults. But we may be asking too much of the students too soon. In our desire to get a great deal of diversified, formal material into comparatively young persons, we have probably overscheduled their time and left them with insufficient occasions to emotionally, as well as cognitively, receive the materials put before them. Perhaps tutorial school arrangements (with students acting as tutors), by increasing the number of "teachers," may permit looser scheduling. Another important step will be to diminish the specialization of teachers, so that students may work with only two or three teachers in the day, rather than four or five. Obviously, the fewer number of teachers cannot cover, in the same depth, the same materials as four or five specialized teachers. However, the word *depth* is misleading, since the current definition of depth may actually foster student disengagement. Perhaps more genuine depth will be achieved by fewer teachers having students for longer blocks of time. Such teachers would be able to occasionally spontaneously reorganize their materials within the longer blocks as student and teacher interest dictates. This arrangement can increase student engagement with the school and its subject matter.

The division of the school day also has important implications for the ability of students to engage in group projects in school or outside school during or after school hours. Group projects imply that groups of students must be able to conveniently arrange to meet by themselves or with a teacher or other adult for planning, discussion, or actual work. If too many students have highly individualized schedules, and a great deal of their time is spent in formal classes, such coordination becomes very difficult. Probably, the solution is for the school to ensure that discrete groups of students have substantially common schedules, including shared classes and shared free time. These groups should be large enough to permit the development of several working subgroups of students. Different theories can be followed in designing the basic groups. They can be based on subclasses within a class, for example, one home room in the freshman class. They can encompass a whole cohort, for example, all freshmen. Or they can be a cross section of several cohorts, for example, twenty-five freshmen and twenty-five sophomores, so that the different age groups may undertake different responsibilities. The scheduling arrangements can also assume that some of the time of the group, for example, one day a week, will be set aside for out-of-school projects. These varied arrangements will be facilitated by lessening the number of different teachers who work with any one student during the day. This change will simplify the matter of scheduling the students' time to assist their work, since the smaller number of teachers will permit greater flexibility in scheduling.

Grouping Students in the School

One thesis of this book is that continuing relationships between limited numbers of children and adults, over rather long periods of time, focused on specified and concrete responsibilities, are extremely valuable to affective learning. Perhaps it should also be recognized, at this point, that such continuing relationships can also subject the children to excessive exposure to poor role models or insensitive mentors or give them inadequate experience in developing personal flexibility. A counterthesis might contend that fluidity in relationships in youth environments may be more desirable than continuity. Of course, the application of any particular thesis can be overdone, but the continuity thesis does not imply severe constraints on students. It assumes that there will be several faculty members directly assigned to the group of students, that many other faculty members will be about in the school, that the peer group will be between twenty and one hundred, and that the possibility of transfer in the school is not ruled out. Finally, the children live at home, with the support and advice of their families. Thus, a school that fosters student-teacher continuity can still allow for some variety in relationships. But the continuity model does imply certain constraints, which assume that children should learn how to develop continuing relationships with adults and peers, and that this learning is worth some degree of tension and risk. The fluidity thesis has a different assumption: that children and adolescents should be assisted to avoid relationships that threaten to cause sustained tension; when interpersonal stress gets strong, emotional and physical withdrawal are conveniently viable options. Educators and parents must form their own opinions as to the comparative value of these conflicting theses in analyzing the current suburban youth environment.

The continuity thesis, when applied to actual school operations, signifies that identifiable groups of students should develop and maintain contacts with specific faculty members throughout their school years. In the elementary school this pattern is already widespread, but it may warrant intensification. The modern high school does not have a strong tradition of such continuity. Students are often assigned to home rooms, and these assignments may keep the same group of students together during their full stay in the high school. But, the home room is typically only an administrative unity to assign each teacher a particular group of students for paperwork, such as recording attendance. The students in the "room" do not necessarily attend classes together; nor are they or their home room teacher expected to undertake common responsibilities as a group. As a result, it is difficult for important ties to be forged as a result of sharing a home room.

The appropriate corrective is to give home room teachers substantial responsibilities for managing the home room students' learning activities, for example, monitoring their out-of-school projects or becoming the teacher regularly assigned to teach their classes. As a result of such patterns, the relationship between the students and their home room teacher will be enriched and affective learning will be fostered.

Affective learning problems are also posed by the American tendency to create larger and larger school buildings. Some of these problems arise simply from the impact of grouping large numbers of students in one or more related buildings. These particular problems will be considered later, in the discussion about smaller school buildings. However, steps can be taken to begin to deal with these issues, short of waiting for the construction of smaller buildings. In essence, these steps focus on dividing the student body into several or more discrete student subunits, so that a three-thousand-student high school is reorganized into six (each containing students from all cohorts) five-hundred-student subschools in the same building area.[4] The more sharply delineated the subschools are from each other, the better they will assist affective learning. Such delineation can be assisted by generally separate administrative and decision-making structures, the demarcation of separate space areas for the students of each subschool, different distinctive names for the subschools, different student dress patterns, different patterns of extracurricular activities, and different student schedules. Such demarcation may enable students and faculty in the subschools to develop learning-community attitudes. Of course, these changes may, in some ways, add certain costs and complexities to school operation—and, once again, we are faced with the reminder that no system will settle all problems and that we usually accept the frustrations of change only after we realize that continuation of present patterns may be even more painful.

Maintaining Attendance
Because the administrators of the school have a responsibility to see that students regularly attend to their personal and collective intra-school obligations, some system for maintaining student attendance must be provided. In order for the system to reinforce each student's sense of group identity, the principal responsibility for monitoring student attendance should rest on other students. In other words, the interdependence of students, through tutoring and group proj-ects, will mean that the absent student will often be handicapping other students in carrying out their cooperative responsibility. If the teachers consistently focus on whether cooperative responsibilities are being met (e.g., are projects being completed, are the tutored students learning), cooperating students will be stimulated to pay at-tention to the regular attendance of their fellow students. Since this means that substantial authority and responsibility will be assigned to students—who will monitor one another—it is pertinent to en-large on this matter at this point. The discussion can serve as a good example of the general principle of enlarging student authority and responsibility, and what it means in actual practice.

One can predict that at first the cooperators will have difficulty with this responsibility, for the current student attitude is chiefly in-difference to the laxness or irresponsibility of other students.[5] The concept that one student should be concerned with the "good citizen-ship" of another will engender predictable discomfort. Students tied to lax attenders will probably urge the teacher to assign them to an-other student or group or demand that the teacher discipline the lax student. Teachers must resist these urgings. The goal of the resis-tance must be to stimulate the students to learn how to work through such difficulties. The teacher should instruct the complaining students on how to improve the performance and attendance of the lax students.

At times poor attendance signifies that the absentee does not understand the material or is under excessive pressure in some other class or subject. The cooperating students should be urged to attempt to discover the basic motives underlying the poor attendance, and see what changes in their conduct can help the absentee improve. Perhaps they are burdening him or her with excessive responsibilities or are using poor tutoring techniques, and the absenteeism is a sign of *their* failure, rather than the absentee's.

Sometimes poor attendance is a sign of noncommitment to a responsibility that should be accepted. Then the cooperating student, who will be penalized by someone else's irresponsibility, must be stimulated and assisted to generate pressure on the absentee, so that he or she accepts responsibilities. The cooperators can be given some authority to assist them in this task. For instance, they can be authorized to subdivide group grades among the group, so that if a five-member group earns a "B" for its project, three of the members can be allotted "A's" by the group and two members, "C's." Or lax group members can be assigned extraordinary and undesirable chores by the group. Finally, both the group and the community have the ultimate sanction of expulsion. This sanction, when applied by the school, has extra force since the expelled student had specifically applied to the learning community for admittance and presumably wants to retain that precious privilege.

It is clear that the matter of enforcing attendance touches on a number of important pedagogical and affective issues. Unquestionably, the students who are monitoring the attendance of other students will require sensitive guidance from teachers. Thus, if the students who are monitoring fail to control the absenteeism by a few lax students, they may find themselves being severely penalized for their failure. Their natural response will be to blame the teacher, rather than themselves or their lax peers. They may develop anger and resentment, become so frustrated as to withdraw from the learning process, or even align themselves with their lax peers against the faculty. The teachers must therefore take care that students are not given a heavier burden of responsibility than they can bear. They must develop a sensitivity to the styles and competencies of their students and be able to sense which groups will need more help, and which less.

Another teacher responsibility created by this process is to assure that the group does not practice gross injustice toward deviants. This involves a fine line. On one hand, the students are young and inexperienced and may unquestionably make mistakes in the punishments they mete out. On the other hand, learning comes from being where mistakes can be made and corrected by living with the consequences. Excessive teacher intervention in the interest of "fairness" may make the members of the group incapable of learning how to be fair, or how to compel others to be fair, when teachers are not around, that is, when they become adults.

This discussion of attendance has suggested how the learning community will help develop new skills in both teachers and students. These new skills will be stimulated, in part, by the apparently simple restructuring of such matters as monitoring attendance. They will also arise out of the stress on ceremony and continuity in the community. Ceremony and continuity will increase the commitment and understanding within the community by stimulating community members to meet responsibilities and by motivating them to learn how to deal with community members who violate the values of the community.

New Kinds of Buildings and Grounds

Before World War II, the British House of Commons was not large enough to seat all its members when full attendance was provoked by an important session; on such occasions, many members were required to stand. The House was destroyed by German bombings in the war. The architects planning its reconstruction proposed a larger building to avoid the former inconvenience. They consulted with Winston Churchill, who expressed disapproval of the proposed enlargement. Churchill contended that it was desirable to maintain an element of drama during important debates, and that the crowd of members standing behind those who were seated contributed to the drama. His suggestion was accepted and the new House was kept to the size of the original. In commenting on the proposal, Churchill said, "We shape our buildings; thereafter, they shape us."[6] Suburban school buildings have a similar significance for their students and faculty.

Smaller School Buildings
Large school buildings are built on the theory that more efficient learning is promoted by bringing great numbers of students and faculty under one roof. Undoubtedly, such arrangements permit the maintenance of teachers with diverse and focused specialties. The

regular and efficient teaching of Russian, ecology, mechanical drawing, and ballet is hard to maintain in a smaller school. But the preceding discussion has made it evident that the very characteristics that make such specialization and diversity of choice possible also create fragmented relations among students and between students and faculty. The specialists present limited amounts of their specialty to large numbers of students as part of an elaborate and diversified learning menu; similarly, the students, during each day or term, are all tasting different combinations of the menu. Few teachers and students stay together for long. The system is both fostered and justified by the existence of large buildings. Without such buildings the arrangements would not be possible, and with such buildings there is inevitable pressure on the faculty to create varied and fragmented programs. The large buildings also compel administrators to view education, in part, as a problem of crowd control: several thousand young people grouped in a small area for long periods of time pose genuine problems in crowd management and safety simply because of their numbers and youthful exuberance. Under these circumstances, a responsible administrator can naturally be driven to make formalized discipline and the maintenance of routine into important objectives.

The long-range answer is smaller school buildings in which adaptive measures can be taken to maintain some of the advantages of scale and specialization. Modern media and learning devices can enable students to tap into physically remote learning sources; specialists can visit, or students can travel from the school. Regardless of the compromise adopted, it must be recognized that a stress on cognitive diversity and faculty specialization can cause a diminishment of affective learning; and many suburban children now have serious deficiencies in this area.

An incidental advantage to smaller schools should be noted: such schools will tend to be nearer to the homes of students. This can make it easier for students and their families to use the school after regular class hours. Furthermore, it may lessen some operating costs, since busing will be less necessary.

Different Layouts and Structures for School Buildings
The school is the home of a continuing community. It should give its inhabitants a sense of possession and belonging, as well as a feeling that previous students have inhabited the community in the past and that other student generations will do so in the future. Such perceptions will strengthen the students' sense of being part of a defin-

able, satisfying cyclic process to which they must make their unique contributions. To attain these effects, the school should include "something old, something new, something from outside the community, something from inside."

The "old" can be the essential structure of the building, which the students will perceive has existed through time. This passage of time can be indicated by symbols and other evidence dispersed throughout the structure: the cornerstone, displays of photographs of earlier classes and student and faculty groups on the wall, trophy cases, an engraved honor roll. The school name should be prominently displayed at the entrance of the school. Whenever the name honors some individual or occasion, the display should include a brief but carefully written statement explaining why this individual or occasion was chosen to be honored. Even if the name is simply descriptive (e.g., Rolling Brook High School), a summary outline of its basic history would be appropriate. There should also be an external bulletin board with notices about future significant activities by the students or faculty, plus announcements about recent important achievements and awards won by members of the school community. In other words, the school should cordially invite the world to be interested in its affairs and should imply that its activities are worthy of interest.

The "new" can be additions and revisions to the basic structure, contributed by the current generation of students, faculty, or outsiders. The additions can be symbolic, such as additional photographs or trophies. Or they can be material, such as additional rooms or substantial reconstruction.

The building itself comes from "outside"; that is, it is typically paid for and largely built by persons outside the learning community. This fact should be explicitly recognized on the property, incidentally providing useful instruction in gratitude. But, over time, the school building will and should receive other contributions from outside the learning community. Some of these additions will be paid for by routine tax-supported expenditures. When this happens, the addition or expense should be appropriately recognized through a ceremony and designation. Other "outside" additions should also be ceremonially recognized and designated.

The "inside" materials are the elements of the building and decorations contributed by members of the learning community. From the first moments of the building's conception to its final demolition, members of the community should help in the processes of building design, construction, decoration, and maintenance. All these acts of

engagement should be recognized in the symbols and traditions associated with the community. The insiders' contributions can be im-
mensely varied: they can make suggestions as to layout and decoration; they can supply labor in the construction process (and that
process should be organized to facilitate such contributions); finally,
when the building is constructed and in use, the learning community can handle certain maintenance and repairs and small-scale reconstruction and additions.

As a result of this combination of old and new, outside and inside,
the learning community will tend to develop a sense of self-identity:
"We are the people who work together within that building." At the
same time, that self-identity will not be egocentric and isolating,
since the building was built and maintained by earlier generations
of the learning community and also by parents, taxpayers, and
school boards outside the immediate community. From recognition
of this support and obligation, the members of the learning community can be led to perceive a sequence of steps that will gradually
lead them from their learning community into fuller participation in
an open and supportive adult world.

New Connections between the Building and Its Environment
The grounds of the building present an often neglected opportunity
for affective learning. In many instances landscaping plans can be
developed that permit students to accept group responsibilities for
maintenance. But a more subtle question arises around the matter
of the permeability between the school and its immediate environment.

On one hand, the school should be differentiated from its external
environment, since it is different, and the students should sense that
it comprises a community. This means that there should be physical
and conceptual barriers between the school and its external community, to remind students they are in school and to remind the world
that these particular youths are students. At the same time, the
school and the students and faculty in it are part of the world, and
the students are growing up to live their adult lives away from
school; it is unrealistic to seek to shut off the school completely from
the external world. These abstract issues distill down to concrete
matters, such as where students shall be permitted to go for lunch
(e.g., in restaurants near school), whether or not they can leave
school between classes, and if strangers should be allowed to casually wander on the premises?

In general, it seems that students should be able to leave the campus, and that strangers could casually visit it, but only if other forces in the school structure already give the faculty and students a significant sense of identity. These other forces encompass a diversity of elements: identifiable student and/or faculty dress patterns; a discrete and recognizable building; a small school; a powerful pattern of school ceremonial life; and a disposition in the surrounding community to accept students and expect responsible conduct from them.

One possible step in handling the off-campus matter is to permit only certain groups of students to leave the campus during school hours, for example, seniors, members of certain honor groups, or freshmen accompanied by seniors. This policy would emphasize that students temporarily leaving the learning community during operating hours were acting as representatives of the community and were expected to act responsibly. Therefore, these students would have to satisfy some significant criteria, such as satisfactory service over a given period of time. Thus, the privilege of going off campus can be a reward for displaying a responsible procommunity attitude.

The preceding discussion has given us a broad sketch of how a revised suburban school might operate. In the next chapter, we will consider the effect of these revisions on the skills, attitudes, and training of teachers.

Administration requires judgment about all things—judgment of priorities. That can be learnt by practical experience, preferably under the tutelage of somebody who already has it. There is no way of formalizing it or reducing it to recipes.
—R. S. Peters[1]

CHAPTER 5
Teaching in Suburban Schools

Teachers in a revised suburban school will have new goals, responsibilities, and authorities—changes that will affect many other elements of their circumstances.

Goals

The revised school will aim to graduate students who are better equipped to assume adult roles than were earlier suburban cohorts. They should have a comparatively high level of affective skills. They will be able to accept responsibility to others in a variety of contexts and to exercise equivalent authority. Further, they will have the essential cognitive knowledge appropriate to their age and status and be able to apply that knowledge in relevant situations.

Teacher Responsibilities

To attain these goals, the teachers in the school must have personal responsibility for the affective learning of a limited and identifiable number of students. They will be mentors for their students, and their mentorship should persist for a prolonged period of time—perhaps during the pupils' entire enrollment in the school. The responsibility may be directly allocated to one particular teacher-mentor for each pupil or, in an environment where a high degree of interteacher cooperation exists, perhaps small groups of teachers (two to three) may be assigned to a group of pupils. Within the teacher groups, informal allocations of personal responsibilities may evolve. But if such group assignments are applied, each group of teachers must be prepared to accept collective responsibility for the shortcomings of any member of their student group.

This allocation of personal responsibility does not imply that the teachers in the school will only have contact with those pupils who are their responsibility. Teachers will also have peripheral contact with a larger pool of students for various cognitive instruction purposes. But their responsibilities vis-à-vis this pool will necessarily be of a more limited nature. Still, even in the case of these peripheral contacts, the teacher will be concerned with promoting both cognitive and affective development.

The concept of responsibility for affective learning needs clarification. It means that the teacher-mentor will be responsible for the pupils' failure to display appropriate conduct, just as a law professor might be held responsible for his pupils' failure to pass some section of the Bar examination, or as parents might be held responsible if their 14-year-old child committed some gross antisocial act. The mentor's responsibility will inevitably arise from the operation of the school. Students will be expected to carry out tasks that will require affective skills: tutor other students; act as members and leaders of groups performing services to the school or external community; or, as representatives of the school community, engage in contacts with extraschool groups. If individual students or groups of students perform these tasks in a clearly unsatisfactory fashion, both the students and their mentors will be subject to criticism or, ultimately, even reprimand or dismissal, for that is what responsibility means on a job. Or, if the students conduct themselves well, both the students and the mentors will be praised and rewarded.

Such an allocation of responsibility will stimulate mentors to attempt to constructively direct the affective learning of their charges. And this is the purpose of the allocation. In the typical contemporary school—in contrast to the revised model—teachers are rarely held *personally* responsible for the affective learning of their pupils. Thus, if a student sells drugs to other students in school, if students engage in vandalism, or if a male student gets a female illegitimately pregnant, often no member of the staff has any personal sense of failure. And, conversely, when a student does display significant constructive affective skills, it is not clear which—if any—teachers should feel a sense of shared pride for that attainment. Without the threat of failure, or the hope of pride, it is difficult for the faculty to strive to foster desirable affective learning. And so, while contemporary faculty members are seriously concerned with preventing antisocial conduct, that concern is generally directed at the moment to the antisocial act on school premises: the drug sale, breaking the window, or sexual foreplay on school property. This limited focus is grossly inadequate. Antisocial acts are usually the outcome of a lengthy progression of developments affecting the student. Those developments can be prevented or controlled only if adults in the school are stimulated to evolve policies and styles that continuously engage the students in useful affective learning. Then, the moment of temptation will be forestalled or resisted.

Some policies to frustrate temptation, which will evolve from the total framework of the school, have been sketched in the preceding chapters. Other policies will provoke mentors to consider how particular students are relating to the overall structure of the school. Are those students learning the appropriate affective skills? Are they enjoying school? Are they acting in a generous and committed fashion? What kind of help do they need? These questions will be asked and answered due to the changed responsibilities of teachers.

At this point, one may realize that these new responsibilities for teachers relate to semimoral questions. Is it right for publicly supported schools to assume such concerns? Are they not properly the exclusive province of the family and the church? Is not neutrality the appropriate role of the school?

Unfortunately, there is no such thing as a morally neutral environment for the young. If children and adolescents spend thirty or more hours a week in the company of adults who are not significantly concerned with questions of community responsibility, or the quality of interpersonal relations, those students are receiving a moral message: morality is not important as a guide for conduct. Even if their parents give a contrary message at home, that message is belied daily in the institution to which the parents have sent their children.

This abstract discussion is nicely illustrated by the reported decline of honor codes in colleges.[2] Such codes provide that exams shall not be proctored, and that students, themselves, should be expected to report students who cheat. The codes are apparently being abandoned because of the unwillingness of students to report violators. Perhaps some of the students attending the schools abandoning the codes come from families which believe that citizens should report persons who break the law. The colleges, by abandoning the code, are "saying" that such an obligation is not significant. They are thus undermining the moral codes of some families.

The revised model school also has another element that relates to the problem of "intrusive" morality. The revised school has been proposed as an alternative, deliberately chosen by the parents and (perhaps) the students. Because it does present such a choice, the school is not thrusting on the students morality that is alien to the values of their family. Furthermore, the parents who are opposed to the school's "values" will have the option to send their child to a school that does not strive to inculcate community responsibility or important, constructive affective learning. In effect, the model will foster the values of the pupils' parents. Conversely, it is inevitable that contemporary public schools—in the nature of their operations—are undermining many of the moral precepts taught by parents at home.

The new responsibilities that the teacher-mentors acquire will subject them to changed modes of supervision. In other words, they will be accountable to their superiors for additional learning outcomes in students. This accountability cannot occur unless their supervisors receive more information about teacher-student relations than they typically do at this time. As suggested earlier, this will mean an increase in the supervisor-teacher ratio and a shift toward more collegial relations between supervisors and teachers, as well as between teachers. Such changes will both increase teacher responsibilities and provide teachers with greater support and counsel. Much of the supervision will be directed at devising better ways of managing groups of students, so that the members of such groups improve their abilities to help one another.

Teachers will have less responsibility for knowing their cognitive subject matter in depth than they do in many contemporary high schools. This lessening of responsibility is a by-product of the school's aim to hire teachers with high levels of affective skills. Of course, an adult may have both high cognitive and high affective skills. However, the higher standards we set, the smaller the pool of persons that are available and/or the more we have to pay for such employees. Because the new school hopes to maintain its costs at a competitive level, it must consciously choose to give more weight to affective, as compared to cognitive, skills in its teachers. But this policy need not have bad effects for students. If some students "exhaust" the teacher's level of cognitive knowledge, they can be put to work tutoring, and thus make use of the teacher's affective knowledge (in managing tutoring) and simultaneously learn a great deal about communication. Furthermore, the school will maintain incentive systems that encourage teachers to stay with the school for years; during those years, the teachers can be stimulated to increase their cognitive skills in appropriate fields, with veteran teachers usually covering the more esoteric material. This approach makes good sense for a variety of reasons: why should one expect a twenty-two–year–old college graduate to be an expert in a cognitive field? And if we have set such expertness as our aim, how much affective learning has the young teacher given up to attain that end?

Teacher Authority

To meet their responsibilities to foster constructive affective learning, mentors will need new authorities over students. First, they will be perceived, in the school, as the natural contact point for all other faculty and administrators who make significant decisions affecting an "assigned" student. Other faculty members teaching an assigned student will periodically be in touch with his or her mentor. It will be understood that the grades given by such instructors will be decided after advising with the mentor. The mentor may even be able to reshape the grade given by an individual faculty member or at least diminish its impact. This authority of the mentor is simply one element of a structure aimed at fostering affective learning—sometimes even over cognitive learning. An anecdote can illustrate the problem:

During the nineteenth century, a group of midshipmen from the U.S. Naval Academy who were about to begin their final academic year were on a summer cruise in the Pacific. Their ship, a sailing vessel, was struck by a typhoon. The crew was ordered aloft to furl the sails so the ship could ride out the storm. The crew hesitated, for the storm made such work extremely dangerous. One of the midshipmen saw the challenge, gave a bold cry, and led the men up into the rigging. The effort was a success, the ship rode out the storm, and eventually it returned to Annapolis. During the next school year, the midshipman who was the first aloft received poor grades in several subjects and was in danger of failing. Then, the faculty recalled what he had done during the storm, and arrangements were made to ensure that he graduated and received his commission. In sum, the school said that, if we are indifferent to bravery and leadership, our students and graduates will be less willing to accept the dangers that flow from such roles. The man who was first up the mast is entitled to something special.[3]

Of course, the principle that school grades should reflect both cognitive and affective learning is still only a general principle. That is, there are still critical issues to be weighed. But the proposition is that the teacher-mentors should have an important say in that process of assessment. By virtue of that authority, they can maintain an appropriate reinforcement structure by which they can meet their own responsibilities for their pupils.

If the mentors are to maintain such a reinforcement structure around the students, they must have a galaxy of benefits and punishments to disperse. The report card and the parent-teacher conference are important elements of this mix, for these communication devices inform the parents of their child's progress. If the parents are satisfied, or dissatisfied, there are many ways they can reinforce their child. Other modes of mentor-parent communication include notes, phone calls, and social contacts. But the mentor-teachers need other tools, too. One such tool is the intimacy that will (or should) arise between the mentors and their students. The intimacy is an appropriate outcome of their frequent and shared contacts over continuing concerns. It will permit the mentors to encourage or discourage diverse student conduct through offering a constructive model, making appropriate remarks, and employing all the other devices that subtle and insightful adults can use to guide the young.

The school structure will also assist the teachers to exercise authority by providing a variety of rewards and punishments that will support the mentors' authority. For instance, significant recognition or prizes can be given to groups of students, or individual students, who have performed important feats. Mentors can be of assistance in helping their students attain such recognition. They can provide advice to their students or try to persuade the award committees that their students are most deserving—just as athletic coaches try to advance their teams and players. But mentors will only undertake such efforts if they feel their students deserve concern. And so students are given extra incentives to win such engagement.

The question of recognition or rewards should be expanded here. Favorable recognition will always be a highly desired and scarce good. It is desired because humans inherently want the praise and attention of their fellows. Sometimes, this want is masked for a variety of personal psychic reasons. Still, it is safe to assume that it can usually be stimulated by judicious management. Recognition is comparatively scarce because we only have limited periods of time to spend recognizing the attainments of others. We can never give all the people about us all the recognition they want. And so we subconsciously ration recognition. Usually, it is rationed via the principle that we recognize persons and conduct that directly and helpfully touch our lives: either we cannot avoid noticing their conduct or the conduct is by some person who is quite important to us, for example, our spouse or child.

But this general principle is quite relative. We may live in an apartment and never see our postman, yet his conduct may "directly and helpfully touch our lives." And so the objectives of our favorable recognition are partly determined by the immediate social and institutional forces, as well as our previous training. Modern schools usually do not stimulate students to give significant favorable recognition to students who develop and display constructive affective skills.[4] Very little student time is set aside for such recognition (e.g., honors assemblies); nor are the school communication and symbolic resources (e.g., student paper, trophies, award plaques) assiduously used for these purposes. Under these circumstances, it is difficult for individual teachers to strive to foster affective learning. But the school can be reorganized to stimulate students to give greater recognition to students with socially desirable affective skills. New awards would be given to individual students and groups. New symbols of excellence can be devised—like the "letters" awarded superior athletes. More occasions can be created at which these awards and symbols, and the conduct they symbolize, are praised before groups of students. These changes can take place within individual classes and student subgroups, as well as on a school-wide scale. As a result, more students will strive to attain these skills, and teachers, who can "teach" students how to display the skills and who have some say in who attains recognition, will find it increasingly easy to motivate students.

The new authorities for teachers that have been sketched obviously give them power to cause greater damages—as well as benefits—for students. This enlarged potential is the reason for the increased responsibilities (and supervision) that teachers will have in the revised school, as well as the growth of parental and community involvement. In other words, the teachers will have more power, but it will be surrounded by more safeguards than exist in current schools. Thus, despite this enlargement, students are probably safer from abuse than they are in contemporary schools. Furthermore, most of the abuse of students that does occur in contemporary schools is committed by other students. It is usually students that sell drugs to other students, who make other students pregnant, or who steal from students or commit vandalism to common property. In the revised school, the new faculty responsibilities and authorities will set in motion new forces to protect students, especially from each other.

The Curriculum Presented by Teachers

The cognitive curriculum being offered in the school will be determined by a medley of forces: college entrance and state legal requirements, the intellectual potential and vocational aspirations of the students, and the needs of the school as a communal institution. These forces will not necessarily always be in conflict. The first two elements listed—college and state requirements, student potential and aspirations—are comparatively familiar to many readers, although experimental program exemptions may permit more flexibility than many persons realize. However, the last element—communal needs—may seem novel to contemporary readers and thus requires some amplification.

At an earlier stage in the book, we discussed the need for maintaining congruence between the curriculum and the students' needs for communal coherence. This discussion has obvious implications for the social sciences (and possibly literature) curriculum of the school. But there are also other community needs. One of these is to foster efficiency within group projects. These projects can require students to develop and apply diverse cognitive and semicognitive skills: receiving and sending communication (both written and oral), bookkeeping, cooking, maintenance of machinery, parliamentary procedure, and library and field research. These skills can properly all be integrated into existing categories of the curriculum. Obviously, they will be better appreciated by students if skillful teachers can time their presentations so they are related to the actual problems the students are facing in their collective responsibilities.

The cognitive curriculum finally offered in the school cannot be simply specified. However, if substantial weight is given to serious collective responsibilities, it is likely that either the cognitive elements will be appropriately related to those responsibilities or these elements will not receive a disproportionate emphasis. If such a balance is maintained, the particular cognitive curriculum that schools or communities choose to apply should largely be a matter for their informed discretion—assuming they are conscious of the extracommunity forces that should be considered in their decision.

Teacher Skills

Teachers, themselves, in the revised school, will need affective skills that are somewhat different than those now usually expected. They will be asked to make a greater commitment to their school than many teachers do at this time. It is not clear whether this commitment will require them to devote more hours to the school each week. However, it is evident that the school will work better if its teachers (and students) have had more continuous experience working together over a number of years. Consequently, the school will establish reward and hiring structures that stimulate teachers to make such prolonged commitments (just as it makes equivalent demands on students).[5] Essentially, the structures will provide significant benefits for teachers who stay employed for prolonged periods and penalties (e.g., surrender of accrued pension benefits?) for teachers who do not choose to stay for some substantial period of time.

Teachers will also be more willing to subject their own work to the analyses of peers and superiors and will be able to skillfully observe and evaluate the work of others. Neither of these attainments is simple. They require resilience, discretion, tact, and a sense of humor. Teachers will also enjoy persistent and involved adult company. In effect, adult relations will become just as important in the new school as adult-youth relations are in contemporary schools.

The teachers will be sympathetic to making collective enterprises work, even if it means short-term sacrifices of the goals of individual students. This personal emotional commitment will enable mentors to communicate, to each member of a student group, that their momentary personal frustrations are being endured on behalf of the group and that the group, at a later date, can be expected to make equivalent sacrifices on their individual behalf. In other words, the priorities of a healthy group are subject to shifts, and the momentary sacrifices of individuals can represent a beneficial long-range trade-off. Only teachers with a sense of the complexities and rewards of group activities can transmit this comprehension to individual students. Many modern teachers may have trouble with this teaching responsibility: they may lack an adequate appreciation of the needs for collective support which all humans have from time to time. And those needs can only be satisfied if each student is taught to offer such support to others.

It will be necessary for teachers to be at ease in having contacts with adults who are not teachers: parents, who want face-to-face information about the school or their children, or out-of-school adults who are involved in cooperative enterprises with students and the school. The teachers will have to respect persons who do not have substantial cognitive skills and attain the respect of other adults who are much older or who earn far higher incomes than do teachers.

The teachers will also have to enjoy having fairly close relationships with adolescents—not relationships of simple equality, but still much closer relationships than often prevail between teachers and students in schools today.

Teacher Rewards

Teachers in the revised school will receive many rewards they typically do not receive at this time. Most of these rewards will be emotional as compared to financial, though the new model should not ask them to accept salaries significantly less than those paid other teachers.

The most important new rewards will flow from the emotional satisfactions generated in the school. Teachers will enjoy substantial collegial relationships with their peers and supervisors. Their work will be understood and judiciously appreciated by parents. The ties that develop in the school, among faculty, between faculty and students, and between faculty and parents, will tend to persist and become richer over time. These relationships will be fostered and enriched by the diverse communal responsibilities generated in the school and between the school and the external community.

Teachers will be constantly stimulated and assisted to maintain their affective and cognitive growth in a relevant fashion. Since the teachers will be asked to cover comparatively broad subject areas, they cannot possibly know all the cognitive subject matter they may try to cover at the moment they are hired. Further cognitive learning may be a requirement of the job. And the learning will be obviously related to the day-to-day needs of the teacher. It will not be a matter of simply collecting postgraduate credits to attain raises.

There will be a stimulating diversity of responsibilities for teachers to choose from. This diversity will permit teachers with different styles to choose different areas of emphasis—supervising the lunchroom group, lecturing on mathematics, being head of the drama committee. Or teachers may switch roles occasionally simply for the stimulation of change. And because a higher proportion of supervisors will be needed, more teachers can choose to eventually shift into supervisory work—although such work will still keep them in close contact with students and other teachers.

The communal spirit of the school can also permit more adaptiveness within the staff, so that responsible community members— when the need arises—will have the support that exists in stable and secure families.

Teacher Training and Selection

It is evident that the system of teacher training should have many elements found in the operation of the model school itself. It will be difficult for the teachers to appreciate the process of community formation and maintenance or the refinement of affective skills unless they have undergone equivalent experiences themselves. Perhaps, if the teachers were students in such a high school, it may be possible for them to pass through a "modern college" and still retain the "understanding" they received in high school. But even if we accept this problematic proposition, most recent college graduates have not passed through a "communal" high school.

As for college, most American colleges maintain programs that are an exaggerated version of the impersonality, transitory contacts, and cognitive focus that are so deleterious in the suburban high school. Thus, it is evident that, if there will be a growing need for teachers trained to work in the new school, significant changes will be required in teacher preparation. The character of these changes can easily be inferred from the preceding material presented on school reorganization. The changes will stress persistent and intense contacts among students and between students and faculty, the development of collective responsibilities for students, and a focus on the attainment of affective skills.

It would be naïve to imagine that changes of this sort will quickly occur in many American colleges. However, there should be no assumption that any of the proposed changes in suburban schools, themselves, will—or should—occur quickly or easily. Thus, it is not impossible to conceive of the gradual changes in suburban schools being accompanied by gradual changes in colleges. Thus, by the time large numbers of teachers are needed for revised schools, a significant number of colleges may have made the needed changes in their programs.

The requirement of teacher certification cannot be ignored. In the long run, it may be necessary for states to revise teacher certification standards to make them more congruent with the new panoply of skills that suburban teachers need. However, once again, in the short run, ingenuity and determination should enable administrators to win approval for carefully developed and well-administered experimental programs. And as the forces for program expansion grow, concurrent changes in teacher certification can be designed, fostered, and promulgated.

In the short and intermediate run, the matter of teacher selection is probably going to be more important than undergraduate training. In other words, most undergraduate schools are not currently aiming to train teachers with the affective skills appropriate to the revised model. Fortunately, those skills are not especially rare among adult Americans in general and are indeed even possessed by many teachers. The problem simply is that the skills have not been learned at colleges of education, in particular, or (probably) at colleges in general. The skills essentially have been acquired by these adults in their progress through life—as workers, community members, youth leaders, or parents or in a myriad of other collective responsibilities. The task of those doing the hiring (or evaluating transfer applications) is to devise and apply employment criteria that will help pick candidates with appropriate affective skills—as opposed to candidates with more cognitive skills. Such criteria should identify applicants whose background reveals that they have the requisite experience and skills. Age can be one criterion of such experience, but it is far from central. Acquiring constructive affective skills is not essentially a matter of the passage of time, but more a matter of how time was spent. A young adult may have already acquired significant valuable affective learning, while much older persons may have maintained themselves in a comparatively isolated individualistic environment. The careful questioning of applicants and the interviewing of references will be essential. The probation period for new employees should also be a significant sorting device. It will be unfair to both employees and the institution to give tenure to significant numbers of persons who will eventually not fit. Thus, the assumption should be that there is no stigma on the probationer who decides—after a responsible look—that the school is not the community he or she wants. Perhaps only two-thirds of the probationers should decide to stay—or be offered permanent work. This comparatively high proportion of failures should be especially likely to occur during the first few years of the school, when it is transforming its abstract conception into a tangible operating reality. After that transformation has occurred, new candidates (and supervisors making decisions) can have a better understanding of what the operation is really about, and better informed employment decisions can be made.

This discussion concludes our school-oriented analysis and prescription; the next chapter will begin our consideration of appropriate improvements in the out-of-school post-industrial suburban environment.

Those were the years when the herring fishing boomed. The fishing industry brought into our town hundreds of people besides the fishermen—curers, salesmen, dealers, coopers, carters, carpenters, fishgirls to gut the fish, and auxiliary workers of various kinds. All was noise and bustle in the normally placid town, the shouted commands as the herring were being unloaded, the Gaelic songs of the fishergirls at their vats, the teasing and ribald comments of the carters as they rattled by, the orders of the wherry skippers as they eased into the piers.
—Robert M. MacIver[1]

CHAPTER 6
Improving Suburban Communities

If some of the preceding suggested changes begin to occur in suburban schools, they will tend to spill over into the surrounding community. Indeed, the changes will not be possible unless a significant proportion of parents in the suburb involved understand and support them. Such a base of public understanding and support will inevitably color the character of suburban community life, even in post-industrial suburbs.

But beyond the matter of school-community congruence, it is also desirable that many suburban communities directly consider their strengths and shortcomings as child-rearing institutions. After all, in Illinois, a typical American state, the school code requires school districts to average 176 attendance days per year. Assuming the school day totals six hours, the average students spend 82 percent of their waking time each year away from school. Obviously, much of the out-of-school time is spent in the community: in streets, parks, neighbors' homes, and stores. The nature of that community can have much to do with the kind of adult the child becomes. This book has emphasized that modern suburban communities have significant shortcomings as environments to aid constructive affective growth. But can anything be done to foster intracommunity improvement?

Public opinion will certainly be a central element in shaping any changes. And, while many adults in modern suburbs are apparently satisfied with their environment, we should not assume that their attitudes cannot be changed by events and careful persuasion.[2] After all, it would be incongruous to contend that couples who would choose to have and raise children would be unwilling to try to change the nature of their environment if they were shown that such environments were seriously deleterious to the children's emotional maturity. Indeed, if many parents did refuse to support apparently necessary changes, there might be logic to considering the passage of laws inhibiting parents from raising children in certain types of post-industrial suburban communities—child rearing is not just a matter of parental taste; such children may eventually develop into burdens on the entire commonweal.

But there are other forces that might foster suburban change, beyond shifts in the opinions of contemporary residents. Like all societies, suburban communities are populated by a transitory pool of residents. Families move, die, or are otherwise replaced. Their successors were raised in different environments and may well have different aspirations for their community. And new suburban developments are regularly being created. In fact, one can conceive that suburban-raised children—when they attain adulthood—may find modern suburbs less attractive than do their city-raised parents. Finally, we might consider that post-industrial adults—who may find the contradictions in their own lives excessive—may increasingly choose to lessen some of those contradictions by making their living areas more like true communities. And so, for a medley of reasons, it is appropriate to suggest some characteristics of modern suburbs that can be changed to help rear children into mature adulthood— and that may also offer unique attractions to some adults.

Security, the Keystone

On the whole, the growth of the suburbs is an extension of continuous patterns of neighborhood shifts that have persistently appeared throughout American history. Security—perhaps also described as emotional convenience—is a central motive underlying these shifts. As older urban neighborhoods "declined"—and acquired neighbors that were "undesirable" to the previous wave of residents—those residents routinely moved on to more remote and secure areas where there was more neighborhood homogeneity.[3] For many years, these patterns of change were essentially urban: people moved from one part of the city to another. Eventually, the city expanded to the limit of its political boundaries, and the auto made more remote travel and wide dispersion of homes possible. As a result, more and more residents moving to attain neighborhood homogeneity eventually reached the suburbs.

Part of the motive for these changes has been physical security: to escape proximate contact with neighbors whose habits we see as physically threatening. Another important motive can be characterized as emotional convenience, which simply means that most humans routinely like to be surrounded with persons from their own class, ethnic group, and age cohort. When we have this homogeneity around us, many aspects of life become more convenient. Things can be taken for granted. We may be pleased with the novelty of sporadic divergent contacts, but we want those contacts to be the outcome of our own choices, as opposed to their being thrust upon us. It will be difficult to generate significant suburban changes unless we frankly consider the implications of these aspirations for security and emotional convenience.

Despite these desires, adults in some environments have been willing to live in comparative proximity with persons from significantly different backgrounds or of varying ages. Indeed, sometimes these patterns of proximate diversity have created more substantial convenience than do patterns of homogeneity. For example, in older cities in the southern states, it was common for black families to live near the upper-class white families.[4] In Europe, lower-class housing is often close to better-off neighborhoods.[5] And in rural towns, persons of different classes are often but just a block or two apart. The fact is that neighborhood diversity is tolerable, and even sometimes convenient, *if there are mediating structures that provide a degree of stability*. The problem is that typical American cities do not provide such structures. As a result, the only expedient for urban residents confronted with excessive diversity is to flee.

At the present time, they flee to suburbs, where they are protected from such diversity by geographic distance and zoning ordinances. But there is no inherent reason why these costly and socially cumbersome shields must be maintained. A modicum of security can be obtained at a lesser social and economic cost.

At this stage, readers should note that I am essentially sympathetic to aspirations to avoid extreme diversity. Humans have an inherent need for order in their environment.[6] Indeed, children and adolescents probably have a special need for such order. Efforts to deprive adults of the power to maintain such order are essentially utopian and may have the destructive and alienating effects that often flow from utopian programs. In this connection, the data about the effects of school desegregation are instructive. The data show that, the more intensely courts and government agencies tried to desegregate urban schools between 1968 and 1972, the swifter the rate of white movement to suburbs.[7] In other words, diversity could not be effectively thrust on people in a pluralistic society. Indeed, one important characteristic of prison is that the inmates cannot choose the people with whom they must spend most of their time. However, significantly, flight from desegregated schools was least in the smallest school districts. There, desegregation actually worked. Apparently, parents in such communities were willing to accept the tensions associated with diversity—if they felt a sense of proximity and identity with the schools involved. However, when the diversity was created in large school districts, with (presumably) remote, larger, and bureaucratic schools, flight occurred. Probably, modern suburbanites can accept higher proportions of diversity than now prevail—if they are given assurance that it will stay within controllable levels. To obtain such assurance, there must be either explicit, predetermined control criteria or a commitment that future changes in the existing levels must be approved by a high proportion of current occupants.[8]

Diversity control policies such as I have just suggested have been traditionally followed by many clubs and other social institutions. These policies permit the institutions to maintain a spirit of easy acceptance within their groups. And people quit excessively diverse communities just to attain such relationships with their neighbors.

Obviously, a variety of obstacles stands in the path of the revised policies I have proposed. The first barrier is simply public opinion. Do any modern suburbanites want to increase the level of diversity around their homes? Of course, the answer to that question must and can be qualified. Not all citizens, or even all modern suburbanites, need to favor diversity for a change to be feasible. Only a small number of sympathetic families would be necessary to foster a few small communities. Then we could see what would happen.

At this time, a few recently developed communities have taken some steps to foster diversity, for example, Columbia, Maryland, and Reston, Virginia.[9] The experiences in these communities will provide data to assist further steps in the direction of diversity. However, for a variety of reasons, these communities cannot be viewed as clear "tests" of the prodiversity changes that have been proposed: the residential patterns of the new communities have been shaped by public attitudes prevailing three to seven years ago (and such attitudes are mutable) and the new communities are not protected from excessive diversity by binding and formal safeguards such as I have proposed. Under these circumstances, we should imagine that the prodiversity steps taken in these communities will be of a very modest nature. But, in any case, the changes that have been proposed will only spread through an incremental process.

The more complex barriers to such experimental communities will be legal and legislative. In other words, can the families entering such communities obtain some "guarantee" that the diversity (which they are prepared to accept) will be kept within certain limits? To attain such a guarantee, the small group of citizens (who are willing to accept controlled diversity) may need the consent of a larger pool of citizens, who will support appropriate legislation or promote constructive judicial decisions.

American society, in the immediate and intermediate past, has displayed some hostility toward the rights of individuals and communities to control their community environments. Various court decisions have struck down exclusionary ordinances, and legislation has conditioned the availability of federal funds on the willingness of institutions and communities to revise, or abandon, their "boundary" systems.[10] Essentially, this resistance has been based on egalitarian premises: each person presumably has an equal right to enter into every community, and groups of individuals cannot permit some to enter and compel others to stay out. Maintaining boundaries by such conduct is regarded as invidious discrimination. Of course, it is unquestionably true that in many ways people are equal, and that in some ways they should be treated as if they were equal. But, at some point, reality must intrude on such aspirations. All healthy humans restrict their circles of friends and associates. And, usually, they base their restrictions on personal and intuitive criteria. While the criteria applied to define communities often change, there seems to be no lessening in the desire of people to control their proximate environment. For example, blacks protest segregation and simultaneously promote black power, black studies, and black caucuses; women criticize sex discrimination and organize female consciousness-raising groups; and ethnics ask for fairer treatment and strive to revitalize ethnic organizations.

One hopes that our antiboundary policies have reached their apogee. Many of their dysfunctional elements are growing increasingly evident: when people cannot control their urban communities, they flee to the suburbs, with destructive effects for both the cities they leave and their children who are raised in homogeneous environments; when people cannot define their immediate shopping or work environment, they become increasingly disengaged from that environment, and the quality of human relationships in stores, offices, and factories declines; and when parents and students cannot define their school environment (and practical circumstances prevent their flight), the school becomes an increasingly impersonal and alienating institution.

As a concrete example, in 1973, only 60 percent of the medical doctors practicing in Brooklyn, in New York City, lived in that borough.[11] Data about earlier proportions of such residents were unavailable, but observers agreed that the figure represented a significant decline. The reasons given for the decline were the doctors' lack of confidence in the public schools, fears about personal safety, and the availability of suburbs as a residential alternative. Presumably, the situation should be bemoaned, since it is inherently desirable for doctors practicing in a community to live there. Evidently, the egalitarian policies that have fostered extreme diversity in the city and its subcommunities have helped to provoke the doctors' flight. Though the situation is unfortunate, it is hard to see how we can *make* significant numbers of doctors choose to live in the city. Some persons who promoted the underlying egalitarian policies that have provoked the flight should take responsibility for this effect. But none of my readers should seriously expect anyone to confess.

Perhaps it is time for us to reconsider exactly how far society should go in compelling enforced heterogeneity. The long-range effect of these policies has been to create even more privacy and homogeneity.

An Economy of Human Exchanges, Not Dollars

All persons and communities—from the individual, or nuclear, family to an entire section of the nation—may be likened to units of economic systems. In such systems each unit engages in "trades" of goods, services, commitments, and dollars with each other. The trades are inevitable, since no one unit is ever completely autonomous. As our society has become increasingly affluent and specialized, and units have become more homogeneous, the need for such trades between units has grown. The trades have increasingly relied on money as the common medium of exchange, as opposed to other valuables.

This proposition—about the increase in monetary trades—may seem so simplistic as to be trite. However, we probably gravely underestimate the proportion of nonmonetary trades that occur even in our society. For instance, parents care for their children; husbands and wives care for one another; volunteer services are rendered by scoutmasters, Little League managers, and political canvassers; auto drivers show courtesy to other drivers and pedestrians; and members of clubs, fraternities, and professions give consideration to their co-members. These actions are "trades," because the implicit understanding is that the persons performing the service have some right to equivalent considerations from other members of the group. Actually, noneconomic trades are one of the means we use to define communities: community members have some pattern of shared values that permits them to assume that other community members will reciprocate their contributions.[12]

Of course, it is true that cultures other than ours give even greater emphasis to nonmonetary trades. And, further, the tendency in our society is for the role of nonmonetary trades to decline. Volunteer services become professionalized, and the professionals are paid. Increasingly, the assumption is that children will meet their obligation to support their aged parents through their payments of social security taxes, and so on. This pattern of decline is likely to be most intense in relatively affluent and homogeneous communities. In such communities residents have the money to buy help, and the restricted, that is, homogeneous, pool of talents means that community members do not have many different skills to trade with each other.

This decline in noneconomic reciprocity, especially in post-industrial suburban environments, has important implications for the young. In adult life, especially for those in more highly skilled work (e.g., executives, administrators, professionals), such patterns of noneconomic reciprocity still form an important element of the job. Tacit understandings, shared conventions, and appropriate personal styles are essential to successfully carry out complex co-operative tasks. And, in work environments, there is often a sufficient diversity of talents and resources (considering the tasks at hand) to make such trades feasible. And so young people are raised in communities where noneconomic trades are scarce, but they are later asked to work in environments where skills in such reciprocal conduct are an important element of success. Perhaps this lack of experience in noneconomic trades is part of the reason why some young people seem to misinterpret the operation of many adult environments. The young from affluent and homogeneous communities seem to often discover simple, economic, and overtly selfish motivations behind the conduct of persons holding authority. Sometimes, such interpretations are correct. But, often, the interpretations are overly simplistic. They reflect a form of paranoia, where a persistent search for devils is conducted, in an effort to explain away allegedly disinterested conduct. In reality, much adult conduct simply represents acts by well-socialized members of a work community who follow community norms vis-à-vis making noneconomic contributions to others—with the assumption that other community members will eventually reciprocate to their benefit. This faith in reciprocal altruism is probably founded in an earlier affective learning experience in a community where such reciprocity prevailed. Modern suburbs do not foster such subtle interpersonal reciprocity, especially in areas involving the young. Thus, it is not surprising that the young misinterpret much adult conduct or find communal expectations about implicit reciprocity highly inhibiting.

In the revised model school that was presented earlier, efforts were made to increase noneconomic trades in the school and between the school and the community, for example, tutoring, parental tithing, and intraschool and school-community service projects. But these school changes will only encompass a fraction of the time of children and adolescents. Therefore, communities should strive to increase the proportion of noneconomic trades that occur within their boundaries, especially trades which involve actions that are tangible and easily comprehended by children.

One change that can encourage such trades has already been referred to: increasing the diversity in the community. Such an increase will enlarge the variety of resources in the community: it may then include plumbers, lawyers, white-collar workers, bankers, and carpenters. Members of such a community will have a more varied capability to help one another.

Steps must also be taken to increase residential stability in the community. Noneconomic trades are more frequent if the contributors realize there will be a day of recompense. But in transitory environments, the beneficiary may not be around long enough to reciprocate. Of course, true altruism is supposedly inspired by selfless good will, but such "selflessness" cannot develop without reinforcing socialization. In other words, there must be relationships that are persistent enough for "selfless acts" to be remembered and ultimately rewarded. Eventually, from such reinforcement, we may inculcate some degree of so-called selflessness; however, even then, we should not expect selflessness to persist without periodic reciprocation and remembrance. And reciprocation and remembrance require some stability.

The proposals about intensifying boundaries in suburban communities bear on the issue of stability and, consequently, affect the frequency of noneconomic trades. If community members have greater control over who enters the community, such control may lessen the rate of leavings. People will have less to flee from. Furthermore, the community may deliberately decide to use potential geographic stability as a criterion for selecting members—just as the revised school strives for such stability among its pupils. One way to foster such stability is to maintain a commitment system for new community members, so they are less inclined to leave after a brief stay.[13] Essentially, the system would establish zoning requirements, or other inhibitions, that provided special penalties for residents or homeowners who moved before some prespecified period of time had passed. Families moving into the community would be advised, in advance of their entry, of the commitment involved.

In the longer run, we must recognize that the degree of explicit personal and family interdependence in the revised community will also be affected by governmental structures and technology. Society increasingly relies on abstract and impersonal modes of cooperation to satisfy our inherent needs for communal support. These social policies are reflected in tax systems, pension arrangements, and diverse municipal services supplied by paid civil servants. The basic data to demonstrate this growth are simple: between 1953 and 1973, the percentage of domestic (i.e., nonmilitary) spending by all levels of government, as compared to the total gross national product, increased from 17.2 to 31.6.[14] This increase, which occurred during an era of increasing prosperity for all social classes, demonstrates that more and more social needs have been transformed from private, family, and community responsibilities into governmental obligations. It is to be hoped that local communities will strive to avoid further intensifying these tendencies and try to enlarge systems that foster interpersonal trades. One example of such a system is the previous proposal for tithing time (by parents) to the school.

Technology, too, is to some degree out of the control of individual communities. If automobiles, homes, and boats are designed so they can only be repaired by experts, or so modular components must be used to replace broken parts, it is difficult for families and small communities to resist such forces.[15] But a consciousness of the problem may create helpful effects. For example, community developers and architects, in planning communities where they hope to foster richer human relationships, may deliberately use designs and materials that invite local maintenance and provoke noneconomic trades, as opposed to using systems that rely on highly specialized skills and resources.

Heterogeneity, Not Homogeneity

Both issues already discussed in this chapter bear on the matter of heterogeneity versus homogeneity. Still, the matter is so important as to warrant direct discussion. In post-industrial suburbs, homogeneity of socioeconomic and cohort groups is fostered by zoning patterns and the style of housing construction, while experiential homogeneity is maintained by the geographic separation of housing from other human activities. The rationale for these separations has already been suggested: to protect suburbanites from the tensions engendered by diversity and to assist certain forms of technologic specialization. While the separation does partially produce these benefits, we must consider the implications of the various forms of homogeneity in some detail.

Perhaps the first observation that comes to mind is the fact that persistent homogeneity is inherently boring. But modern suburban adults presumably satisfy their need for novelty via their auto-based mobility and their heterogeneous work environments. In a way, home is their place for sameness. However, policies fostering extreme homogeneity still create certain serious dysfunctions that directly affect adults. These dysfunctions are in addition to the indirect adult burdens caused by the effects of modern suburbs on the children.

Structures that encourage intracohort homogeneity imply that young adults (in their early twenties) and older adults (nearing retirement and after retirement) will be discouraged from living in child-rearing communities.[16] But both these classes of adults might obtain many advantages from policies that encourage greater intercohort contacts. Young adults can gain a richer appreciation of the nature of the married life and parenthood that probably lies before them (unquestionably, the young adults will see more and differently when they are in their twenties living close to child-rearing families, as compared to what they see as children and adolescents). In other words, they will receive important knowledge. The near-retirement and postretirement citizens may gain important satisfactions from participating in the intergenerational transmission of experience and values.[17] They may participate through assisting in schools and in community youth-oriented programs—or even merely by being active members of neighborhoods containing significant proportions of children and adolescents. The transmission will be informal, incidental, and anecdotal, but it should communicate important affective knowledge to the young. Essentially, the elders will be "teachers."

This suggestion that teaching—as compared to learning—is the central role of the old is at variance with many contemporary themes about the role of the aged, for it consciously implies that younger persons have more to learn from the old than the old from the young. The idea that the old should teach is consonant with the roles taken by the old in most traditional societies. Of course, in our society, we are often presented, via the media, with the picture of some elderly person enrolled in college and still seeking cognitive knowledge. Such pictures, and the accompanying texts, implicitly overvalue the acquisition of such knowledge and fail to give appropriate weight to the valuable knowledge already possessed by many older persons. A more sensible policy would seek to foster the image of older persons instructing students and teachers. Such an appreciation of the affective teaching capability of the old might give greater satisfactions to the old, make better use of manpower, and increase the affective knowledge of the young.

The promotion of greater cohort heterogeneity in suburbs may also serve broader social interests than those of the particular individuals and the age groups involved. Nationally, we have been witnessing a steady growth of the divorce rate, and we are becoming increasingly concerned about the forms of care for the elderly that our society should evolve. Both of these broad problems are related to the issue of intercohort isolation. If young adults are not routinely brought into contact with older, stable married families, or if the old are isolated—or isolate themselves—into age-segregated communities, it becomes harder for each of these cohorts to receive, or ask for, the counsel or help of other cohorts. But America—which is a community—cannot ignore the national problems generated by cohort isolation. The whole society is affected by the tensions that may be generated by these patterns. We all suffer some from the problems of children from one-parent families, share the frustration that typically flows from broken marriages, and feel guilt and sorrow when the aged live out their years lonely and ignored. We cannot walk away when large proportions of individual Americans experience such distress. And, if we cannot walk away, we will strive to encourage community structures that make the problems less likely to occur. These structures can foster greater cohort heterogeneity in communities.

The roots of socioeconomic segregation are not quite the same as those of cohort segregation. Cohort segregation is largely due to the attitudes of cohorts who stay "out" of particular suburbs—although, if they did want to get "in," they would discover that few facilities (and an uneasy welcome) were available to them. Socioeconomic segregation is largely the product of the exclusionary desires of suburbanites, reflected both in explicit policies and in the paucity of housing for diverse economic groups. Of course, socioeconomic segregation is ultimately the product of the flight to the suburbs discussed earlier. The harmful effects of such segregation on suburban children have already also been discussed, and a remedy has been proposed, that is, systems that permit the establishment of parameters about permissible diversity in a community. Perhaps the only additional observation that should be offered is that such controlled desegregation would be beneficial not only to contemporary suburban children but, presumably, also to children from lower socioeconomic classes, who have also suffered the deprivation that flows from being reared in a homogeneous environment. And the benefits to lower-socioeconomic children may ultimately work to the benefit of the whole society. After all, the affective skills that these children acquire through childhood and adolescence in diversity can lead to their becoming more productive citizens. Incidentally, it should be mentioned, at this point, that the "mixing" of upper-middle-class and lower-class children is not necessarily aimed at producing warm relations among all members of these classes. Indeed, the students' divergent home backgrounds may well generate some interclass tensions. More-affluent children may verbally "put down" their lower-class opposites, who may respond by threatening physical violence—or the scenario may begin from the other end. Still, if the diversity is within manageable limits, and the school community is fairly cohesive, such exchanges can still be quite productive. Although one important affective skill is learning to live with diversity, we are not expected to like all elements of that diversity; we must just like parts of it and manage the rest. We cannot learn about either interclass tolerance or friendship unless diversity is present and is kept in a disciplined framework.

The relationship between homogeneous post-industrial suburbs and technologic specialization is difficult to dissect. The technology, a highly efficient means of producing material goods and other benefits, is reflected in a variety of institutional patterns: shopping centers, drive-in banks, medical complexes, and industrial parks. These specialized activities are usually located at central sites where the high rates of usage justify their specialized activities and substantial overhead costs. However, the institutions are usually remote from homes, except via auto travel, and thus the young are deprived of important learning experiences that come from routine contact with public and private institutions. Furthermore, this remoteness discourages many suburban adults from developing a sense of identification with their surrounding geographic area: one just cannot feel a sense of loyalty to a shopping-center catchment area. Perhaps it is time we recognize the high social costs generated by these technological efficiencies. As we become conscious of these costs, we may evolve changes in expectations and legislation that may moderate the momentum of our technology.

Youth, a Manpower Resource

Society is filled with important, unsatisfied community needs: dirty streets; communities in need of beautification; elderly people who deserve help and company; employers who have many productive tasks to be done but cannot afford to pay the federally required minimum wage, or find it unprofitable to hire unskilled young persons at that rate. At the same time, many young persons are bored with school, and/or need hands-on experiences, as well as authority and responsibility for tangible, cooperative work.

We are told that the gap between the work that needs to be done and the affective learning needs of the young cannot be bridged, since (*a*) there are no systems to mesh the young with the needed work, or (*b*) it is more important that the young stay in school, or (*c*) we cannot hire young workers (especially at pay rates below the minimum wage) until all out-of-work adults are employed. Still, we should try to narrow that gap.

Giving the young responsibility and authority in community projects and paid work can be fostered locally and on a national level. The discussion of these issues that follows will not distinguish between these alternatives; it will be directed at the basic objections that have just been presented. Presumably, if these general objections are settled, each locality (or the entire nation) can foster such youthful engagement with work and community projects via the most appropriate modes at their disposal.[18] These modes will vary according to the political and social structure of the entities involved: park districts may design youth involvement projects tied to park maintenance, localities may require local employers to hire predetermined percentages of young employees, schools may give credit for community services, or the federal government may revise its minimum wage laws. But before such concrete steps are taken, the general objections must be considered.

The absence of "systems" to bring together the young and work is, in one sense, an easily satisfied objection. We must change the situation. The fact is that throughout most human history, and in most societies, youths have made significant contributions to the work and service performed in communities. The distinctions that are drawn between youth and productive activity in our society are actually an anomaly. It is difficult to believe that plans and systems could not be developed to revise such a situation, if there were large-scale support for such a change. The change could not occur quickly, but incrementalism is a good idea in this area. We must design systems that balance between the romantic idea that the young have the skills and idealism to save us and the overly protective view that fails to make significant demands on the young, by giving them inadequate responsibility or authority. Of course, such casual proposals mask immense problems in planning. However, those problems are different from serious intellectual objections which would need to be founded on the theme that we should not try to increase the role of youth in work and community service, even if it were technically feasible.

But the discussion of the systems to increase on-the-job experience for youths should include a sketch of some work situations that foster better affective learning.[19] Strong reinforcement systems—covering both positive and aversive reinforcement—and arrangements for reporting results are important. In other words, children and youths should be stimulated to do things correctly and should be able to see whether they are doing things right or wrong. Attractive and constructive role models should be available. These may be either adults or simply older—and comparatively mature—youths, but they should have incentives to develop significant contacts with the young, and their contacts should often persist over periods of time. If possible, there should be a relationship between the work and the youth's schoolwork. The job responsibilities should also gradually give the participants an opportunity to exercise some authority over other youths and adults. Part of the work should be in uncompensated community service (though lack of compensation does not mean there should be no recognition) and part in typical paid employment.

Of course, this sketch represents an ideal. It will be difficult to integrate all these elements into one situation, especially since our first-hand experience in developing such work is limited. One barrier to such design will be our misunderstanding of the work "responsibility." All too often, we confuse it with "authority." Authority means the power to act or to compel others to act. Responsibility means the willingness to personally accept the consequences that flow from good or bad action. Unfortunately, many jobs designed for youth—especially in the public service area—do not have immediate, tangible consequences for the youths concerned. The responsibilities in many such jobs are too amorphous and abstract for youths to feel any connection between their work and its outcomes. As a result, some youths employed in such jobs leave work with a diminished capacity for productive activity. The jobs have actually taught them destructive affective learning: how to loaf and con. To avoid these pitfalls, careful job design is critical.

Another problem tied to the issue of job design is that the process of design requires talent and that the operation of such jobs—which are essentially learning environments—will need the skills of able adults. In other words, the total effort will have significant new economic costs. But teaching people usually is costly. Parents make huge investments of time in their children, and schools cost money, as do libraries, newspapers, and on-the-job training programs. Thus, an important aim of a good design will be to create systems that spread costs and provide widespread benefits. Of course, different systems of cost diffusion will be needed in the different types of communities which foster the programs—ranging from small neighborhoods to large national agencies. The benefits generated for the adults may be as much emotional as economic, for helping a young person to grow up can be rewarding as well as demanding.

If we have systems to help the young into work-type responsibilities, we should not be deterred by the fear that their schooling, especially their compulsory education, will be disrupted. The importance of formal education in post-industrial society is rather problematic.

Unquestionably, effective adults in our society must possess relatively high levels of cognitive skills. But it is not clear that these skills must be attained largely beween the ages of six and twenty, or that they can only be attained in traditional schools. Furthermore, it seems likely that the discontinuities between school and adult-type responsibilities that do exist in our society may even handicap cognitive learning. Much of the school learning seems apparently unrelated to the students' future adult life. Of course, school materials cannot—and should not—always be immediately relevant to the aspirations of students. Indeed, important learning often involves elements of deferred gratification. But, stressing the ultimate appreciation of relevance can be overdone; if a student, while attending school, is brought in touch with a variety of adults and adult experiences, it is likely that these contacts will lend greater day-to-day relevance to any well-constructed curriculum. In sum, work-type programs for the young need not seriously undermine overall formal learning. Such programs might only (*a*) postpone some formal learning until later in life, (*b*) provide greater incentives for some formal learning during youth, and (*c*) stimulate schools to cut out some formal learning which is truly irrelevant.

The problems generated by competition for jobs between youths and older workers are complex. But analysis is helped if we divide these problems into short- and long-run concerns. In the short run, any actual or potential job in the labor market is usually pursued by several candidates. When one candidate is hired, other competitors feel that they might have gotten the job if it had not been for their competition. And so job competitors do what they can to keep other people out of the labor market. As a result, any effort to increase youth responsibilities or authority through assigning them work that may arguably be done by someone else will be resisted. And, since the potential resisters are often organized into labor unions, they generally can mobilize considerable political force.

The preceding short-run analysis is not necessarily an accurate portrayal of the situation. After all, tens of millions of immigrants have entered America since the early nineteenth century. Most of them managed to find work, and American-born workers have also generally prospered during the same years. Indeed, when the "stealing jobs" argument is applied to school-age youths, its ultimate illogic is disclosed: the only way to prevent beginning workers from becoming job stealers is to prevent them from ever growing up— keep them in school forever, then they will never be able to take anyone's job. But who pays for the tax costs of anyone's schooling besides employed workers? And who pays the costs generated by people who cannot earn their own living? Of course, the truth is that all newly employed workers, whether natives or immigrants, take jobs from other competitors, use their wages to buy and consume the goods produced by other employed workers, and produce goods that other workers can then afford to buy. In other words, the long-range effect of the growing labor pool has been greater overall production and larger markets. The discomfort of individual workers who occasionally have found themselves beaten out by some lower-paid person has been more than compensated for by the general increase in the welfare of all, including large proportions of union members.

Unfortunately, the social benefits promoted by increased competition in the labor market—and consequent enlargement of the work force—are broadly diffused. The injuries promoted by increasing labor competition are sometimes apparent, but always easily imagined by out-of-work employees. And so a great deal of potential resistance exists to measures that may increase youth employment by (apparently) threatening some adult jobs. The effect of this resistance on overall public opinion can be moderated by broad-gauged analyses—such as has just been presented. However, the inevitable tensions that are produced by significant unemployment ensure that the resistance to increased youth employment will be substantial anytime there is a comparatively high level of adult unemployment.

Despite this foreseeable resistance, a diversity of tactics can be used to diminish its impact. The logical flaws in the "stealing jobs" argument should be carefully explained, so that growing numbers of the public appreciate that increasing jobs for the young usually means that the overall pool of adult jobs will concurrently expand. Political measures to increase youth employment should generally be advanced during periods of comparatively high adult employment, though the changes promoted should be in forms that will persist if employment downturns do occur. Legislation to stimulate youth employment can be promoted at both local and national levels. This flexible approach may enable change proponents to encourage such legislation in some communities, even though the resistance may be intense in other regions. Employment can also be fostered in volunteer jobs, where youth service may be viewed as a form of recompense—by the young—for the free schooling they are receiving from the community. Some of these jobs can involve activities that are not being handled by anyone at this time, and thus the youths are no threat to anyone's employment. Perhaps the final point to be made is that the youths whom we isolate from affective learning, by policies that foster youth unemployment, are actually our own children. And, there was no sense in having them if we support policies that keep them imprisoned in childhood.

In the performance of these duties, I was often late for school, but the master, knowing the cause, forgave the lapses. In the same connection I may mention that I had often the shop errands to run after school, so that looking back upon my life I have the satisfaction of feeling that I became useful to my parents at the early age of ten. Soon after the accounts of the various people who dealt with the shop were entrusted to my keeping so that I became acquainted, in a small way, with business affairs even in my childhood.
—Andrew Carnegie[1]

CHAPTER 7
Being a Suburban Parent

There are many reasons why the extrafamily environment surrounding children in post-industrial suburbs is not helpful to sound socialization to adulthood. The suburban parents' power to change that environment is limited, since many shaping forces are beyond family control. Still, there are areas of conduct in which individual families may have some influence and in which collective action by groups of families can produce desirable change. This chapter will discuss how parents can make decisions that can be helpful to their children in these matters.

The first principle is that children's relationships with other persons and public institutions—such as institutional religion—will be substantially determined by their parents' attitudes toward these institutions. This principle can generate complex ironies. Sometimes, parents' aspirations or needs stimulate them to adopt attitudes that can discourage their children from identifying with these institutions. Such negative parental attitudes may be based on motives unrelated to their aspirations for their children—for instance, parents may withdraw from contact with neighbors because they build their social life around friends at work. However, regardless of the motives, parental attitudes may still have important effects on their children's extrafamily relationships—in the example just given, the parents' friendship patterns may handicap the child from developing easy relations with neighborhood adults. Sometimes, parents' attitudes (which affect the nature of the child's environment) arise from deliberate decisions to raise their child in an environment different than that to which they were subjected. Of course, the basic emotion underlying this aspiration—to give our children more than "we" had—is commendable. But we may not always recognize the "real" effects of our own childhood environments or see how even certain apparently unpleasant aspects of our childhood contributed to unique strengths in our own personalities. And so an important objective of this chapter is to suggest how extrafamily persons and institutions may benefit our children— and to imply ways that equivalent patterns in our children beneficially shaped our own adult lives. From this analysis, we may arrive at a fuller understanding of what environments are really good for growing children. That may stimulate us to reorder our patterns of personal and institutional relationships, to enable our children to attain healthy adulthood. T. S. Eliot undoubtedly had a like theme of rediscovery in mind when he wrote:

We shall not cease from exploration
And the end of all our exploration
Will be to arrive where we started
And to know that place for the first time.[2]

Necessarily, any reordering—for the benefit of children—will be a compromise. After all, we are not only parents rearing children, but also wage earners, spouses, and individuals seeking personal satisfaction in our work and friendships. Still, an outline of some major environmental factors affecting sound child rearing can supply us with useful information that can help us to make better informed compromises. Indeed, we may even discover that some child-related conduct changes that, at first, seem personally painful to us may, in the long run, promote changes that significantly enrich our individual lives. In other words, just because we have planned to do something one way does not mean that such a decision is in our personal interest. The decision may be just the result of transitory anger and inadequate information.

Relatives

Children are helped to maturity by continuing relations with persons of different ages under varied circumstances. Obviously, the relatives of a child's parents—their parents, cousins, brothers and sisters and their children—are a valuable pool for providing such experiences. But we are not only concerned with the child knowing of the existence of these relatives or seeing them occasionally; we also want to promote routine and continuing contacts. Then, intense interaction can occur, and children can learn how to conduct themselves when they are close to persons of other ages and backgrounds. Such learning is facilitated by the existence of family ties, which creates tolerance on both sides. Then, if difficulties arise, the ties serve as stimuli to working things out, as opposed to cutting and running.

The quality of child-relative relations is inevitably affected by the quality of parent-relative relations. If the latter are weak or poor, it will be difficult for significant child-relative relations to develop. The decisions are made in the early stages of the marriage, when the future parents (who are also former children, siblings, and cousins) establish the principles that they expect will control later contacts with their relatives. Sometimes, recently married couples, to demarcate the independence they hope will characterize their married status, take steps that isolate them from their parents or other relatives. And, of course, sometimes parents of recently married children fail to give them an adequate sense of independence and freedom from intrusion. Parent-relative relations are also continuously reshaped by the decisions made by both parties throughout their lives. For instance, decisions about where people live can easily revise the nature of relationships.

American culture does not provide an easy body of conventions to guide newlyweds and their parents (and, often, other relatives) in structuring and restructuring family relationships. The traditional mother-in-law jokes suggest that the essential pattern is too much intrusion by the bride's mother, but the line between intrusion, thoughtfulness, and love is not easy to draw. We might just as easily conceive a body of jokes about the desperate insecurity of new husbands, which they direct against their bride's mother.

The quality, as well as frequency, of contacts between relatives and children is relevant. Beginning contacts between generations probably go best when they have to do with getting something done—as opposed to just exchanging talk. As contacts become more comfortable, and shared values are revealed, then personal talks can become satisfying. But, at first, activity is a helpful bridge—people working in the kitchen; going to the zoo; playing a sport together; sharing a hobby or, perhaps, visiting someone at work; sewing; shopping; fixing the house; and, of course, babysitting by a relative, a natural way of getting relationships started.

Parents may not realize the need of such bridging structures between children and relatives because their own interpersonal relationships with their parents or siblings do not usually require such "bridges." Thus, grandparents and their own children may quite comfortably come together for the simple, overt purpose of visiting. However, these adults forget that earlier in their relationships—when they were, respectively, parents and young children—there were many years when their contacts were pervaded with bridging factors. It is just this intense past history which makes such bridging unnecessary between them now. But grandchildren do not automatically inherit the shared understandings existing between adult relatives. The understanding must be learned.

Developing and maintaining such relationships can take as much, or more, learning for adults as for children. After all, if the growing child has never had experience with adult contacts except his parents, the parents have never had the experience of raising a child—and then they complicate the process by bringing their parents onto the scene in an intimate and routine fashion. Grandparents (and other relatives, too) can be uncomfortable about being close to their own children's child rearing and still being expected to maintain a degree of tact. Again, grandparents may be uneasy about developing vital relationships with grand-children. They are usually lovely to look at, or to talk to briefly, but it is another thing to organize one's work, play, or house-chore patterns so that the grandchildren have meaningful roles. But without such reorganization, in the long run, there is not a basis for more substantial exchange. The grandparents can give money or presents and receive a "Thank you," but this material exchange cannot create the base for emotional intensity.

The process of developing relationships is greatly complicated by post-industrial affluence and technology. There are simply fewer natural occasions for people to overtly cooperate with one another to get tangible things done. People need human contact as much as in the past, but such contacts are less sustained by the tangible need for cooperation. Thus, the first stages of the contact process become more self-conscious and difficult. But since relationships between children and relatives (especially grandparents) seem so inherently desirable for people on both sides, perhaps grandparents should deliberately seek to develop activities that facilitate such contacts, just as adults might take up tennis, golf, or bridge if they moved into a neighborhood where that activity was what brought people together.

Religion

Institutional religion can play an important part in stimulating attitudes and values in children that can assist them to attain healthy adulthood. For instance, many formal religions are iden-tified with structured systems of conduct and useful and re-sponsible guides for day-to-day conduct. Furthermore, religious institutions often are highly supportive of intergenerational activi-ties: children attend many religious services with adults, adults and children are involved in Sunday school, and intergenerational social and service activities are common.

Children's religious interest is highly dependent on their parents' attitudes. As a minimum, the parents must vigorously support the children's involvement. But verbal support and demands usually are not enough. Unless the parents make religious attendance and observance a significant force in their own lives, it is unlikely that the children will be significantly engaged in religion. Of course, such unengaged children may still describe themselves (or their family) as Christian or Jewish or whatever. However, this formalistic acceptance cannot supply the emotional engagement, and the occasions for personal interaction, that arises from routine attendance at services or observance of religious obligations. Parents may feel that it is inappropriate for them to determine their children's religion and may be reluctant to deliberately shape their children's religious preferences. They may believe that the children should make that decision for themselves when they are older. However, such withdrawal by the parents is simply another form of choice making for children. The parents' own nonreligious participation or failure to involve the children in religion is evidence to the children that their parents do not believe that religion is a vital matter. Of course, this indifference to the children's religious involvement is antithetical to the spirit of most religions, and, after all, we do not give children choices about attending school, seeing doctors, or staying clean. Assume that the children have been receiving this message about religious indifference for fifteen or twenty years. Then, they are figuratively asked to make up their own minds. But, by that time, it is very unlikely that they will disregard the intense example of indifference given by their parents. For better or worse, it is impossible for parents to avoid significantly shaping their children's religious attitudes. The only issue is whether the parents will be conscious of the power they are exercising.

The religious preferences of parents are largely determined by family traditions and personal philosophies. Still, some families who are prepared to make religious commitments may have some degree of choice. If such a choice is being exercised, parents should recognize the form of religious involvement likely to be most helpful to children. Essentially, children are especially affected by religions that stress physical involvement of the believers in religious practices and symbolism and that proffer a simple and clear-cut system of beliefs and values. Physical involvement includes such activities as singing and the repetition of prayers by the congregation; attendance at frequent religious services; promotion of household prayers, such as grace before meals; dietary restrictions; or maintenance of certain expectations about appropriate dress for services. Clear-cut systems of belief make direct statements about what forms of conduct are right and wrong and what are the consequences of different forms of conduct. Such systems can be better perceived if we consider their converse: subtle, ambiguous, and abstract religions that demand high self-assurance and conceptual skills among their believers.

One might imagine that ceremonial, clear-cut religions such as I have described can engender guilt and fear fantasies in children, as well as trigger ecstatic imaginings. But that is part of the point. These impacts are the inevitable outcomes of religious systems that reach children at an emotional level. Values and a sense of belonging to a community are also both largely transmitted at such a level. Thus, a religion that fails to stimulate significant fantasies may also fail to engage the child's emotions. As a result, the child seeks other resources to provoke such engagement. And so some children assiduously attend vampire movies, explore astrology, experiment with drugs and danger, and otherwise test fantasy outlets. Such outlets are oftentimes not managed by adults or designed by persons who have the child's welfare in mind. And, thus, if we neglect to guide children to religion as a world for fantasy outlets, we make it likely they will find dangerous outlets on their own.

Religions that we might characterize as "child satisfying" have styles that diverge from the preferences of many sophisticated, modern adults. Formerly, many adults did not have such "sophisticated" attitudes toward religion and were able to accept religious modes that simultaneously were useful to their children. Formerly, too, some religions simultaneously maintained themselves at two levels—one simple, physical, and direct, the other subtle and abstract—and met both adult and child needs. Judaism and Roman Catholicism are examples of such religions, where simplicity, on one hand, and abstraction, on the other, were supplied for different audiences. Still, for most of history, even such complex religions assumed that all believers—novices and sophisticates—would first accept the religion at its simplest level. The seeker for complexity simply added complexity to the simplicity. Today, when a religion turns toward abstraction, it frequently abandons vital ritual and ceremony.

Incidentally, the focus of both physical involvement and conceptual simplicity assumes that the child's religious involvement, to the extent possible, will not be interdenominational. An interdenominational approach, despite the institutional needs it may satisfy, will tend to lessen the child's sense of religious focus. And that focus helps the development of strong and reassuring religious identities in children. Once again, we have the dichotomy of religious patterns that may be useful to adults but present disturbing ambiguity to children.

Work

The parents' work, and the way they relate to it, can have a powerful effect on children's attitudes and affective skills. Of course, the major determinants of the children's reaction may be beyond the immediate control of the parents: the parents' skills, the labor market, and so on. However, there is often still room for choices.

Parents may have some choice in whether to accept work in jobs, or for employers, that stress geographic mobility and frequent transfers. Such mobility patterns may handicap their children in developing persisting, intimate ties with other persons—either adults or children. This limitation of contacts to the nuclear family can significantly lessen the children's opportunities to acquire important affective skills. Of course, if the choice is transfer or starve, then the decision is simple. But sometimes parents, and potential parents, choose to accept an employment structure that stresses mobility because the level of income they will attain will enable them to offer certain advantages to their children. To the extent that such benefits for children are a motive, parents should recognize that many drawbacks for children are also generated by the process.

In any event, when moves must frequently occur, parents should make efforts to maintain sources of transitional stability: for instance, persistent affiliation or re-affiliation with one religious denomination or persisting employment with an employer who generates a sense of collective identification among employees and their families.

Children should acquire some sense of the nature of their parents' work. If their mother is a housekeeper, gardener, and/or clubwoman, it may be easy. Indeed, in such cases, the assumption should be that the children will assist her in many of her activities, for that is how one really gets a feel for things. However, if one or both of the parents work away from home and/or the neighborhood, it becomes difficult. But, again, involvement and understanding are still to be desired, wherever possible. Unfortunately, the work of many parents is not easy for children to understand, visit, or find interesting. Still, it is probably better for parents to err on the side of overinvolvement than to keep the work remote and undiscussed. Perhaps older children can occasionally be taken on business trips—with side visits to the zoo or ball park. Or they can be taken to lunch with a colleague. Maybe the company can be stimulated to run a children's visiting day. Union meetings are probably not closed to children. Does the company have annual picnics? Relatives and friends of the family may also be persuaded to take your children along when their work may be interesting to the children.

The Community

The community is the geographic area in which the family lives, but, actually, it is comprised of a number of concentric communities of growing size and complexity. The smallest community might be the block or street on which the family lives. The largest community could be the largest geographic area an adolescent might conveniently visit within the day using public transportation. As children grow older, we want them to have access to continuously enlarging communities that provide them with constructive, diversified, and more demanding and rewarding experiences.

Constructive experiences offer children incentives to test and acquire new affective skills. Those tests should be graduated in such a fashion that not too great a challenge is presented to the children at any one time. Diversity implies that the persons and agencies in the community display enough variety to stimulate children to learn a variety of skills. Diversity is exemplified by a wide variety of age groups in the community; a variety of shopping facilities—both small, owner-managed stores and larger chains; a variety of housing arrangements—private homes, apartments, and townhouses; and, finally, a variety of ethnic and socioeconomic groups.

Of course, all this variety can never exist on the family's home street. And this is the significance of the concept of concentric communities: some of the areas that are easily reached by children and adolescents—but are not near the home—can provide the desirable variety that can never be next door.

Another element of the community is the forms of structured youth activities that it provides: Little League, Scouts, and so on. These activities can be occasions for children and adolescents to test and learn interactive skills under the guidance of adults. One force that undoubtedly will affect children's involvement in such activities is their parents' own commitment to assist, as volunteers, in promoting such activities. And so the combination of available activities and parental involvement can make this community resource highly useful to children.

In talking about adult-sponsored youth groups, one caveat must be uttered. These groups can perform valuable services. They can be especially helpful if they bring together youths and adults from different socioeconomic backgrounds and thus supply the young participants contact with the challenges of diversity. However, the groups are not a full substitute for other kinds of extrafamily contacts between youths and adults, such as those that might occur between relatives, on a job, or within a congenial and diversified neighborhood. The youth groups are handicapped because they often meet on scheduled occasions, the children frequently need to be car-pooled to the gathering, and the adults involved often do not live near to all the children. Child-adult interaction in such groups is often constrained by the formal structure. This remark is no criticism of dedicated adult volunteers involved in such activities or the many valuable services they supply. It simply is a recognition of why a community with many such activities may still have serious shortcomings in youth-adult engagement.

The physical challenges in the environment can also be another important community resource to assist affective learning. Challenges might include flooded quarries, swamps, woods, and frozen lakes in the winter. Such challenges, if they are fortuitously patterned, can provide children and adolescents with occasions to test their judgment and courage in situations in which there are manageable risks: mistakes are likely to be awkward rather than deadly, but judgment can gradually be refined through attempting successively more difficult challenges.[3] Sometimes, young adults and older children can act as mentors to younger children who want to be initiated through such tests. In contrast to such graduated tests, we can conceive of environments in which there are few or no physical risks or those in which there are only occasional but very dangerous tests (such as living beside a busy unfenced highway). Neither of these alternatives can facilitate useful affective learning—in one case, children are bored and may engage in reckless experimentation; in the other, death or sudden, drastic injury does not facilitate learning. The proposal that environments should have semidangerous features that are available to children may be upsetting to some parents, but growing up is inherently a process of testing and exploring. If there are no natural challenges about, children may strive to develop artificial substitutes, which may be far more dangerous than those found in a natural environment.

The community also consists of the local social and service activities that may involve children and adults. Some adult clubs make a deliberate effort to engage children and adolescents in social activities sponsored by the groups. Other clubs establish service programs that permit adolescents to render volunteer services. And, once again, we must keep in mind the dichotomy between simply turning resources over to children and adolescents, as compared to establishing and monitoring guidelines which provide goals and structures for the participants. Such structures should not prevent youths from participating in planning, but the structures do mean that children and adolescents who regularly receive resources from others should be held accountable for what they do with those resources. It is only when adolescents are self-supporting financially that they are entitled to completely decide how to spend important resources. And, by that time, they are no longer adolescents, but adults.

In-the-Family Policies

Many in-the-family policies can importantly shape children's affective learning. In general, these policies should aim to diversify the character of interaction within the family. As a result, children will be better able to first experience, in their family (a comparatively secure environment), some of the learning experiences they will later face away from home.

Probably the most basic of these experiences is the discovery that generous love can be coupled with demands. Or, stating it otherwise, parents who love any one child still have many other competing loves and obligations, and the loved child must temper his or her demands and expectations to mesh with the other needs and loves of the parents. This discovery of "tempered love," and how to live with it, can assist children to perceive of society as an environment that loves and sustains them—but, still, this love proffered by society requires them to display a sense of proportion and to accept appropriate responsibilities.

Essentially, parents temper their love by asking children to make certain adaptations. And so, in addition to love, the family presents demands that are helpful and instructive to children. In the past, many such demands naturally arose out of the patterns of life.

There were just never enough resources to go around, and many things needed to be done. As a result, there was a need for everyone to share and to pitch in. Some natural demands still arise today. For instance, since overtired infants and young children can make life uncomfortable for everyone, such children must be sent to bed at an appropriate time in order to make life decent for others, as well as themselves. Children are sometimes upset when such to-bed rules are enforced. Perhaps they mistake being put away for an absolute deprivation of love. One hopes they eventually will learn (at a subconscious level) that they are still loved and that their parents, despite their love for the children, also must have some free time.

But despite the natural affective learning demands that still arise in most families, it is probably desirable to further enrich the in-the-family learning environment. The efforts at enrichment will face one basic problem: making sure that children learn can be unpleasant for the teacher. As a result, the parent giving the instruction must strain to overcome the anger, confusion, and resentment of the child. This unpleasantness is especially aggravated in post-industrial family environments, for in such environments the necessary learning often cannot be related to an immediate and tangible need—like how to catch a fish to eat—but only to more abstract issues, like getting dishes clean so there will not be germs around. As a result of this potential unpleasantness, we may avoid making learning demands on children unless they are dramatically necessary. Unfortunately, in our comparatively affluent modern environment, we can all too often get by without demanding real cooperation from children. For example, if a child keeps an extraordinarily messy room, and we believe this is irresponsible, we can simply keep the door closed and ignore the situation. In smaller homes, where less privacy is possible, we cannot ignore such disorder, and so we compel the child to develop better habits. If some eloquent modern social reformer wanted to lessen parents' tolerance for sloppy children's rooms, that reformer could preach forever about the matter but not generate much change in parents' conduct (except to stimulate some guilt). However, assume the reformer could compel all parents and children to live in different parts of a large common room, or have two or more children share the same room. Then, the reformer might expect that far more parents would strive—and succeed—in teaching neatness and responsibility to their children.

And so reasonably affluent parents are constantly faced with a tension between postponing useful learning demands on children and making such demands in the face of resistance. Some strategies can be helpful. One is for the parents to collect allies. Be in touch with persons and institutions that typically assume that such demands should be made on children and that supply satisfactions to parents and children who conduct themselves this way. Appropriate churches, community youth activities, sports groups, and friends and relatives can all be helpful. Try to live in a community that inevitably makes such demands on children—where they can travel by public transportation, where varied neighbors make diverse demands.

Another strategy is to identify issues of general principle and settle those. Such general principles can focus on discipline, allowances, household responsibilities, family contacts, and the media.

Discipline exists in the extrafamily world to assist and encourage cooperation and to make communal life possible. The discipline in the family must generally replicate extrafamily discipline, or family life will be unpleasant and the matured child will eventually be ill at ease in adapting to adult community life. In addition, since children do not always know how to protect their own interests, discipline must be maintained so that adults have the power to satisfy their parental responsibilities to their children.

To encourage cooperation in the family, discipline must require the children to moderate their desires to permit other family members to obtain satisfactions. But in many modern families, activities can be organized so that, in the short run, the family can comfortably exist without the children being forced to moderate their many demands. Cooperation is less necessary. But even in comparatively affluent families such nondiscipline policies do not work in the longer run: moments must arise when the child is told "no," in the interest of making group life worthwhile. The problem is that a much delayed "no" may come with extraharshness because of its unfamiliarity. Thus, reasonably balanced discipline must be maintained even in affluent families in the interest of the family.

Even more important than the immediate interests of the family are the long-range interests of the child. If the family's disciplinary style is too sharply different from adult or community life, the child may not learn appropriate affective skills. For example, adult life is and must be surrounded by rules and powerful conventions. Adults are expected to discover these rules, generally follow them without question, sometimes differ with them and ultimately obey them, sometimes differ with them and manage to get them changed or revoked, sometimes break them and accept punishment, or sometimes break them and avoid punishment. But adults who expend their energy by quarreling with almost all rules are wasting their time, just as adults who unquestioningly accept all rules are also probably acting unsoundly. In-family discipline must strive to replicate this adult world. Even if parents could give children everything they ask for, we would be wise to set up an environment of scarcity, so that rules could arise and our children would learn to usually just obey them but sometimes quarrel with them, change them, or break them and accept punishment.

If we look at the adult world around us, we see that obedience to rules is the widespread norm. For each much criticized violation, there are hundreds of acts of conventionality and rule observing. Indeed, most of the public outcry we often hear about some breach arises because we assume that rules will be observed. If the media were compelled to report every act of conventionality or rule observing that occurred, as well as the acts of rulebreaking, 99.5 percent of the reporting would be about observance. Because observance must be the norm in any community, a substantial degree of simple, unquestioning obedience is a valuable characteristic to acquire. Without that characteristic, the child or adult will devote a great deal of energy to fruitlessly disputing the many expectations that life sets upon us. Therefore, family discipline—especially in affluent environments where circumstances cannot substitute for family demands—must contain a significant proportion of "no's" that are accepted without great difficulty. Otherwise, the children will be encouraged to use whining and malingering as basic tools of persuasion, but these tools cannot work very well away from family living. Furthermore, such conduct can exhaust the emotional resources of the parents. This is not to say that parental "no's" should never be explained, or even moderated or revoked. However, such a process should typically mirror the circumstances in which "no's" are sometimes moderated in adult life. In such instances, polite, reasonable, persistent questions are asked. The objector uses judgment and tact, offers compromises, and makes it clear that he or she is usually willing to take "no" for an answer. Indeed, it is just this willingness to usually accept a "no" that makes the adult objector most effective; people who are constant objectors quickly lose credibility.

The modes of punishment for rule violation in the family—critical words, deprivation, physical blows—are far less important than the spirit: love, plus a determination to maintain the community and protect the rights of *all* members. In sum, children are punished to protect others, to enable the parents to meet parental responsibilities, and, finally, to protect the children themselves. Administering discipline is not a happy experience and may even signify earlier mistakes by the parents. Still, there is no reason to feel guilty about the basic proposition that the children's immediate desires are only one of the parents' concerns. Ultimately, that fact must be learned by healthy children and adults, for if parents cannot state this fact comfortably—through their conduct and words—the children will have difficulty learning this vital lesson. Such ignorance is not good.

The discussion of discipline can be an occasion for demonstrating the relationship between family and community attitudes and the acquisition by children of laudable characteristics. Let us take the characteristic of pride. Pride is the desire to maintain a certain status in the eyes of others, or at least in our own eyes, but it is also the willingness to accept the *consequences* of having that status. Thus, proud workers or professionals believe they are competent, think their work should be admired, and are willing to strive to do their jobs well. In the historic past, the proud man was someone who wanted certain treatment from others and was willing to duel to compel others to give him that regard.

If one has the desire for status without the willingness to accept consequences, many problems arise. When the brake of consequences is lost, our desires are almost unlimited, guaranteeing a great degree of personal frustration. Furthermore, most of us do not want to be associated with persons who have high aspirations but little pride. These persons are constantly generating aspirations for themselves, having those aspirations frustrated because they are unwilling to really do the work or accept the discipline involved, and then letting their resentment at their loss spill over into their personal relations. Children call such persons crybabies; adults see them as chronic whiners and complainers. But if people who lack pride drive us away, people with pride are usually attractive. In practical affairs, we want to be around persons who think their work is good and want to strive to improve it. Such people are proud. In social matters, prideful people have strong aspirations but keep them under control and are relatively predictable, since their willingness to accept consequences means that they cannot go around aspiring everything. These characteristics are nice to have in friends—they give them a little vitality, which makes them interesting, and some predictability, which makes relations manageable.

Pride can partly be an outcome of family discipline. But a discipline that instills pride must apply the principle that a child's aspirations for attention and status must eventually generate consequences for the child as well as satisfactions. Usually, the consequences will involve the child's acting in a responsible fashion—doing chores, dressing in a particular manner, accepting certain restraints. But assume the child demands status without accepting the consequences: that is, the child wants attention and praise but rejects responsibilities or breaks family rules or understandings. Such a child lacks pride. In such cases, pride can be fostered by compelling the child to accept consequences—that is, punishment. Thus, the principle is maintained that, will it or not, there should always be strong consequences for strong aspirations. Even a child who persistently must be disciplined for some form of conduct, and still persists in that conduct, may be learning to accept the consequences of aspirations. Of course, in particular situations, such persistent obstreperous conduct by a child can have other implications that should be considered. But on the whole, the imposition of discipline, despite the immediate resentment some children show, need not be an especially disturbing experience, for children can acquire pride only in an environment with demands and consequences. The generation of these consequences is one way we show love.

The principles underlying financial allowances for children are important. Regardless of the parents' level of income, the allowance should be at a level that will increasingly stimulate the children to take good care of property, save money, and seek to earn more money through becoming engaged with extrafamily activities. The fact that the children are occasionally deprived of some good or experience they want (and that the family can afford to give) is far less important than the fact that such deprivation may stimulate the children to invent ways of overcoming that deprivation. Essentially, the allowance, and other presents the children receive, is too high if the children do not generally take good care of their possessions, are not driven to save, or are not, as they mature, stimulated to try to find work to earn more money. No matter what we do for our children, important forms of deprivation are inevitable in adult life; the key thing we can teach them is how to resolve the challenges set by that deprivation. But that lesson cannot be taught unless the children are first exposed to deprivation—that is, not being able to get all the things they very much want. Now, it should be admitted that one solution, for children, to deprivations by their parents is to bother their parents so much they give in. This tactic displays persistence, which is a useful form of adaptation. However, the forms of persistence which often work with parents —badgering, bad manners—are not usually adaptive in most other deprivation environments.

Allowance also ties in with the matter of gifts. If children receive a great many gifts, they have less stimulus to care for their possessions or earn outside money. Thus, gifts from all relatives and family friends must be related to the degree of maturity displayed by the child.

Household responsibilities are an evident area of cooperative learning. Inevitably, this important area has declined in importance with the growth of technology and affluence: there are just fewer ways in which a modern youth is needed around the house. Still, some remedial action can be taken. Parents may choose to forego certain modern equipment—dishwashers, power mowers, sprinkler systems—just to provide children with occasions for cooperative learning. A family garden can be a productive project for children. In such a project, it would be far better to have a small garden—to grow either flowers or produce—that was carried through with comparative success than a more elaborate one that was abandoned in mid-stream. In any event, the aim should be to grow products that are either eaten or used to beautify the home. If a first, small project is successful, it will have planted the "seeds" for more elaborate efforts the next year.

Whenever decisions are made to assign responsibilities to children, it will be better if the occasions establish environments in which children and parents work together, rather than structures that have the children going away to do certain jobs. Parental participation offers active role models for the children and establishes a natural system of supervision. Even with modern equipment, there are some chores to be done. As children grow older, they should be increasingly involved. Ultimately, we might expect that a high proportion of the household chores should be done by the children, especially if both parents work or are involved in serious community activities. In other words, the children's contribution to maintaining the house is their work, just as the parents' contribution is largely the money they earn. Because children, like all "citizens," should contribute to their home community, it is probably undesirable to pay them for most household chores. Parents do not get paid for washing the dishes, why should the children? Furthermore, if payment for household chores becomes too convenient a source of wages for children, they will have less stimulus for seeking work away from home. Why work for strangers, when they can work for their parents? And yet a major parental goal should be to stimulate the children to seek outside jobs and experiences. For the children, the aim of such experiences will be to earn money; for the parents, the goal will be to give the child or adolescent new interactive experiences which cannot occur at home.

Children and parents should maintain frequent and regular contacts with one another. Of course, such family contacts are inevitable between parents and infants, but circumstances may make them more infrequent as the children become older. A typical occasion for such contacts might be the evening dinner. Other occasions might be devised, but the principles of frequency and regularity should be observed. As a result of such patterns, children will recognize that they (and their parents) are expected to routinely have tactful, humane contacts with one another, regardless of the other distractions that have arisen. Such patterns of contact are inevitable in significant social situations, and the family dinner table—or some equivalent gathering—is a natural place for children to acquire some of the affective skills involved. There may be other times when there are exceptions—not the way things usually are, and not the product of some minor distraction, but a significant special occasion.

The media—particularly television—are an extrafamily influence that can shape children's affective learning.[4] At the same time, they can supply important learning benefits. Putting it simply, it is important to closely ration this resource. The television shows that children watch and the total amount of time they are permitted to watch should both be restricted until sometime in adolescence, when basic habit patterns are established. This is not the place to articulate principles for evaluating children's shows. But the basic rule is that parents should know what their children are seeing and should be thinking about the relationship between such shows and their children's conduct. The total amount of viewing time is probably more important than the particular shows watched: the most harmful effect of the medium may be to deprive children of the stimulus to do things on their own or to interact with others. If children are using the screen to escape boredom, it may be better for them to become bored and try to learn what else to do about it.

One philosophical theme that has pervaded this discussion of family conduct is the concept of scarcity. It has been expressed in terms of limitations, restrictions, demands, and discipline. That stress may seem incongruous. Our society is comparatively affluent, and even modern children make rather limited material demands. In other words, many of us can afford to buy the things our children want, and many of us feel that most adult Americans can expect to always have their vital material wants satisfied. Why, then, this emphasis on scarcity and control? Because we all have emotional needs as well as material ones. We want others to give us attention, love, and consideration. But each other person in the world has only a limited amount of these valuables available for distribution. No one can give love and attention to everybody, for that attempt would lead to self-immolation. Thus, emotionally stable people only distribute love and courtesy to persons who "deserve" it. The standard of deservingness we establish ensures that not too many justified love demands are pressed on us. As a result, we can meet them.

This discussion of the deservingness tests established by others may engender resentment in us: "Who are these people, to say they won't love me or be courteous to me?" But it is certain that almost all of us, ourselves, apply such tests. We must. Naturally, we tend to say that the deservingness tests *we* apply are appropriate and reasonable. But it is predictable that the tests we apply are such that we rarely choose to give most of our love—our time, attention, or money —to remote persons and institutions that give us no satisfaction. If we do find ourselves tricked into practicing such grotesque generosity, we become angry and change our deservingness standards. Then, the former objects of our consideration become "undeserving." They must either change or be deprived of our consideration.

It is appropriate to recognize the conflict between the concept of deservingness and the concept of "right." We are entitled to our rights regardless of whether we have been good or bad: even a guilty person has a right to a lawyer. And one may say that children always have a right to love from their parents, despite their bad conduct. Society will always be a blend of deservingness and rights, of things we must earn and things that should not be taken away from us. However, because the fairly comfortable family can afford to give children many "rights"—as opposed to insisting on deservingness— children may assume that the world is equally filled with rights, but very few duties. This is an illusion.

In a family, the first criterion of deservingness is the familial relationship. Our children "deserve" our love, unless they commit some unimaginable offense, but, the farther they go outside the family, the more difficult it becomes for children to meet the deservingness tests that are applied—they are going into an environment where there must be a scarcity of love. That environment need not be hostile, but it is often indifferent. To find courtesy and love in that environment, the growing children (or young adults) must establish deservingness. They must display tact, tolerance, control, and judgment to appropriate persons, in order to receive affection or, at least, respect.

In sum, regardless of the material affluence in the world, once we leave our families we will have to seek the affection we need. And, unless the family creates an artificial microeconomy of limited material resources and affection, we will not learn the skills needed to deserve the affection of significant persons. We will be unloved and lonely, or only receive the love of unstable, self-destructive people.

What It All Means

Raising children in a post-industrial suburban or affluent environment takes more kinds of some work and attention than in the past. Many conventions and institutions that were naturally available to help parents have decayed, been cast aside, or made obsolete through the advance of technology. In the long run, society will be better off if new conventions and institutions are created to more adequately assist parents. But when such conventions and institutions arise, they may make demands that make us uncomfortable— because those conventions and institutions will not just involve the creation of new professions; they will require all of us to reorganize our lives, since healthy child rearing can never be conducted by a group of professionals acting on their own.

Until these changes occur, parents will have large areas of freedom and, consequently, responsibilities. The situation presents a wonderful opportunity for the display of human talents. In this era, our children are uniquely "ours," the product of our choices and policies. If we may make some mistakes under the pressures placed on us, we can also have greater pride in the virtues our children develop as a result of the concern and attention we give to the management of their environment.

We should finally recognize that many patterns of conduct proposed in this chapter will encourage continuing relations among parents, their relatives and friends, and their children. This continuity will be facilitated by policies to increase the congruence of religious values held by children and their parents. In the short run, these developments may create discomforts for parents who had different expectations about their own adulthood and their child-rearing plans. Ultimately, we may discover that such patterns of continuity —within the larger family, with friends, and between parents and children—not only will benefit the children, but also can make our own adult lives far richer. And so, as a result of doing things to benefit our children, we may also reap unexpected benefits for ourselves.

The upbringing of young people at the present time conceals from them the part sexuality will play in their lives.
—Sigmund Freud[1]

CHAPTER 8
Education and Sexual Identity

So far, this book has made no reference to the issue of sex role identification: how will young males and females, in the revised suburban environment, learn their prospective adult sex roles, and what sex roles will they—and should they—learn? Questions about the issue of sex role identification have generated considerable controversy in our time.[2] Although the issue is not uniquely suburban, it is particularly related to the effects of post-industrial environments. The evidence suggests that criticism of traditional sex role identification patterns has arisen more often among affluent families—and such families will tend to live in suburbs.[3] It would be unrealistic to present a lengthy treatment of affective learning without accepting the responsibility to relate that discussion to the learning of sexual identity.

This question must be approached with extreme tentativeness, for it is fraught with uncertainty. While the previous sections of this book have dealt with complex problems, human societies have had considerable experience in socializing their children to the styles of adulthood lived by most members of the society. Essentially, these societies have relied on systems that bring young people into intimate contact with diverse adults and/or have created microcosmic communities in schools that have some relevance to the existing world. Of course, phrases like "intimate contact with diverse adults," and "created microcosmic communities" represent relatively general principles. It is not easy to move from such generalizations to concrete implementation, but, still, the principles have been tested.

The issues of sex role identity in the post-industrial society may be another matter. To some degree, it is proposed that children should learn sexual identities that are not widely practiced by adults in society today[4]—and that may have never been widely applied in previous societies or cultures.[5] Thus, the proposal for a revised youth environment—to the extent the preceding interpretation is fair— raises novel problems. We do not have significant numbers of mature adult role models to place before students, nor do we have a clear image of an actual, operating society that we wish to replicate or model in school.

Obviously, proposals for revision have the ability to stimulate vexatious conflicts. We may try to escape such ambiguity by opting to defend traditional sex role identifications and simply rejecting arguments for change. Unfortunately, such an approach is unrealistic. The traditional sex role patterns assumed by women have been undergoing a continuous process of social and psychic erosion. Technology, affluence, and modern institutions have been central forces underlying this erosion, which presents us with a historically unique challenge.

The Erosion of Traditional Sex Roles

Technology has created an enormous number of devices to lighten and simplify household chores or to enable them to be efficiently done by away-from-home systems and processors. As a result, it is increasingly possible for a household to be efficiently managed by a wife who has out-of-the-home responsibilities and who does not have household help.[6] Technology has also diminished the role of physical labor in productive work. Thus, physical strength and endurance—characteristics that are more intense in males—are less important in getting most of the work of the society done. Affluence has made it possible for increasing proportions of households to afford a great variety of labor-saving systems. It has also permitted adults—both males and females—who do paid work to have shorter work hours and to have time to both be employed and do housework. Modern institutions have increasingly taken responsibilities away from the household and neighborhood and allocated them to private and public institutions, ranging from dry cleaners and food processors to hospitals, schools, and social welfare agencies. The transfers of responsibility have occurred through a variety of means. Activities have been shifted to new physical structures: from the home to the hospital, plant, or school. Roles have been assumed by new types of people: they have been taken from relatives, or friends, or neighbors and assigned to paid employees. And new mediums of exchange have evolved: previously, female neighbors in a community might often assist one another's families, but the increasing pattern is for women to hold paid jobs and help to provide the lost "assistance" through paying taxes.

As a result of these post-industrial changes, many traditional feminine responsibilities—child care, care of the sick, food preparation, housekeeping—have left the home and neighborhood.

The final major force for change has been the prolongation of human life: mature females are now expected to live many years after their chidren have left home. The median death age of the white female cohort born in 1900 was 65; the projected median death age of the equivalent cohort born in 1970 is 78.[7] This prolongation has made it more appropriate for females to consider significant away-from-home roles.

Simultaneously, successive generations of young females have been removed—for substantial periods of time in schools—from the home environments that have molded traditional sexual identities. In a historic sense, schools are "new" environments: that is, prolonged schooling (i.e., 12 years) for almost all children and adolescents is a comparatively new phenomenon; it has probably not existed for longer than two or three generations in any significant human society. Before that time, schooling was briefer or restricted to limited groups or to persons who showed special inclinations.

In schools, girls do not see females engaged in housework, cooking, or caring for young children. The formal work of the school is learning cognitive skills, which are viewed by the adults in schools as important. Females are assigned essentially the same cognitive responsibilities as males and perform them just as well. The school gives little formal regard for excellence in traditional feminine activities. The adult females that the students see in schools are wage earners, holding, in the eyes of the students, comparatively prestigious positions. It is not surprising that successive generations of females socialized in such an environment begin to show increasing dis-ease over assuming traditional feminine responsibilities.

The phrase "successive generations" deserves some amplification. Each generation of both males and females in industrial and post-industrial societies has been subjected to more prolonged school than the previous generation. And each such generation, partly as a result of its school-learned affective characteristics, has transmitted a somewhat different message about the essence of femaleness to its children than it received from its parents. The "message" supporting traditional female roles has thus been successively weakened through the intensifying "defeminization" of parents' values and the prolongation of their daughters' formal education. The message has received further support from the effects of technology and the modern systems that we have sketched.

The problem is that we have a better idea of the sex roles we may be leaving than the ones we are going toward. But we must try and have some idea of where we are going. The affective learning transmitted to children today can help to shape their conduct twenty and thirty years from now, and that future conduct should bear some plausible relationship to the world around them. And so we have a responsibility to engage in social forecasting and to use such forecasts as data to assist our process of improved systems to assist sex role socialization.

Principles for Forecasting

Plausible social forecasts are largely based on principles derived from historical or cross-cultural experience. The past may not repeat itself, but if something has happened once, it may happen again; if it has never happened, it still may occur but repetition is more probable than any unique occurrence. The proposed changes in sex role learning can have ramifications for many elements of adult life. We have had an enormous amount of experience with some of these elements. Let us consider the implications of the history of four of them: heterosexual attraction, marriage decisions, child bearing and rearing, and career effectiveness. From this consideration we can derive principles to assist forecasting.

Heterosexual attraction has been a historic human motivating force. When adults of different sexes are brought in close contact for prolonged periods, we assume that such attraction will occur, unless powerful conventions or other boundaries act as constraints. Usually, social groups try to develop such conventions (e.g., marriage, the value of chastity) to diminish social tensions. Most individual members of these groups sympathize with these inhibitions, since the inhibitions protect the sanctity of love and marriage, which evolve from vital sexual relationships. Furthermore, society aspires to marital stability, since it assumes that stable parental sexual relationships foster better child-rearing systems, and society—as well as the immediate parents—has an interest in the healthy growth of children.

But there is persisting tension between this desire to stabilize sexual relationships and the transitory temptations—that occur to many humans—to breach sexual commitments in the interests of conquest and novelty. However, probably most of the persons that engage in such breaches still support the principle of stability; they just object to its application in their particular instance.

The tension between stability and novelty in sex relations is common to perhaps all societies, and diverse systems have evolved to foster necessary constraints. While modest levels of evasions of these systems have occurred in all societies, general maintenance of these constraints is the norm. Social conventions, which provide expectations that govern contact between males and females or define situations where male-female contacts are inappropriate, are a typical system for fostering such constraints. For instance, a variety of conventions and circumstances have discouraged sexual instability among males and females in paid employment. Sometimes, there were definable differences between the work typically done by males and females at the same work site, and such differences created barriers to certain forms of intimacy. Sometimes, only small proportions of males or females shared the work typically done by members of the other sex, and these people had undergone an arduous screening process; as a result, the "intruders" were well equipped to maintain appropriate distance. And, finally, some kinds of jobs were reserved solely for members of one sex. Any great increase in the working contacts between males and females, or change in the character of those contacts, will erode conventions based on other patterns of relationships. Such an erosion can be destabilizing. In the short run, the erosion will win many sympathetic adherents, partly due to its subconscious appeal to the widespread human desire to "cheat," in hopefully painless ways, in significant sexual relationships.

New conventions can evolve that will maintain sexual stability under conditions of comparative proximity and intimacy. However, conventions are understandings shared by groups of persons, and, within larger groups, it is more difficult for conventions to arise or evolve, unless they are shaped around discrete, readily identifiable principles. The more complex, original, or subtle the convention, the more slowly it will appear, or the more limited its area of acceptance.

The bearing and rearing of children has been an important source of gratification for females, in particular, and families, in general. This proposition can be countered by survey research data which show that married couples recall their preparental state as their most satisfactory and by the evidently increasing number of persons who express a desire not to rear children.[8] But the proposition must first be considered at a high level of abstraction. The proposition implies that humans have an inherent need to participate in the process of generational transmission: to feel that, in some way, they are contributing to a continuous social system and that their contribution will, to some degree, persist after their death. Child rearing has been a major means of participating in that process.

If this general proposition is accepted, then the discrepant data can be dealt with. The parents (who told researchers that their preparental life was happier) still chose to have children, although they had ample evidence around them as to the effects that might result. Perhaps such families concluded that "happiness" may be only transitory if the acquirers do not see their pleasures tied to some social purpose. Furthermore, the research done on marital happiness does not include the married couples who did not have children and got divorced. There will always be a few couples who "should" be married and who "should not" have children. But studies focused on only married couples do not include the persons who "should" have had children, did not, and got divorced. As for the contemporary adolescents and recently married adults who propose to avoid child bearing, we will see how long those aspirations persist.

None of this is to say that all women must bear children or that families must plan their lives around children. However, if we abandon these conventions on a large scale, it will probably be necessary for large numbers of adults to be supplied with other structures to enrich and shape their lives. The structures must provide strong emotional gratification, generate powerful identities, and endow participants with significant prestige.

Children's sex role learnings have often facilitated their later efforts at mate selection. As a result of such learnings, members of each sex in a society or cultural subgroup develop assumptions about the sex role expectations of prospective mates and, concurrently, shape their own aspirations and attitudes in the light of those expectations. This process has facilitated mate selection and the persistence of marriages, since it has created pools of males and females with roughly harmonious aspirations. If the sex role aspirations of males and females become diverse and fluid, mate selection and marriage will become extremely complicated. Persons of marriageable age will become less sure of whom they want to marry or of how they will act after they are married. And, after marriage, husbands and wives will find themselves beginning arduous explorations of who they are and what they want from each other. In many cases, the outcome will lead them to conclude that they do not want each other.[9] Meanwhile, children may have been born, or other commitments made.

Personal commitment is a central element to successful careers, whether the careers involve child rearing or paid employment. Commitment is crucial because important responsibilities are inevitably difficult; commitment provides the emotional cement which stimulates us to stay with the challenge when the going is tough, as we pass through dilettantism on to mastery. Commitment is facilitated by structures that limit the number of choices people must make and the variety of alternatives they must choose from. Frequent choices frustrate commitment because they limit the pressure on us to attain true mastery in any one career: we can always hope that the next alternative will prove more auspicious. A variety of alternatives complicates and prolongs the act of commitment: there are just too many avenues for us to adequately investigate, investigation becomes overlong, and the ultimate choice is marred by uncertainty.

As a result of these factors, arrangements that increase the number or complexity of career decisions that adults must make will engender substantial frustration. One traditional system for preventing such frustration has been the conventional division of labor in marriage: child rearing and peripheral paid jobs for the wife, while the husband has central work and economic support responsibilities. Although this division has simplified the decision-making process, it has not removed all uncertainty: for example, sometimes child rearing has taken priority over moving for career considerations, and sometimes vice versa. But the division has helped family members perceive where their personal commitments lay. It has stimulated individual family members to master their own personal responsibilities, and it has encouraged healthy interdependence within families. Any changes that increase the variety of commitments which individual family members make, or that ask them to select from a diversity of commitments, will make it harder for people to keep commitments, or will stimulate them to postpone (or avoid) commitments.

The Principles and Some Proposed Reforms

Any analysis of some of the proposed sex role changes is complicated by the variety of change proposals that are presented and the vagueness that attaches to many of them. We are told the changes strive for "equality," but we know that that simple word encompasses complex ideas.[10] Furthermore, such phrases as "the elimination of sexism" simply beg the question, since it is not always clear what conduct is sexist. Still, for the purposes of analysis, perhaps we can assume that the changes—insofar as they will affect school practices —aim at immediately revising school practices so that male and female students are prepared to live in an adult society where no predetermined distinctions are made in marriage or work roles on the basis of sex differences.[11] If this reform were carried out, what effects might we forecast, in view of the principles we have just considered?

In the short run, the proposed changes might be implemented in schools. Fortuitously enough, schools are environments peopled largely with relatively inexperienced (in the affairs of life) asexual students, who are often too young to engage in courtship or child bearing and who have not yet fully entered on their careers. Of course, students do display some sexuality, but this conduct is often inhibited because they live at home and because the academic structures of the school inhibit much intimacy; for example, male and female students usually do not car pool to school, share private offices, or work together on the night shift. Indeed, in school it is natural for males and females to dress and look the same—jeans, long hair—while sex differentiations in dress and personal appearance are typical among adults integrated into mainstream society. Schools do ask some commitments of students, but such demands are modest compared to the demands that employers and clients make on people to whom they pay money, the demands that infants or young children can make on parents, or the intense personal demands that spouses make on one another.[12] In other words, sex, courtship, marriage, and career usually become far more intense for students after they leave school.

The problems that may be generated by the proposed changes will become more apparent when ex-students and public and private institutions attempt to apply the underlying principles in adult life. Males and females will be indiscriminately assigned to work together in tasks that isolate them from routine observation by adults. Young adult males and females, who want both careers and children in marriage, will engage in courtship and discover that they are each uncertain as to how they will arrange such a prospective mix in their individual lives, and are doubly uncertain of how they can make plans with another equally ambivalent person.[13] Traditionally, courtship was a period for "making plans together"; but planning must center on some agreed certainties. Couples will marry with the assumption that they will avoid or postpone child bearing and organize their life around that commitment. Then, at a later date, one member or another of the couple may decide that simple togetherness is dull or shallow and that work has insufficient emotional reward. And complex differences may arise—at a late date in the marriage —as to what the couple really wants from life. Finally, our differently socialized adults may be engaged in making a living (and perhaps concurrently child rearing) and realize that employers and customers in many jobs—especially many interesting jobs—demand high levels of sacrifice from employees. Those personal sacrifices may spill back into the marriage, as unusual work hours are established or demands are made that require away-from-home travel or acceptance of transfers.

There are writers who have contended that human beings will

prove adaptable to the changes implicitly sketched above. One article summarized much of the literature on social forecasting in the following terms:

The literature rather consistently characterizes twenty-first century society and its components in terms of impermanence, transiency, ephemerality, marginality, instability, novelty, and value conflict. . . . In the midst of this vortex of change, the individual will have increasingly become challenged to organize his life around transience, to endure discontinuities and disjunctions, and to withstand ego-flooding from an environment explosive with sensory stimulation. His personality will have begun to become change oriented, and he will be evolving a Mutable Self. *. . . His interpersonal contacts will have generally become briefer, . . . He . . . will have become less affixed to social forms outside of primary contacts, although he will have a commitment to humanity as a whole.*[14]

These abstract forecasts can be supplemented with concrete examples of the complexities proposed by decreasing adult sex role differentiation. In New York City, protests arose when policewomen were assigned to ride as partners to males in police prowl cars.[15] One principal group of protesters comprised the wives of the male police officers who might receive such assignments. The wives contended that the new options obtained by the policewomen made their marital status insecure—and is it unreasonable to suspect that prolonged intimacy between members of the opposite sex under conditions where great trust may be generated might stimulate sexual attraction? Or, as another example, an article in the *New York Times* described a married couple deeply committed to sexual equality, who determined to continue their careers and simultaneously raise their child.[16] The couple—both successful lawyers—hired a full-time female maid at $135 per week. The couple were participants in a panel, "Real Adult Life," presented to some college students. Finally, another article on two-career families characterized the role demands in such marriages as "extraordinary."[17]

At this moment, it is obviously impossible to determine the degree to which "androgynous education"—to use the phrase applied by one equalist—will create excessive gaps for students between school and adult reality.[18] Of course, when students leave school for adulthood, marriage, and work, a natural corrective process may occur. Males will discover that they grow jealous when their wives or fiancées go to a professional conference with a male colleague, and the wife simply asks why should she "discriminate" when her professional colleague is a male?[19] Females will become confused when their husbands expect them to earn a decent income and simultaneously want them available for routine child-care help. Such conflicts may stimulate the development of more realistic attitudes, but, despite this potential for self-correction, it is desirable to avoid substantial gaps between school curricula and adult reality.[20] When such gaps occur, we talk about "irrelevance." And irrelevance engenders cynicism, confusion, and boredom. These are poor commodities to foist on the young in the interest of encouraging social change.

Unfortunately, the proposed changes in sex role socialization that have just been criticized are a response to a genuine social challenge. The objectives of sex role socialization that previously obtained in our society are tending toward obsolescence as a result of the post-industrial changes that were sketched earlier. In other words, if the school tried to strive toward those obsolete objectives— or strove to regress toward those patterns—that process, itself, would tend toward irrelevancy. And so the challenge before our society—and our schools—is to revise the traditional patterns of sex role socialization but to simultaneously keep those revisions within the bounds of realistic social forecasting.

The Principles and Realistic Forecasting

We should assume that, in the future, as in the past:
1. Adults will want substantial sexual fidelity from their spouses and will support conventions that foster such loyalty.
2. Adults will want permanent commitments from their spouses and will strive to avoid marriages that are largely experimental. In other words, marriage will not become an important system for transporting youths from adolescence into adulthood; two immature personalities will not necessarily transform one another into adults but may simply make each other very unhappy. And while marriages must leave room for learning and development, they must also be rooted in a base of shared maturity. Otherwise, they will generate a great deal of unhappiness.
3. Adults will continue to want to make significant, personal, and identifiable contributions to the process of their society. Unless large-scale systems for personal sublimation evolve (e.g., monasteries, nunneries), successful child rearing will be an important means of fulfilling those aspirations.
4. The consumption of goods and services will continue to be an im-

portant goal of the society: adults will generally aspire to obtain valuables, such as air travel, air conditioning, psychotherapy, and schooling. To buy these goods, adults will need to acquire substantial and scarce skills. As a result, adults will have to display commitment in the face of frustration and ambiguity.

The preceding items replicate values that have prevailed in the past. But there is a new value that also must be recognized: females will increasingly aspire to significant roles apart from their household responsibilities. The reasons for the development of this value have been suggested earlier. Of course, females have frequently been an important of community activities and/or members of the labor force. However, this tendency will intensify.

Our society must integrate its previous values with the changed sex roles of females. It is impossible for us to forecast how this integration will occur, but we can assume that the process will take a great deal of time. Also, we cannot expect each change to be ideally integrated with its appropriate counterpart. Thus, this disjointed change will provoke considerable tension.

But even with these qualifications, it seems likely that far too much emphasis is being placed on fostering change through revising (*a*) the explicit patterns of sex role socialization practiced in schools and (*b*) the incentives that determine the number of working women and the kinds of jobs they occupy. Essentially, these changes have more to do with raising the expectations of women than with creating systems which will enable them to lead fuller lives. The expectations they generate are at great variance with other recognized social values. It is time to foster changes in sex role responsibilities that have greater integration with other social values. In other words, some parts of the change process should be slowed down or reversed, while others need speeding up.

A better designed system of sex role differentiation would give greater emphasis to a number of considerations. It would recognize that sex will frequently be a factor in structuring work situations— not because of widespread male or female incompetency, but because conventions must evolve that protect parties from the effects of heterosexual attraction. Although such conventions will necessarily require some "discrimination" based on sex differences, they would not necessarily prohibit males or females from doing particular work but would attach conditions to such assignments. Those conditions may eventually handicap members of one sex or the other who wish to practice an activity, but the handicaps should not be insurmountable to reasonably motivated persons. However, there will be handicaps and nominal inequality.

More constructive affective learning will be required as preparation for marriage. The preparation will not be intellectual, but experiential. And not so much sexual, but rather in persisting intimate social environments where the participants are provoked to (a) live out (and try out) some of their individual role aspirations in a relatively accelerated fashion and (b) integrate their own role aspirations with those of their associates. It will take considerable imagination by planners to inject realism and motivation into this process, but the effort can succeed. The "graduates" may be able to approach marriage with a better sense of their own aspirations. At the same time, society must continue to encourage marriage as an institution for structuring human life in a rewarding fashion. The stability and gratification fostered by marriage are in the interest of the community and the individual. Therefore, social pressures that encourage marriage must be sustained, and prolonged, widespread self-exploration (i.e., noncommitment) must be discouraged.

New arrangements for child rearing must be developed.[21] Such arrangements will leave principal responsibility with the nuclear family but encourage the development of more ancillary services to parents. The arrangements may also assist husbands who wish to accept greater child-care responsibilities. Of course, many neofeminists have made equivalent demands. However, many of their proposals—such as widespread, free day-care services—are extremely expensive. Any systems that are applied on a large scale will require more imagination in their design in order to make the costs more bearable or to allocate the costs more fairly. For example, the new systems might make heavy use of school children in handling child-care responsibilities or enable pools of parents to share their child-care responsibilities.[22] However, those pools will not diminish the quantity of the parents' child-care responsibilities, but simply make the responsibilities slightly more flexible. In other words, parents who want to have children and also work will have significant extra costs or will have to give up something.

Society will need to make its commitment systems more explicit and continue to foster commitment. Points of choice for determining careers and personal styles must be more explicitly labeled, and persons faced with choice should be assisted in discovering the pertinent information. Gradually increasing pressures should be directed at encouraging commitment, and significant rewards established to stimulate commitment—and significant punishments maintained to penalize those who breach, or substantially postpone, commitments. The commitments need not stimulate persons to pursue affluence—they may just as well pursue community service, or religious experience—but once a course has been adopted after deliberation, the actor must be under pressure to see it through and accept the consequences as well as the rewards.

The preceding general discussion related to a diversity of topics and systems for structuring social life. It encompasses such matters as marriage and divorce law, tax policy, laws governing employment policy, and, most importantly, the conventions established by employers and social groups. The appropriate changes in these systems —if they evolve—will evolve slowly.

Many of these suggested changes seem to be in conflict with the obvious social currents surging around us. However, the conflicts of the moment do not necessarily represent definitive social forces. There is a historical analogy that may be enlightening: For many years in the late-nineteenth and early-twentieth centuries, righteous Americans—particularly upper-middle-class reformers—strove to regulate alcoholic consumption through prohibition and even succeeded in passing a constitutional amendment.[23] The problem these reformers were concerned about was a genuine challenge. Alcohol was a threat to the social order and helped cause serious injury— often to innocent bystanders. However, reform via prohibition was a failure and may have even aggravated the problem. In our time, we are still striving to develop laws and conventions that more effectively deal with the challenge of alcohol. Perhaps we would be further along if national prohibition had not been advanced as a remedy, and we had had the insight to accept more incremental methods. This analogy suggests that a similar focus on incrementalism and changing conventions—as opposed to broad legal pressures— may be equally appropriate vis-à-vis sex role change.

Undoubtedly, some readers may also raise at this point the feasibility of the about-to-be-proposed changes given in the various federal regulations and laws prohibiting inappropriate sex "discrimination" in federally assisted school districts. The inhibitions generated by those provisions can be dealt with in several ways. The provisions only apply if the school district receives federal funds. At the present time, federal funds provide an average of only 7 percent of the expenses of American school districts.[24] Obviously, the proportion in some districts is much smaller. While we occasionally see newspaper articles about the impact of the removal of such funds (the district will lose tens of thousands of dollars unless it does such-and-such), the articles rarely mention that such sums still only amount to about 5–10 percent of the district's budget—or even less. Sometimes such articles also dramatically laud the effectiveness of the endangered programs. But if the programs are that good, the district ought to be able, over two or three years, to phase them in on its own without the aid of federal money. Frankly, it seems that the publicity generated by such articles is typically stimulated by administrators and other district employees—and, perhaps, a few engaged parents who have a special investment in the programs—who are hoping to frighten the bulk of the district's parents into accepting some generally unpopular or irrational rule. Indeed, most objective evaluations of the federal educational programs have not reported the dramatically effective outcomes that are often suddenly discovered when the jobs of the district staff are threatened. In sum, it is profoundly unfortunate that the national government has been able to "purchase" so much control over the lives of local parents and children for comparatively so little money. It is equally unfortunate that local systems have been so willing to be bought.[25] But, fortuitously, we are now only 7 percent out of control; if we work at it, we can begin to buy our way back. Even if a district is forced, temporarily, to accept federal regulations telling parents what sexual identities they must give their children, there is still considerable leeway. As already noted, the current rules will surely change; they are highly susceptible to political and philosophic pressures. Forming subschools, in which parents voluntarily and deliberately make choices (typically with their children's support) is one such pressure device. Such a development might well withstand a court test. Furthermore, the development could surely win widespread public support which would have many beneficial repercussions.

Fostering Realistic Sexual Identities

Sex Grouping
The school should give greater recognition to the real sex role differences that exist and that will persist. It should not continue to treat students as essentially asexual creatures. There are areas where appropriate changes can occur, for example, dress-code requirements, noncoeducational schools or courses. Community service responsibilities, to some degree, can also be divided along sex role lines. The more extreme manual work in school service activities can be reserved for males. Perhaps services to older adults by school children

should be broken down along sex lines, with males caring for males and females caring for females.

The school can give consideration to traditional feminine arts, for example, cooking, needle work, home handicrafts. Some teaching responsibilities for these skills can be undertaken by mothers, and awards can be given to female students for excellent performance. There can be school competitions in which mothers and daughters work together to produce such products. Fathers can be stimulated to undertake similar roles with their sons in traditionally male activities.

Of course, it is true that the "value" of some of the traditional feminine arts has been undermined by technology; for example, premixed foods have made cooking skills less necessary. But the values of many activities are largely the result of attribution. If humans choose to grant acclaim to some activity—whether it is ability at football, juggling, or piano playing—persons with that skill will receive praise. And who is to say that skill at making a soufflé for others to enjoy is less valuable than being a good engineer or bank clerk? Thus, a great variety of abilities can give their possessors satisfaction—if distinctions are made between degrees of skill and if more skilled people are rewarded with attention. Incidentally, an important element in the reevaluation of feminine arts is a growing level of connoisseurship in males as well as females. Schools can help to stimulate such connoisseurship.

The sex role divisions generated in the school need not replicate those that are made, or may be made, in the adult world. The divisions are partly symbolic, to demonstrate that men and women are not exactly the same. The ways in which these differences may be reflected can change from place to place, but the fact of difference remains. It should not be forgotten.

Commitment
The school can communicate the significance of commitment and how that challenge can best be approached. The previous discussion on school administration emphasized how commitment will be an important element in student school-enrollment decisions. But beyond the matter of enrollment, there are many other elements of school programs by which students can be presented with the opportunities and demands of commitment.

The general characteristics of such occasions are easy to articulate. Choices, of gradually increasing complexity and significance, can be placed before students: for example, whether to participate in certain extracurricular activities or take certain elective courses. Students should be helped to acquire adequate information before making commitments and to understand the implications of commitment. However, such efforts should still recognize that commitment always looks different on the far side of the line. Students who choose certain obligations, and meet them, can receive special recognition, and students who avoid commitments can be continuously provoked toward engagement. Students may renege on commitments, but such withdrawal will be associated with penalties of increasing seriousness.

Some of the potential commitments should be related to sex role issues. For example, assume certain activities or patterns of conduct in the school are labeled as especially appropriate for males or females. If a student of the opposite sex wishes to participate, such participation can be possible. But the participation should be related to a network of consequences—some of which may be uncomfortable. A female in an elementary school who wants to be on the boys' basketball team may also be required to wear male clothes in school and to graciously accept any derision that is associated with her special status. If a male is interested in working closely with young infants in a community service project—when such work is usually assigned to females—appropriate restrictions might be placed on his conduct. In other words, the school will distinguish between the exercise of a legal right—which will be formally protected—and the informal sanctions that frequently are applied against persons who exercise such rights. Such informal sanctions will always exist and are one of the costs of commitment. Ultimately, the school should not aim to foreclose certain kinds of unusual commitment. It merely wants to ensure that the commitment costs are not concealed from inquirers. When there is such openness, the committed person is then stimulated to accept—with a degree of philosophical distance —the drawbacks, as well as the rewards, of his or her choice. And this acceptance is one of the elements of commitment, for, to bring up an old saw, "You can't have your cake and eat it, too." There may be some parallels between the approach proposed and the British tradition of toleration of eccentric personalities. In Britain, such characters are not necessarily rewarded or encouraged. However, if they are prepared to accept some of the social costs that flow (to them) as a result of their eccentricity, the society is likely to give them a degree of tolerance. But eccentricity is not painless. It makes demands on society, and the society can reasonably be expected to receive some reassurance or deference from such characters.

Obviously, we are asking the school to participate in drawing fine lines—between attaching real costs (as well as benefits) to commitment and severely penalizing all innovative conduct. There is no assurance the lines will be "correctly" drawn, but there are some safeguards. There should be a substantial degree of parental choice about the school program (or the alternative school students attend), and parents should be comparatively well informed about the program. In addition, the school will frankly confront the issue of commitment and its implications: the issue will not be swept under the rug, with vague language about indefinite exploration or painless choice. Even the use of such means to avoid the tensions of commitment represents a commitment with resultant consequences, but there is not always discussion about the "costs" associated with a commitment to postponement, drifting, and dilettantism.

Marriage

It is hard for students to acquire realistic views of the nature of marriage. Their intimate experience with married couples is severely limited, and teachers, the nonfamily adults that are usually before them as models, are constrained to leave most of the personal details of their marriages out of the sight of students. Given the casual nature of modern student-teacher contacts, such constraint is appropriate. But there are some steps the school can take.

Students can be sent out to interview married couples, to develop biographies of marriages.[26] Adults may be reluctant to be revealing in such exchanges, but teachers can help students develop conventions to help ensure a reasonable degree of discretion. And students, also, might be taught to police each other, to maintain appropriate confidentiality. Giving students such self-policing structures can assist important affective learning.

Students can participate in simulations that mirror some of the satisfactions and demands of married life: budgeting, the character of responsibilities to in-laws and children, the mutual emotional support that spouses are expected to provide to one another.[27]

The school can show it believes that married, heterosexual life is the desirable norm for adults. Its staff can be composed of persons who are married or have "traditional" reasons for being unmarried, such as being young and single, or widowed. It can decide not to hire or retain divorced, unmarried persons. It can actively discourage illegitimacy and overt homosexuality among its students and/

or faculty.[28] If student-teacher relations become more stable and significant, teachers can make more of their family life visible to students.

Teachers can cultivate student relationships which encourage students to turn to them for advice about courtship. Such relationships will become more justified if the school develops the type of staff described in the preceding paragraph. After all, an apparently well-adjusted married person is likely to be better prepared to give courtship advice to a student than is a homosexual or a lonely divorced person.

Spreading Child Care
The school can help spread child-care responsibilities over a broader base. We have discussed ways that older students—of both sexes—can assume greater responsibilities for the care of younger children, both in school and in the community. Both fathers and mothers of children enrolled in the school can also be expected—by the school—to assume responsibilities toward their children. Report cards can be signed by both parents, and both parents can be expected to participate in school meetings and other activities or to take turns in such participation.

Women as Community Builders
Many segments of this text have emphasized the need for deliberate acts to strengthen the quality of community in post-industrial environments. Women may be well qualified to play an important role in this matter, especially in residential communities. Area residents themselves, and not just paid transitory specialists, can make important contributions to policies on these issues. Adults who are in and around their homes during the day can contribute special perspectives as to what should be changed and what maintained in order to foster community. In particular, there is a long-standing American tradition of volunteer workers, especially females, helping to sustain community cohesion. At this moment, this tradition is under attack as a form of exploitation—as if we can only help our friends and neighbors for money. But paid workers can also bring a degree of formalism and remoteness that is alien to the forms of community we hope to revive. It is to be hoped that our restructured school will train a generation of female activists who can both rear their children and help to analyze and structure their family's community environment into a wholesome microcosm.

Life Patterns
Students can be provoked to realize that not all major adult commitments—marriage, career, and child rearing—need to commence at almost the same time. It may be quite feasible for a woman to marry, rear a family, and then (as the children mature) enter into a career —and even go to college at that time. However, such a course requires a comparatively high degree of self-assurance, in order to comfortably postpone—and then take up—her career. This assurance can be assisted if the school puts plausible arguments and models before students. The school, for example, can suggest to female students that college can be postponed without one being damned for life, that it may be better to go to college after rearing children. Or the school can offer, as models to students, the examples of some of its own teachers who have gone into late-in-life careers. The school can also offer extra hiring credit or seniority to such mothers for the experience they have accrued from child rearing and homemaking.[29]

The school can also revise its employment structure in order to permit husbands and wives to cooperate more effectually in child care. Both spouses can be hired as teachers, with the understanding they will take turns covering a common pool of teaching obligations.

Conclusion

Significant changes in female sex roles are inevitable. But some elements of these changes are moving at such a disjointed pace that excessive social tensions are likely. In part, the proposed school revisions aim at slowing down some aspects of the change. Simultaneously, the school should strive to assist society by speeding up some elements of the process of sex role changes, such as placing new life patterns before students and involving more children of both sexes in child-care responsibilities.

We hear it advocated, by those erroneously labeled progressive, that far from pushing their children, adults should make no demands on them—which satisfies neither child nor adult, and deprives the child of both the experience he craves and the adult leadership he needs.
—Bruno Bettelheim[1]

CHAPTER 9
Summing Up

This book has given some attention to works of modern social science. Still, it has made no explicit reference to one of the important areas of scientific endeavor: evaluation. That silence has been advertent, but the question of evaluation must now be discussed.

Any important endeavor must be subject to occasional careful and deliberate scrutiny. We can call such scrutiny evaluation. And, in that sense, of course the melange of innovations that have been proposed should and will be evaluated as they are tried. The evaluations may even be done by persons with a somewhat dispassionate interest in the enterprise being evaluated. But the word *evaluation* has assumed a meaning, in our time, that goes beyond critical or impartial scrutiny, or even systematic reporting. Essentially, it has come to mean a scrutiny based on the scientific analysis of the effects produced by an activity. In the case of learning, these effects are changes in the cognitive or affective knowledge of persons affected by the activity or innovation.

Sometimes distinctions are made between formative and summative evaluation.[2] The first is concerned with the intermediate effects of an enterprise, and such information can be used to improve the ongoing operations of the enterprise, while summative evaluation aims to determine whether or not the end outcomes meet the final objectives of the enterprise. But, despite these significant distinctions between the two types of evaluation, both types essentially aim at measuring outcomes—the effects produced. The measurements may be made at a final or intermediate stage, but the same outcome-focused process is involved.

It may not be beneficial or important to have such outcome evaluations applied to the proposed innovations. Indeed, such evaluations may seriously mislead people.[3] The innovations, if tried, would aim to produce large-scale changes through a slow and incremental process. In any brief period of time (say two or three years), many factors may confound the measurement of such changes: the innovations may be handicapped by inevitable start-up problems; there may be disputes as to the appropriateness of the instruments used; the innovators may deliberately change the outcomes they are aiming for, as a result of their own learning from the operation; the short-run changes may be too small for plausible measurement; or innovators or critics may be equally biased—in different directions—in interpreting the data. Finally, at this time, an efficient measurement methodology may not exist to do the job, and it may take generations to perfect the methodology. But we may not be wise to hold up an important innovation until such a methodology is created.

Many contemporary social scientists have developed a good understanding of the limits of outcome evaluation (as applied to large-scale social experiments) through the controversies surrounding the many social programs launched in the 1960's.[4] In the case of school programs, the desired "outcomes" have largely been achievement test scores. Such tests admittedly encompass a limited range of important school outcomes. But even when this arbitrary and constricted outcome has been accepted as a goal, enormous controversies have arisen over the validity of these evaluations. Questions have been raised as to what factors in schools, families, and communities are related to these outcomes, and what is the extent of such relationships.[5] And thus, after over fifty years of research with instruments that are relatively accurate in measuring reading and mathematics learning, we are still quite unsure how much to manipulate what school variables to affect such scores. If we have all these problems measuring reading ability, imagine the confusion surrounding affective learning outcomes, such as "honesty," "tact," "persistence," or, finally, "good character."

The preceding analysis may be distressing, for it leaves one with the feeling that nothing can be done to assure some rational control over the proposed change process. But this is not the case. Reasonably effective safeguards can be developed, if we escape from the conceptual limits generated by an excessive reliance on outcome evaluation.

An appropriate evaluation arrangement should first focus on the *process* to which participants are subjected, as compared to the outcome produced. The essential assumption will be that important learning outcomes—either affective or cognitive—can only come from a process that rewards the incremental development of such outcomes and places role models before learners. The "process evaluation" proposed will focus on identifying and analyzing the reinforcers and role models available to learners. These reinforcers and role models should be congruent with the affective characteristics the system aims to produce in learners. Let us take a concrete example. Suppose we wish to evaluate the effectiveness of the system for "teaching" students to be honest under pressure: to tell the truth when it counts. A thorough outcome evaluation would be based on a "test" of such honesty: the test should appear to be a real-life situation to its subjects. That test would be administered to students about to enter the school and to graduates. The ultimate evaluation would try to see what changes in pertinent conduct, if any, occurred to such students. Incidentally, if the students were to be in the system for several years, the outcome evaluation might also have to pre- and posttest a control group of nonstudents, to ensure that any changes that occurred to the graduates of the system were not largely the result of the passage of time, compared to the effects of the system. Obviously, the design and operation of an evaluation arrangement to effectively carry out this task would be costly. In contrast, process evaluation would stimulate perceptive observers to see if the system was (*a*) putting students in situations where they were asked to tell the truth (e.g., by maintaining a student-enforced honor code), (*b*) providing the students with role models of honest conduct, (*c*) gradually increasing the demands for honesty placed on students, and (*d*) rewarding honest students and punishing dishonest ones. Essentially, a process evaluation would say that, if these steps are occurring, we will infer that the system is teaching honesty under pressure.

The suggested evaluation plan may seem skimpy to some social scientists and administrators. But it may represent a realistic understanding of social processes. Many powerful and successful human institutions and social systems were designed long before the development of modern outcome evaluation techniques and the aspirations we have attached to such techniques. For example, the United States of America, the Society of Jesus, and the American public school system all represent designed social systems that were planned, developed, and have persisted without heavy reliance on modern outcome measures. The planners and developers of these systems—the American founding fathers, Ignatius of Loyola and his colleagues, Horace Mann and his allies—gave first consideration to what they viewed as general principles governing human conduct. Of course, these large systems provided for built-in reporting of results. However, their reporting processes were infinitely more subtle than simple reliance on outcome measurements. And, indeed, heavy reliance on outcome data may even lead to a misunderstanding of the more profound issues involved in managing large social systems.

A process-oriented system of educational evaluation will revive certain "proverbial" elements of evaluation that have been referred to earlier. In other words, many traditional proverbs—"As the twig is bent, so the tree inclines," "A rotten apple spoils the barrel," "Like father, like son"—are process-focused modes of evaluation. They were important conceptual tools for evaluating socialization systems concerned with the development of character. Presumably, as schools gave growing emphasis to cognitive goals, these tools fell into decay, since they do not directly bear on the teaching of reading or mathematics. Furthermore, the development of instruments that could measure some cognitive skills shifted discussions of educational policy from the issues of affective learning and character to issues relating to test scores and cognition.

This decline in the importance of process-focused—or proverbial —evaluation has deprived us of a valuable evaluation tool, for we are less able to analyze many recent important educational developments. For instance, interest in affective learning is not extinct. There is a body of contemporary literature concerned with affective learning, and that literature is part of a persisting tradition.[6] However, the contemporary literature has often been colored by a strong sympathy with extreme individualism and romanticism. Indeed, it is evident that such literature—and, presumably, the "free" schools and diverse programs created in response to that literature—does not stimulate the development of cooperative and coping skills. We can reach this conclusion because the *processes* prescribed by the literature do not reward significant cooperation or punish excessive individualism. Furthermore, free or open schools are rarely able to routinely place substantial and varied adult role models before their students. It is true that some of these open schools do send their students out to community work, but often the responsibilities generated are poorly defined and the students' contacts with profit-oriented environments are very modest. And, yet, most employed adults in America work in profit-structured environments. In other words, process evaluation shows us that contemporary free and open schools are unlikely to create adults who help other people or develop true communities—regardless of the rhetoric that surrounds such schools.

There are also signs of a powerful and persistent public interest in what is essentially traditional education. Or at least that is a plausible interpretation to give to the great public concern with lack of student discipline in schools.[7] And there are some signs of intellectual support for such concern.[8] Good student discipline is an element of affective learning; however, many "traditionalists" make frequent reference to a reemphasis on the "3 R's" or individual responsibility. These remarks generate a peculiar irony: the contemporary traditionalists may fail to understand the key elements of tradition. Some of this confusion is suggested by the following extracts from a typical "letter to the editor" about school issues: "It appears that both the purpose of education and teaching methods in our local schools have been changed drastically . . . 'Group assignments' were given, deemphasizing, if not discouraging, individual effort, responsibility, and incentive. Four-letter-word contemporary writings replaced classics in English classes. The twin 'how-to' courses, sex education and drug education, were added to the curriculum. . . . I quote Theodore Roosevelt, 'To train a man in mind and not in morals is to train a menace to society'; and Abraham Lincoln, 'The philosophy of the classroom is the philosophy of the next generation.' "[9]

Although the letter writer is concerned about conduct and fostering responsibility, she implies that individual assignments and cognitive focus are the keys to social responsibility. More probably, social responsibility is fostered by well-designed collective responsibilities and affective learning situations. It is likely that the learning systems that surrounded Theodore Roosevelt and Abraham Lincoln gave emphasis to such learning. Perhaps the contemporary traditionalists have mistakenly concluded that affect always means romanticism and individualism. They have failed to see that *feelings* also include patriotism, loyalty, honesty, and persistence. And so it may be important to evaluate contemporary experiments in "traditional schooling" via an analysis of the reinforcers and role models placed around students. The analysis may reveal that many such experiments are generating useful affective learning—or it may show that such schools fail to make constructive affective learning demands on their students or to place significant role models before them.

Some Immediate First Steps for School Administrators

First steps can be made more constructively if administrators, or persons directly concerned, can set quantitative and time targets. For instance, "within three years, the average student in the school will spend two hours a week acting as a student in prosocial activities." "Prosocial" can be defined as action by which the student goes to some trouble to make other persons feel good: tutoring, helping to maintain a flower garden, delivering messages, participating in the presentation of a play for the amusement of others, or assisting in fund raising. Statistically, the standard deviation about the average of two hours' participation should range from 1.5 to 2.5 hours per week. Thus, about two-thirds of the students would put in between 1.5 and 2.5 hours a week: the activities are not all done by a small group of eager beavers. It should also be understood that these activities are generally performed with the same concern for excellence that should pervade the school's academic program.

Once a target of this sort is set, a great deal of planning must get underway. How are these activities to be supervised, defined, and publicized, and how are students to be reinforced into them? What mix of compulsion (and compulsion is used in many school and community activities) and voluntarism is appropriate? How are teachers to be trained and supervised for their new roles? How is the advice of parents and students to be collected and assimilated during the planning stage? How is the development of the "plan" to proceed over the three-year phase-in period: where should things be at the end of the first year?

Administrators might determine to improve school assemblies, in order to intensify school spirit. How frequently are assemblies held and how long do they last? What proportion of school time do they use? How are they planned? Do they have substantial constructive affective content? Do they appropriately use music, symbols, costumes, and the contributions of diverse school community members—from the students to the janitors to the members of the school board? Do they stimulate their audiences to laughter, tears, or ecstasy? Do they tie the school together, and the school to the world? What kind of help can improve the situation? What plan can be devised? Is there sense in devising subassemblies in addition to school-wide affairs?

School rules often can use improvement. Do they articulate students' rights as well as obligations? For example, do they say things like "A student has a right to feel safe in school, and, therefore, students who endanger others will be reprimanded and punished"? Are both these said side by side so that students can see the connection between repression of antisocial acts and the protection of individual rights? Is antisocial conduct defined with enough precision so that students can tell what they should not do? Are copies of the rules generally available to teachers, students, and parents? Is the punishment system clearly articulated and enforcible, or is it, practically speaking, ineffectual? Is it clear that parents will be notified of violations of rules committed by their children?

Efforts can be begun to create smaller continuing student-teacher communities in large schools. Quantitative goals are helpful: so many students and so many teachers will be spending so many hours working with each other in a small, defined group by a predetermined time, and this group will continue together for so many years. These "communities" must define their aims, prepare statements of purpose and rules, inform students and parents, obtain signed consents, and learn how to work together. Unquestionably, issues will arise about recruitment, admissions, expulsions or resignations, scheduling, supervision, reinforcers, the provision of a definite locus of operation, and the relationship between the subcommunities and the larger school they inhabit.

Businessmen and service clubs can be enlisted to find more out-of-school responsibilities for students. Again, quantitative goals must be set. So many students by a predetermined time will average so many hours a week in activities of the following character. And, of course, some system of quality control must be designed—apropos to both the employers and the students—and parental support solicited and obtained. Whether the jobs should be paid or un-paid—or what mix of the two is necessary—will surely be an issue. Further, the relationship between the students' school program and their out-of-school responsibilities will become pertinent.

Criteria for graduation can be examined, as well as criteria for giving graduates recommendations for college acceptance. Even if these criteria are to be changed—after extended discussion with parents, staff, and students (at the high school level)—the underlying academic program must be reevaluated to see if the revised criteria are realistically related to the package of activities put before the students. In other words, there is no point in saying "all graduating students must have spent so much time doing such-and-such in a satisfactory manner" unless there are opportunities for such activities and forewarning to students about their obligations.[10]

Time and Change

A vast and complex medley of proposed changes has been presented. Readers may wonder: can any significant proportion of the changes be brought to pass, since they run counter to many current trends? To respond to that question, we must separate the transient from the persistent and enlarge our time horizons.

Many of the social analyses that are presented to us today are essentially reflexive emotional responses to tension-generating structures in post-industrial society.[11] But tension does not usually engender careful perception, though it does create pressures for dramatic and immediate action. And so tension is likely to stimulate superficial and ephemeral intellectual fads. Like other forms of fads, they may expire as quickly as they appear—despite their brief moment of stylishness. Trends do not always represent the intellectual tides that shape our social environment. During the late 1960's, many white American public leaders talked about the "oppression" of blacks. Of course, whether blacks were actually oppressed during that period is a question of vast complexity. But, regardless of that complexity, the language of oppression became popular terminology. Then, most whites, and many blacks, became increasingly concerned with riots and other disorder in ghettos. Citizens, and some leaders, began to suspect that telling people they were oppressed might be an incentive for riot or might handicap the suppression of riots. Some leaders began to change their vocabularies and some, who did not change, became less prominent as leaders. I suggest that the language of oppression was promoted by some whites, not because of complex philosophical analyses, but because such terminology enabled them to treat with black frustrations in simple, immediate, and dramatic terms. The language permitted them—as well as many blacks—to release latent anxiety through the verbal expression of aggression. "Oppression" has expired as a popular or intellectual issue. But, the underlying anxiety within certain classes of articulate whites may still persist. However, it may be possible, over time, to persuade anxious people to adopt more thoughtful responses to their anxiety.

In any event, the immediate popular appeal of an analysis among American intellectuals and writers is not necessarily a sound test of its staying power. If we must make social forecasts—and we cannot escape that necessity—it is probably sounder to base our estimates more on our personal analyses of persisting human motives (seasoned with a good dose of cross-cultural and historical perspective). Forecasts grounded in such a perspective will take a cynical view of the infinite mutability of humans or their drive for novelty and of proposed societies where people display an immense tolerance for ambiguity and confusion.

Realistic forecasts will tend to assume that people want a significant degree of certitude and social stability and that their children need roots and environments that gradually develop important affective skills. If we are creating physical environments (i.e., modern suburbs) that frustrate these ends, we should expect that adults will gradually see the error of their ways and set about fostering constructive change. Eventually, many Americans will develop a better perspective of the unhealthy effects of post-industrial environments on the young—just as we have reconsidered our views on energy consumption, race relations, and the appropriate role of higher education in our society. This improved public perception will not develop quickly. We have spent a long time getting where we are, and it will not be simple for us to turn around. But some incrementalism is not all to the bad. While it is easy to develop change proposals that apparently are responsive to the problem, it is difficult to say what combination of what proposals is best for some community or region at any particular time. Proposals must be gradually developed, tested, analyzed, and refined, at the same time society is reconsidering its current aspirations.

Incidentally, while we cannot count on serendipitous events, we should not be amazed at their occurrence, or neglect to seize unexpected opportunities. For instance, American attitudes toward post-industrial suburbs may tend to change as and if our energy shortage gradually intensifies. After all, post-industrial environments are basically high consumers of energy, using large amounts of it to "buy" privacy and time via reliance on the automobile, detached homes, and a vast array of gadgets and home conveniences. If the economic costs of energy continue to mount, we may be driven to design and construct suburban communities where homes, stores, businesses, schools, and the residents themselves are all nearer to each other. While the motives for such a shift may not directly relate to child-rearing concerns, they may very well have valuable constructive side effects. Indeed, those effects may be magnified if the designers of these changed environments are conscious of some of the propositions urged in this book. For, if we are going to live in greater proximity, and rely more on each other, it can be helpful if this new-old environment is perceived in an appropriate ideological framework.

This process of testing and refinement may not involve many deliberate, conscious, and funded experiments. It may just as well mean that schools and communities, on their own, may simply begin to try some different ideas—just as some of them probably are doing at this moment. Such a process of trial and error will gradually lead us to improvement—or it will tend to demonstrate that the proposed ideas are inherently unsound. Essentially, a similar process of trial and error was attempted during the late 1960's and early 1970's by people who wanted to foster communes and free schools. Apparently, those experiments demonstrated that the proposed systems were usually not good ideas. Or, at least, the ideas did not catch on. One need not say that these experiments failed, since (if we treat them as true experiments) they did test an idea. The idea failed, not the experiments. A similar process of trial and error may be appropriate for improving post-industrial suburban environments. Perhaps this idea will not fail. But the process will take persistence and vision.

This book implies that the problem of improving post-industrial child-rearing environments may remain a public issue throughout the lives of many of the readers. But that should be neither surprising nor discouraging. We live in a vast country; democratic processes rely on persuasion. The assumption is that debate and conflict produce better and more persisting reform. And, therefore, most important and creative major systemic changes have required persistent, incremental promotion. Still, the scope of the challenge is not the crucial problem. The question is whether we have large ambitions. If our aspirations are large enough, there are many allies and social forces that can be mobilized in support of appropriate changes.

Notes

Preface

1. Louis H. Masotti and Deborah Ellis Dennis, *Suburbs, Suburbia, and Suburbanization: A Bibliography* (Evanston, Ill.: Center for Urban Affairs, Northwestern University, 1973).

1. Why Worry about Suburban Children?

1. George C. Homans, *The Human Group* (New York: Harcourt and Brace, 1950), p. 315.
2. Unless otherwise indicated, throughout this book the term "suburb" will refer to those parts of Standard Metropolitan Statistical Areas which are not included in "central cities" by the Bureau of the Census. Other definitions can be proposed, but this one is generally accepted and will satisfy the needs of this work.
3. U.S. Bureau of the Census, *Statistical Abstract of the U.S., 1974* (Washington, D.C.: Government Printing Office, 1974), p. 17.
4. U.S. Bureau of the Census, "Regional Metropolitan Projections," in *Population Distribution and Policy*, ed. Sara Mills Mazie, Papers Prepared for the Commission on Population Growth and the American Future, vol. 5 (Washington, D.C.: Government Printing Office, 1972), p. 274.
5. David Riesman, "Leisure in Post-Industrial America," in *"Abundance for What?" and Other Essays* (Garden City, N.Y.: Doubleday, 1964), pp. 162–182.
6. Daniel Bell, *The Coming of Post-Industrial Society: A Venture in Social Forecasting* (New York: Basic Books, 1973).
7. Robert Goldston, *Suburbia: Civic Denial* (New York: Macmillan, 1970), p. 21.
8. U.S. Department of Transportation, *1972 National Transportation Report* (Washington, D.C.: Government Printing Office, 1972), pp. 45, 69.
9. U.S. Bureau of the Census, *Statistical Abstract of the U.S., 1972* (Washington, D.C.: Government Printing Office, 1972), pp. 886–887.
10. Northeastern Illinois Planning Commission, *Suburban Factbook, 1973* (Chicago: Northeastern Illinois Planning Commission, 1973), p. 44.
11. Regional Plan Association, *Growth and Settlement in the U.S.* (New York: Regional Plan Association, 1975), p. ii.

12. Northeastern Illinois Planning Commission, *Suburban Factbook*, pp. 31–33.
13. Ibid., pp. 21–25.
14. Commission on Population Growth and the American Future, *Population and the American Future* (Washington, D.C.: Government Printing Office, 1972), p. 32.
15. For an imaginative discussion of the issue of contradictions, with special reference to suburban child rearing, see John R. Seeley, R. Alexander Sim, and Elizabeth W. Loosley, *Crestwood Heights: A North American Suburb* (New York: John Wiley and Son, 1963).
16. For a useful and careful sketch of a contemporary high school environment, see Philip A. Cusick, *Inside High School* (New York: Holt, Rinehart and Winston, 1973).
17. See, e.g., Bruno Bettelheim, *The Uses of Enchantment: The Meaning and Importance of Fairy Tales* (New York: Knopf, 1976).
18. U.S. Department of Health, Education, and Welfare, Public Health Service, personal communication, 1976.
19. U.S. Department of Justice, Law Enforcement Assistance Administration, *Sourcebook on Criminal Justice Statistics, 1973* (Washington, D.C.: Government Printing Office, 1973), p. 168.
20. San Mateo County, Department of Public Health and Welfare, *Summary Report, 1976, Surveys of Student Drug Use* (San Mateo, Calif.: Department of Public Health, 1976).
21. U.S. Bureau of the Census, *1970 Census of the Population, Characteristics of the Population, California* (Washington, D.C.: Government Printing Office, 1973), vol. 1.
22. U.S. Department of Justice, *Crime in the United States, 1972* (Washington, D.C.: Government Printing Office, 1972), p. 124.
23. U.S. Department of Health, Education, and Welfare, National Institute on Drug Abuse, *Marijuana and Health, Fifth Annual Report* (Washington, D.C.: National Institute on Drug Abuse, 1975), p. 63.
24. U.S. Department of Health, Education, and Welfare, Public Health Service, *Second Special Report on Alcohol and Health*, preprint ed. (Rockville, Md.: National Institute on Alcohol Abuse and Alcoholism, 1974), p. 128.
25. Yankelovich, Skelly, and White, *A Study of Cigarette Smoking* (New York: Yankelovich, Skelly, and White, 1976), 1:36.
26. U.S. Department of Justice, Law Enforcement Assistance Administration, *Sourcebook on Criminal Justice Statistics, 1974* (Washington, D.C.: Government Printing Office, 1975).
27. U.S. Senate, Committee to Investigate Juvenile Delinquency, *Our Nation's Schools*, 94th Cong., 1st sess., preliminary report (Washington, D.C.: Government Printing Office, 1975), p. 4.
28. U.S. Department of Health, Education, and Welfare, Health Service Administration, *Approaches to Adolescent Health Care in the 1970's* (Washington, D.C.: Government Printing Office, 1975).
29. U.S. Department of Health, Education, and Welfare, Public Health Service, *Trends in Illegitimacy, U.S., 1940–1965*, ser. 21, no. 15 (Washington, D.C.: Government Printing Office, 1968); U.S. Department of Health, Education, and Welfare, National Center for Health Statistics, *Monthly Vital Statistics Report* 24, no. 11, supp., February 13, 1976.

30. Department of Justice, *Crime in the United States*, 1972, p. 124.
31. President's Commission on Campus Unrest, *Report* (Washington, D.C.: Government Printing Office, 1970), p. 387.
32. "Nine Radicals on Most Wanted List," *New York Times*, November 28, 1970, p. 13.
33. Douglas Heath, *Growing Up in College* (San Francisco: Jossey-Bass, 1968), p. 63.
34. Dean R. Hogue, "College Student Values," *Sociology of Education* 44 (1970): 170–197.
35. Milton B. Freedman and Paul Kanzer, "Psychology of a Strike," in *Student Activism and Protest: Alternatives for Social Change*, ed. Edward S. Sampson and Harold A. Kron (San Francisco: Jossey-Bass, 1970), p. 155.
36. Daniel Yankelovich, *Changing Youth Values in the 70's* (New York: John D. Rockefeller 3rd Fund, 1974), p. 16.
37. Goldston, *Suburbia*, p. 21.
38. Herbert J. Gans, *The Levittowners: Ways of Life and Politics in a New Suburban Community* (New York: Random House, 1967), pp. 190–198; idem, *People and Plans: Essays on Urban Problems and Solutions* (New York: Basic Books, 1968), pp. 137–151.
39. James B. Conant, *Slums and Suburbs: A Commentary on Schools in the Metropolitan Area* (New York: McGraw-Hill, 1961); W. G. Mollenkopf and S. D. Melville, *A Study of Secondary School Characteristics as Related to Test Scores*, Research Bull. 56–6 (Princeton: Educational Testing Service, 1956).
40. Christopher Jencks, *Inequality: A Reassessment of the Effect of Family and Schooling in America* (New York: Basic Books, 1972); Sarane S. Boocock, *An Introduction to the Sociology of Learning* (Boston: Houghton Mifflin, 1972), pp. 245–251.
41. James S. Coleman, "Education in Modern Society," in *Computers, Communications, and the Public Interest*, ed. Martin Greenberger (Baltimore: Johns Hopkins University Press, 1971), pp. 116–132.
42. Apropos of this erroneous confusion of emotional maturity with intellectual and physical capability, a recent report observed: "For a variety of reasons, including better nutritional, parental, and medical care, and better housing, children in the United States are maturing more rapidly . . . . the self-conscious character of this adolescent culture is evidence of its experiential maturity. . . . While the evidence is not conclusive about the occurrence of emotional maturity," the report finally recommended that "secondary schools need to adapt to students who are maturing earlier in many ways" (U.S. Department of Health, Education, and Welfare, National Panel on High School and Adolescent Education, *The Education of Adolescents* [Washington, D.C.: Government Printing Office, 1976], pp. 25–29). Obviously, the exact meaning of the word *maturity* as used in the report is obscure. Clearly, it encompasses physical maturity, but, presumably, the schools should be even more concerned about the *emotional* maturity of their students; and it is on precisely this question that the report, in its "fine print," becomes vague. The term "experiential maturity" is absurd. The data cited earlier in the text obviously reveal a great deal of "experientially mature" conduct among

adolescents: drug use, venereal disease, delinquency. However, such conduct is usually presumed to be evidence of *emotional immaturity.* That is, it is stimulated by the need for immediate gratification without heed for future consequences.

43. John Dewey, *Democracy and Education* (New York: Macmillan, 1916), p. 6.
44. Teena DeVaron, "Growing Up," in *Twelve to Sixteen: Early Adolescence,* ed. Jerome Kagan and Robert Coles (New York: Norton, 1971), p. 339.
45. Edward A. Wynne, "Learning and Competition and Cooperation," *Educational Forum* 40, no. 3 (March 1976): 279–288.
46. For a broader consideration of such issues, see, e.g., Lewis S. Feuer, *The Conflict of Generations: The Character and Significance of Student Movements* (New York: Basic Books, 1969); Kirkpatrick Sale, *SDS: Ten Years toward a Revolution* (New York: Random House, 1973).

2. *How We Attain Adulthood*

1. Orrin E. Klapp, *The Collective Search for Identity* (New York: Holt, Rinehart and Winston, 1969), p. 220.
2. For discussions about the impact of talented but alienated people, see Louis J. Halle, *The Ideological Imagination* (Chicago: Quadrangle Books, 1972); Howard Mumford Jones, *Revolution and Romanticism* (Cambridge, Mass.: Belknap Press of Harvard University, 1974); Irving Kristol, "Utopianism, Ancient and Modern," *Alternative,* June–September, 1974, pp. 5–9; and Edward Shils, "Of Plentitude and Scarcity," *Encounter* 32, no. 5 (May 1969): 37–57.
3. Quoted in Robert A. Nisbet, *Tradition and Revolt: Essays Historical, Sociological, and Critical* (New York: Random House, 1968), p. 25.
4. Edward L. Thorndike, *The Psychology of Wants, Interests, and Attitudes* (New York: Appleton-Century, 1935), p. 212.
5. Some of the principles involved in such an analysis are articulated in Homans, *Human Group.* See also Bruno Bettelheim, *A Home for the Heart* (New York: Alfred A. Knopf, 1974); Erving Goffman, *Behavior in Public Places: Notes on the Social Organization of Gatherings* (New York: Free Press, 1963); and B. F. Skinner, *Beyond Freedom and Dignity* (New York: Alfred A. Knopf, 1971).
6. For a basic work, see Neal E. Miller and John Dollard, *Social Learning and Imitation* (New Haven: Yale University Press, 1941).
7. Gallup Poll, "Students Still Favor Teaching Careers," *Chicago Sun-Times,* May 12, 1974, sec. 4, p. 8.
8. R. Mugo Gatheru, *Child of Two Worlds: A Kikuyu's Story* (Garden City, N.Y.: Anchor Books, Doubleday, 1964), p. 20.
9. See, e.g., Rosabeth M. Kanter, *Commitment and Community: Communes and Utopias in Sociological Perspective* (Cambridge, Mass.: Harvard University Press, 1972).
10. A good discussion of techniques for creating such a sense of identity is found in Klapp, *Collective Search for Identity.*
11. W. Lloyd Warner, *The Living and the Dead* (New Haven: Yale University Press, 1959), p. 245. Consider also the secular and rational spirit

portrayed in Seeley, Sim, and Loosley, *Crestwood Heights*, a study of an upper-middle-class suburb.

12. For a consideration of these themes, see James S. Coleman, "New Incentives for Schools," in *New Models for American Education*, ed. James W. Guthrie and Edward A. Wynne (Englewood Cliffs, N.J.: Prentice-Hall, 1971), pp. 72–90. For a sketch of a more traditional school, see Jacquetta Hill Burnett, "Ceremony, Rites, and Economy in the Student System of an American High School," *Human Organization* 28, no. 1 (Spring 1969): 1–10.

13. Bureau of the Census, *Statistical Abstract of the U.S., 1974*, p. 34.

14. See, e.g., Roger G. Barker and Paul V. Gump, *Big School, Small School: High School Size and Student Behavior* (Stanford, Calif.: Stanford University Press, 1964).

15. Amos Hawley, *Human Ecology: A Theory of Community Structure* (New York: Ronald Press, 1950), pp. 248–252.

16. Robert Wood, *1400 Governments* (Cambridge, Mass.: Harvard University Press, 1961).

17. See, e.g., Bernard Berelson and Gary S. Steiner, *Human Behavior: An Inventory of Scientific Findings* (New York: Harcourt, Brace and World, 1964), pp. 512 ff.

18. For a useful discussion, see James S. Coleman et al., *Youth: Transition to Adulthood*, Report on Youth of the President's Science Advisory Committee (Chicago: University of Chicago Press, 1974), pp. 127 ff.

19. Margaret Read, *Children of Their Fathers: Growing Up among the Ngoni of Malawi* (New York: Holt, Rinehart and Winston, 1968), pp. 2–3.

20. Richard K. Nelson, *Hunters of the Northern Ice* (Chicago: University of Chicago Press, 1969), pp. 385–388.

21. See, e.g., Berelson and Steiner, *Human Behavior*, pp. 245 ff.

22. See Gans, *Levittowners*, "Levittown Is 'Endsville': The Adolescent View," pp. 206 ff.; idem, *People and Plans*, p. 195; Social Research, *Suburban Teens: Their Problems and Needs*, Report for Palatine Township Youth Committee (Chicago: Social Research, 1972): "the major problem is the lack of activities in an extremely affluent community for young people" (p. 27).

23. Ann Vernon, reviewing Maria W. Piers, *Growing Up with Values* (New York: Parents Magazine Films, 1974), in *Curriculum Review* 15, no. 4 (October 1976): p. 225.

24. For a general discussion of these issues, see the issue on values education, *Phi Delta Kappan* 56, no. 10 (June 1975).

25. For a review of the research, see Robert Hogan, "Moral Conduct and Moral Character," *Psychological Bulletin* 79 (1973): 217–232.

26. For some discussion of the "division of authority" between parents and society, see Edward A. Wynne, "Accountable to Whom?" *Society* 13, no. 2 (January–February 1976): 10–37.

27. See, e.g., Roger G. Barker and Phil Schoegan, *Qualities of Community Life: Measurement of Environment and Behavior in an American and an English Town* (San Francisco: Jossey-Bass, 1973), esp. pp. 405–408; Roger G. Barker and Herbert F. Wright, *One Boy's Day: A Specimen Record of Behavior* (New York: Harper and Brothers, 1951).

28. See, e.g., Curtis K. Statfield, *From the Land and Back* (New York:

Scribners, 1972).

29. Barker and Gump, *Big School, Small School*, pp. 154–159.
30. See, e.g., Andrew Carnegie, *Autobiography of Andrew Carnegie* (Boston: Houghton Mifflin, 1924); Robert M. MacIver, *As a Tale That Is Told* (Chicago: University of Chicago Press, 1968); and Arthur M. Schlesinger, *In Retrospect: The History of a Historian* (New York: Harcourt, Brace and World, 1963).
31. See, e.g., Claude Brown, *Manchild in the Promised Land* (New York: Macmillan, 1965); Kenneth B. Clark, *Dark Ghetto: Dilemmas of Social Power* (New York: Harper and Row, 1965); Herbert J. Gans, *The Urban Villagers* (New York: Free Press, 1962); and Gerald D. Suttles, *The Social Order of the Slum* (Chicago: University of Chicago Press, 1968).

3. Administering Suburban Schools—I

1. Lucien Price, *Dialogues of Alfred North Whitehead* (New York: Mentor Books, 1954), p. 113.
2. Henrietta S. Schwartz, "Contrived Role Playing and Attitude Change," presented at the annual meeting, American Education Research Association, February 5, 1973.
3. Dewey, *Democracy and Education*, p. 416.
4. Thomas Hughes, *Loyola and the Educational System of the Jesuits* (New York: Charles Scribners, 1892); Bettelheim, *A Home for the Heart*; George Richmond, *The Micro-Society School: A Real World in Miniature* (New York: Harper and Row, 1973).
5. For a general history of these developments, see Lawrence A. Cremin, *The Transformation of the School: Progressivism in American Education, 1876–1957* (New York: Alfred A. Knopf, 1961). See also idem, *Public Education* (New York: Basic Books, 1976).
6. John Dewey, *Experience and Education* (New York: Macmillan, 1938).
7. For a criticism of Dewey's psychology by one of his contemporaries, see William F. Ogburn, *On Culture and Social Change, Selected Papers*, ed. Otis D. Duncan (Chicago: University of Chicago Press, 1964), pp. 295–297.
8. See, e.g., Julian Weber Gordon, *My Country School Diary* (New York: Dell, 1946).
9. See, e.g., John Dewey and Evelyn Dewey, *Schools of Tomorrow* (New York: E. P. Dutton, 1915).
10. Raymond E. Callahan, *Education and the Cult of Efficiency* (Chicago: University of Chicago Press, 1962).
11. National Commission on Marijuana and Drug Abuse, *Drug Use in America: The Problem in Perspective* (Washington, D.C.: Government Printing Office, 1973), p. 111.
12. David W. Minar and Scott Greer, eds., *The Concept of Community: Readings with Interpretations* (Chicago: Aldine, 1969), p. 130.
13. Skinner, *Beyond Freedom and Dignity*; Thorndike, *Psychology of Wants, Interests, and Attitudes*.
14. Wallace Brett Donham, *Education for Responsible Living: The Opportunity for Liberal Arts Colleges* (Cambridge, Mass.: Harvard University Press, 1946), p. 107.

15. See, e.g., James V. Downton, Jr., *Rebel Leadership: Commitment and Charisma in the Revolutionary Process* (New York: Free Press, 1973); Klapp, *Collective Search for Identity.*
16. See, e.g., James S. Coleman, *The Adolescent Society* (New York: Free Press, 1961); Cusick, *Inside High School.*
17. See, e.g., James Herndon, *How to Survive in Your Native Land* (New York: Simon and Schuster, 1971); Neil Postman and Charles Weingartner, *Teaching as a Subversive Activity* (New York: Delacorte, 1969).
18. Talcott Parsons, *Essays in Sociological Theory*, rev. ed. (New York: Free Press, 1954), p. 42.
19. Byron G. Massialas, "The Inquiring Activist," in *Political Youth, Traditional Schools: National and International Perspectives* (Englewood Cliffs, N.J.: Prentice-Hall, 1972), p. 245.
20. Russell F. Farnen and Dan B. German, "Youth, Politics, and Education," in *Political Youth*, ed. Massialas, p. 176.
21. Rupert Wilkinson, *Gentlemenly Power* (London: Oxford University Press, 1964), p. 197.
22. Ibid., p. 40.
23. Carnegie, *Autobiography*; Benjamin Franklin, *The Autobiography of Benjamin Franklin* (New York: Macmillan, 1966).
24. National Commission, *Drug Use in America*, p. 104.

4. Administering Suburban Schools—II

1. Barker and Gump, *Big School, Small School*, p. 196.
2. Leo W. Simmons, *The Role of the Aged in Primitive Society* (New Haven: Yale University Press, 1945), p. 175.
3. H. F. D. Kitto, "The Polis," in *Concept of Community*, ed. Minar and Greer, p. 72.
4. P. B. Dierenfield, "Personalizing Education: The House System in England," *Phi Delta Kappan* 56, no. 9 (May 1974): 605–607.
5. See, e.g., Edward A. Wynne, "Learning about Cooperation and Competition," *Educational Forum* 40, no. 3 (March 1976): 279–288.
6. Rhoda Thomas Tripp, ed., *International Thesaurus of Quotations* (New York: Thomas Y. Crowell, 1970), p. 31.

5. Teaching in Suburban Schools

1. R. S. Peters, *Ethics and Education* (London: George Allen and Unwin, 1966), p. 316.
2. "Students Find College Honor Codes Losing Favor," *New York Times*, April 12, 1975, p. 11.
3. I cannot recall the source of this anecdote, which I read in a naval history.
4. See, e.g., James S. Coleman, "New Models for School Incentives," in *New Models for American Education*, ed. Guthrie and Wynne, pp. 70–90.
5. For a useful discussion about the factors affecting occupational commitment patterns of teachers, see Blanche Geer, "Occupational Commitment and the Teaching Profession," *School Review* 74 (1966): 31–47.

6. Improving Suburban Communities

1. MacIver, As a Tale That Is Told, p. 29.
2. For assessments of the attitudes of adult suburban residents, see, e.g., Bennett M. Berger, Working Class Suburb: A Study of Auto Workers in Suburbia (Berkeley: University of California Press, 1960); Gans, Levittowners, and idem, People and Plans.
3. Leo F. Schnore, "On the Spatial Structure of Cities in the Two Americas," in The Study of Urbanization, ed. Philip M. Hauser and Leo F. Schnore (New York: John Wiley, 1965), pp. 347–398; James W. Hughes, ed., Suburbanization Dynamics and the Future of the City (New Brunswick, N.J.: Rutgers University, Center for Urban Policy Research, 1974).
4. Alma F. Taeuber and Karl E. Taeuber, Negroes in Cities (Chicago: Aldine, 1965).
5. Anthony Downs, Opening Up the Suburbs: An Urban Strategy for America (New Haven: Yale University Press, 1973), p. 2.
6. For an extended consideration of this proposition, see Homans, Human Group.
7. For an outline of the pertinent literature on this issue, see James S. Coleman, "Response to Professors Pettigrew and Greene," Harvard Educational Review 46, no. 2 (May 1976): 217–224.
8. As an example, see the proposal presented in Downs, Opening Up the Suburbs.
9. See Louise Reemer, New Towns: A Bibliography (Columbia, Md: Wild Lake Village Branch Library, 1974).
10. For an indication of some of the issues and litigation relating to this complex issue, see, e.g., Belle Terre v. Borras, 416 U.S. 1 (1974); Boris I. Bittker, "The Case of the Checker-Board Ordinance: An Experiment in Race Relations," 71 Yale Law Journal 1387 (1962).
11. Murray Schumach, "40% of Brooklyn Doctors Live Elsewhere," New York Times, June 5, 1975, p. 29.
12. For some discussion of nonmonetary trades, see William F. Ogburn, "Southern Folkways Regarding Money," in Culture and Social Change, pp. 197–206.
13. See Kanter, Commitment and Community.
14. U.S. President, Economic Report of the President, 1974 (Washington, D.C.: Government Printing Office, 1974), pp. 249, 265, 328.
15. Consider the suggestion that automobiles should be designed to facilitate home repairs by adolescents in Paul Goodman, Growing Up Absurd (New York: Random House, 1960), p. 78.
16. For a general treatment of the segregation of the old, see Matilda White Riley and Anne Foner, Aging and Society, vol. 3, A Sociology of Age Stratification (New York: Russell Sage Foundation, 1972); see also Matilda White Riley, "The Perspective of Age Stratification," School Review 83 (November 1974): 85–91.
17. See Simons, Aged in Primitive Society.
18. For some discussion of these issues, see Coleman et al., Youth.
19. These principles are amplified in Harry F. Silberman, "Involving the Young," Phi Delta Kappan 56, no. 9 (May 1975): 596–600; Edward A. Wynne, et al., Management Internships: A New System for Youth Sociali-

zation and Learning, Report to the National Institute of Education (Chicago: College of Education, University of Illinois, 1974).

7. *Being a Suburban Parent*

1. Carnegie, *Autobiography*, p. 14.
2. T. S. Eliot, "Four Quartets: Little Gidding," in *The Complete Poems and Plays* (New York: Harcourt, Brace and World, 1952), p. 145.
3. See the discussion in Donald Barr, *Who Pushed Humpty Dumpty? or, the Education of a Headmaster* (New York: Atheneum, 1971), p. 51.
4. It is notorious that the extensive research on the effect of television on children is still inconclusive. For some data, see, e.g., Eli A. Rubenstein, George A. Comstock, and John P. Murray, eds., *Television in Everyday Life*, Background Papers, Surgeon General's Scientific Advisory Committee on Television and Social Behavior, vol. 5 (Washington, D.C.: Government Printing Office, n.d.).

8. *Education and Sexual Identity*

1. Sigmund Freud, *Civilization and Its Discontents* (London: Hogarth Press, 1930), p. 123 n.
2. For some materials discussing this issue, see, e.g., Judith M. Bardwick, *The Psychology of Women: A Study of Biocultural Conflicts* (New York: Harper and Row, 1971); Maren L. Carden, *The New Feminist Movement* (New York: Russell Sage Foundation, 1974); Lawrence H. Fuchs, *Family Matters* (New York: Random House, 1972); Joan Huber, ed., *Changing Women in a Changing Society*, special issue *American Journal of Sociology* 78, no. 4 (1973); Myron Lieberman, ed., *Women in Public Education: Education and the Feminist Movement*, special issue *Phi Delta Kappan* 55, no. 2 (1973); Eleanor Emmons Maccoby and Carol Nagy Jacklin, *Psychology of Sex Differences* (Stanford: Stanford University Press, 1974); Terry N. Saario, Carolyn K. Tittle, and C. N. Jacklin, "Sex Role Stereotyping in Public Schools," *Harvard Educational Review* 43 (1973): 386–416.
3. For information on the status of typical neofeminists, see, e.g., Carden, *New Feminist Movement*, p. 20; J. Freeman, "The Origins of the Women's Liberation Movement," *American Journal of Sociology* 78, no. 4 (1973): 792–812.
4. For some statements on these aspirations, see, e.g., Pauline Bart, "Why Women See the Future Differently Than Men," in *Learning for Tomorrow: The Role of the Future in Education*, ed. Alvin Toffler (New York: Random House, 1974), pp. 33–55; Lieberman, *Women in Public Education*; McGraw-Hill, *Guidelines for Equal Treatment of the Sexes in McGraw-Hill Book Company Publications* (New York: McGraw-Hill, 1974); Saario, Tittle, and Jacklin, "Sex Role Stereotyping." See also U.S. Department of Health, Education, and Welfare, *Regulations Relating to Sex Discrimination Issued Pursuant to Title IX, Higher Education Act of 1972* (Washington, D.C.: Government Printing Office, 1976).
5. For some discussion about sex role differences that continue to persist

across cultures, or among diverse species, see, e.g., George Gilder, *Naked Nomads: Unmarried Men in America* (New York: Quadrangle, 1974), pp. 92–105; Steven Goldberg, *The Inevitability of Patriarchy* (New York: Morrow, 1973); Corrine Hutt, *Males and Females* (Baltimore: Penguin Books, 1973); Harry F. Harlow, "Sexual Behavior in the Rhesus Monkey," in *Sex and Behavior*, ed. Frank A. Beach (London: Wiley, 1965); Margaret Mead, *Male and Female: A Study of the Sexes in a Changing World* (New York: Dell, 1968), esp. p. 168; John Money and Anke A. Ehrhardt, *Man and Woman, Boy and Girl: The Differentiation and Dimorphism of Gender Identity from Conception to Maturity* (Baltimore: Johns Hopkins University Press, 1972). For a somewhat different emphasis, see, Maccoby and Jacklin, *Psychology of Sex Differences*.

6. There are some data indicating that the total amount of time housewives spend in household chores has not significantly decreased over time (Joann Vanek, "Time Spent in Housework," *Scientific American* 231, no. 5 [November 1972]: 116–122). However, it seems likely that at least one force for this stability has been an elevation of the standards applied (by full-time housewives) to evaluate "good housekeeping." In other words, a modern working wife may keep her home as well as did the typical fulltime housekeeping wife of forty years ago; this is not to say higher or lower standards of housekeeping are better, but simply to emphasize that the "per hour productivity" of housewives has probably increased.

7. U.S. Public Health Service, *Vital Statistics of the U.S., 1970*, vol. 2, *Mortality, Part A* (Washington, D.C.: Government Printing Office, 1974), table 5.4.

8. Jessie Bernard, *The Future of Marriage* (New York: World Publishing, 1972), pp. 56–58; Karen S. Renne, "Correlates of Dissatisfaction in Marriage," *Journal of Marriage and the Family* 32 (1970): 54–67.

9. For a contrary prediction, based on approximately the same data, see Betty Yorburgh, *The Changing Family: A Sociological Perspective* (New York: Columbia University Press, 1973), pp. 194–195.

10. Some of the complexities generated by demands for simple equality are suggested by the issues raised by the following traditional patterns of conduct: Higher life insurance rates for males than for females of the same age. Sex-segregated college dormitories. Employers who are reluctant to hire females for jobs that require costly and lengthy training, if the applicants state they propose to bear children in the next year or two. Prisons that segregate male and female convicts. Schools that establish different performance criteria in physical education for males and females. Branches of the armed services that refuse to assign females to certain jobs. Unmarried females who expect their dates to walk or drive them home at night.

11. Some of these proposals are discussed in Lieberman, "Women in Public Education"; McGraw-Hill, *Guidelines*; Saario, Tittle, and Jacklin, "Sex Role Stereotyping"; see also Department of Health, Education, and Welfare, *Regulations*.

12. See, e.g., National Commission, *Drug Use in America*. The Commission said, "For ever increasing numbers of our youth, we have postponed by many years the stabilizing influence of earning one's own living. In the

sheltered atmosphere of the college campus, however, the risks for the
student of experimental and recreational drug use are minimal compared with the potential consequences of such behavior for a job holder"
(p. 135).
13. For some discussion of these problems, see Fuchs, *Family Matters*.
14. Louis A. Zurcher, Jr., "The Poor and the Hip: Some Manifestations of
Cultural Lead," *Social Science Quarterly* 53, no. 2 (September 1972):
360–362. The footnote for the section of text quoted contained twenty-
three separate references to forecasting and futurist literature. For a
more pessimistic view of an unstable, utopian future, see Edward A.
Wynne, "Utopianism and Education," *Journal of Educational Thought*
10, no. 3 (December 1976): 169–178.
15. "Wives of Police Protest Use of Female Partners," *New York Times*, June
21, 1974, p. 29.
16. Judy Klemesrud, "College Students Think Ahead," *New York Times*, April
22, 1975, p. 26.
17. Mary Belove, "For Married Couples," *Wall Street Journal*, May 13, 1975,
p. 1.
18. Saario, Tittle, and Jacklin, "Sex Role Stereotyping," p. 415.
19. As an example of the rediscovery of the obvious, consider the following:
"Increasingly, the separation of sex from affection is being discovered
by the avant-garde of sexual liberation to result in frustration, tension
and jealousy" ("Sexual Revolution Cooling," *New York Times*, January
30, 1975, p. 20, quoting sociologist Amitai Etzioni).
20. Perhaps some of the complications are suggested by the following anecdote: "One long interview [on a television 'special'] is with a married
couple in St. Louis. She is a policewoman; he works for the telephone
company in an office full of women and has taken over much of the
work of keeping house and raising the children. They both profess that
they would never return to the old 'sexist' way. But the viewer learns that
the interview was filmed last October and the couple filed for divorce in
November. . . . The special seems determined to be positive, valiantly
upbeat" (John J. O'Connor, "TV Review," *New York Times*, January 1,
1975, p. 62).
21. See, e.g., Dennis R. Young and Richard R. Nelson, *Public Policy for Day
Care of Young Children: Organization, Finance, and Planning* (Lexington, Mass.: Lexington Books, 1973).
22. For some suggestions, see Eugene Litwak and Josefina Figueira, "Technological Innovation and Ideal Forms of Family Structure in an Industrial Democratic Society," in *Families in East and West*, ed. Ruben Hill
and Rene Konig (The Hague: Mouton, 1970), pp. 348–396.
23. For one interpretation of the social significance of the temperance movement, see Joseph R. Gusfield, *Symbolic Crusade: Status Politics and the
American Temperance Movement* (Urbana: University of Illinois Press,
1963).
24. Ralph B. Kimbrough and Michael Y. Nunnery, *Educational Administration: An Introduction* (New York: Macmillan, 1976), p. 293.
25. For a more extended discussion of the issue "who should control," see
Wynne, "Accountable to Whom?"

26. For an example of a book based on student interviews on another topic, see Eliot Wigginton, ed., *The Foxfire Book* (Garden City, N.Y.: Doubleday, 1972).

27. Joan Libman, "Marriage Can Be a Trying Course," *Wall Street Journal*, June 9, 1975, p. 1.

28. It is true that some current court decisions have enlarged the power of teachers to retain their jobs, even if they adopt practices and positions that are unpopular or statistically abnormal (Jim Montgomery, "Breaking the Mold," *Wall Street Journal*, January 28, 1975, p. 1). The question is Do teachers want to be persons who have influence on students and can act as role models for them? If they do, then society will ask them to display responsibility and restrict their conduct. Conversely, if teachers are not expected to influence the affective conduct of students, their personal conduct is less material.

29. For some discussion of structures to foster a greater degree of child-care sharing among parents, see Pamela A. Roby, "Sharing Parenting: Perspectives from Other Nations," *School Review* 83, no. 3 (May 1975): 415–432.

9. *Summing Up*

1. Bruno Bettelheim, *Children of the Dream* (New York: Macmillan, 1969), p. 60.

2. Benjamin S. Bloom, *Handbook on Formative and Summative Evaluation of Student Learning* (Chicago: McGraw-Hill, 1971).

3. One of the reviewers of the manuscript of this book pointed out that the proposed school could be at least partially evaluated legitimately and relatively inexpensively through comparative statistics: there should be declines in vandalism, discipline problems, truancy, and drug incidents; SAT and ACT scores should at least stay stable. There is much to recommend this suggestion. Ideally, the school would have a far more positive impact than only producing order and stabilized cognitive learning. Still, meeting the statistical tests just presented might stimulate many observers to recognize that other good things are implicitly happening.

4. Peter H. Rossi and Walter Williams, eds., *Evaluating Social Programs: Theory, Practice, and Politics* (New York: Seminar Press, 1972); Carol H. Weiss, ed., *Evaluating Action Programs: Readings in Social Action and Education* (Boston: Allyn and Bacon, 1972); Henry W. Riecken and Robert F. Boruch, eds., *Social Experimentation: Method for Planning and Evaluating Social Intervention* (New York: Academic Press, 1974).

5. Harvey Averch et al., *How Effective Is Schooling?* (Santa Monica, Calif.: Rand, 1971); Don Davies, ed., *Do Teachers Make a Difference?* (Washington, D.C.: Government Printing Office, 1970); Robert E. Klitgaard and George R. Hall, *A Statistical Search for Unusually Effective Schools* (Santa Monica, Calif.: Rand, 1973); Theodore W. Schultz, *Investment in Human Capital: The Role of Education and of Research* (New York: Free Press, 1970).

6. John Bremer and Michael von Moschizisker, *The School without Walls* (New York: Holt, Rinehart and Winston, 1972); Philip H. Coombs, *New Paths for Learning for Children and Youth* (New York: International

Council for Educational Development, 1973); Allen Graubard, "The Free
School Movement," *Harvard Educational Review* 42 (August 1972):
351–373; A. S. Neill, *Neill! Neill! Orange Peel: An Autobiography* (New
York: Hart, 1972); Roland G. Paulston, *Non-Formal Education: An An-
notated International Bibliography* (New York: Praeger, 1972). For some
history of affect-oriented education in the early twentieth century, see
Cremin, *Transformation of the School*; idem, *Public Education*; Patricia
A. Graham, *Progressive Education from Arcady to Academe: A History
of the Progressive Education Association, 1919–1955* (New York: Teachers College Press, 1967).

7. The Gallup Poll reported that a national sample of adults believed that
lack of discipline was the major issue facing public schools. It has been
the principal issue for seven of the eight successive annual polls on
public views of school issues (George H. Gallup, "Eighth Annual Gallup
Poll on Public Attitudes Toward Education," *Phi Delta Kappan* 58, no. 2
[October 1976]: 187–201).

8. See, e.g., Thomas Sowell, "Black Excellence—the Case of Dunbar High
School," *Public Interest* 35 (Spring 1974): 3–21; Cornelius J. Troost, ed.,
Radical School Reform: Critique and Alternatives (Boston: Little, Brown,
1973).

9. Mrs. B. Dixon Hollard, "Our Changing Schools," Letters to the Editor,
Chicago Tribune, July 7, 1974, sec. 2, p. 2.

10. Obviously, another book could be written which would provide more de-
tailed and concrete suggestions about how to carry out these proposals
in an effective manner. But the few paragraphs presented here should
at least convince readers that the suggestions are capable of being treated—at one level—as administrative responsibilities, divided into concrete components and planned for in the same way as are curriculum
revisions or changes in the athletic program. Of course, these "technical
plans" will also be surrounded with immense emotional difficulties (in
many schools), but the major aim of the book has been to provide leaders and participants with a rationale for confronting such barriers.

11. For some discussion of this proposition, see Edward C. Banfield, *The
Unheavenly City Revisited: A Revision of the Unheavenly City* (Boston:
Little, Brown, 1974); Ronald Berman, *America in the Sixties: An Intellectual History* (New York: Harper and Row, 1970); Irving Kristol,
"Utopianism, Ancient and Modern," *Alternative*, June–September, 1974,
pp. 5–9; Edward Shils, *Selected Essays of Edward Shils* (Chicago: University of Chicago Press, 1972); Wynne, "Utopianism and Education."

Index

adult life: central challenges of, 44; definition of maturity in, 28–29; effects of immaturity in, 44–46; emotions in, 18

affective learning: and commitment, 102; defined, 31–32; impact of grades on, 138; impact of large buildings on, 128; modern trends of, analyzed, 211; and natural learning, 58–61; and negotiating, 32–40; and pride, 179–180; relationship of, to learning environments, 46–58; and sex roles, 187–206; and skills of parents, 112; and supervisor-subordinate relationship, 105; teacher responsibility for, 133–134; undesirable forms of, 40

affluence: as barrier to learning negotiating skills, 35; as cause of erosion of traditional sex roles, 189; contrasted with limitations on emotional support, 182–183; effect of, on in-family learning, 176; and mental health, 49; in modern suburbs, 9

aged persons: role of, in schools, 114; as teaching resource, 157

alcohol, youth and, 20

alienation: as related to nationality and individualism, 91–92; youth, acts of, 19–22; youth, attitudes of, 21–26; youth, relationship of, to suburbs, 29

allowances, learning implications of, 180

altruism, as affected by reinforcement, 155

alumni: as involved in school ceremonies, 95; more in-school roles for, 103–104; significance of, to students, 104–105

androgyny, relationship of, to education in sex roles, 196–197

art, role of, in ceremonies, 95

athletics, as means of teaching affective skills, 55–56

attendance, monitoring student, 125–127

attitudes: as elements of affective learning, 31–40; as signs of youth alienation, 21–26

authority: of teachers, in improved school, 137–140; of the young, defined, 160–161

Barker, Roger G., 111

basics: back to, 211–212; contrast of, in traditional and post-industrial school, 30

Bettelheim, Bruno, 207

boredom: as caused by homogeneity, 157; of suburban adolescents, 64

boundary: with reference to school community, 127–131; social, around residential communities, 151–152

buildings, appropriate, 127–131

bureaucracy, in schools and communities, 78–79

Carnegie, Andrew, 165